Southern Biography Series

William J. Cooper, Jr., Editor

Archibald Grimké

Archibald Grimké

Portrait of a Black Independent

Dickson D. Bruce, Jr.

Louisiana State University Press
Baton Rouge and London

Copyright © 1993 by Louisiana State University Press
All rights reserved
Manufactured in the United States of America
First printing
02 01 00 99 98 97 96 95 94 93   5 4 3 2 1

Designer: Amanda McDonald Key
Typeface: Bembo
Typesetter: G & S Typesetters, Inc.
Printer and binder: Thomson–Shore, Inc.

Library of Congress Cataloging-in-Publication Data

Bruce, Dickson D., 1946–
    Archibald Grimké : portrait of a Black independent / Dickson D.
Bruce
        p.   cm.—(Southern biography series)
    Includes index.
    ISBN 0-8071-1796-X (acid-free paper)
    1. Grimké, Archibald Henry, 1849–1930. 2. Afro-Americans—
Biography. I. Title. II. Series.
E185.97.G8B78   1993
305.896′ 073′ 092—dc20
    [B]   92-42703
                                                              CIP

Excerpts from items in various archival collections are quoted by permission of the Charles H.
Chesnutt Collection, Fisk University Library Special Collections, Fisk University; the Moorland-
Spingarn Research Center, Howard University; the South Caroliniana Library, University of
South Carolina; the William L. Clements Library, University of Michigan; the William Monroe
Trotter Collection, Mugar Memorial Library, Boston University.

Frontispiece: Archibald Grimké, early in the twentieth century. Archibald Grimké Papers,
Box 39–40, Folder 789. Courtesy Moorland-Spingarn Research Center, Howard University.

The paper in this book meets the guidelines for permanence and durability of the Committee on
Production Guidelines for Book Longevity of the Council on Library Resources. ∞

This is Anna's book.

Contents

Illustrations

William Monroe Trotter
Roscoe Conkling Bruce
Mary White Ovington
Ulises Heureaux
O. G. Villard
Wendell Phillips

Preface

The story of Archibald Grimké, in its bare outline, is well-known to many American historians. Born a slave in South Carolina in 1849, one of three sons of a slave owner and a mulatto nurse, Grimké was also the nephew—initially unknown to them—of two of the most noted abolitionists, champions of racial equality and women's rights, the famous Grimké sisters, Angelina and Sarah, who had long since left South Carolina and settled in the North to work against the institution of slavery. Despite his slave origins, Grimké received some education in Charleston both before and after the Civil War and then, with his brother Francis, attended Lincoln University in the years immediately following the war. While there, he was "discovered," in a sense, by his noted aunts, who quickly accepted him as a member of their family and sponsored his further education, through Harvard Law School. He went on to a career as a racial activist and a writer.

The romance of Archibald Grimké's story is obvious and real. His life in slavery paralleled accounts found in antislavery autobiographies; the coincidence of his relationship to the famous sisters, and of his discovery by them, sounds like something out of a nineteenth-century novel. As both an activist and an intellectual, moreover, he became a notable figure during the tumultuous period of American race relations following Reconstruction and for the next half-century. Active in party politics beginning in the 1880s, he was, in the 1890s, an American consul to the Dominican Republic. Throughout his career, his advice and friendship were widely sought by other leaders, white and black, in the battle against racism and racial discrimination. And he was an influential participant in the early twentieth-century debate over philosophy and tactics that has come to be identified, simplistically, with the conflict between Booker T. Washington and W. E. B. Du Bois. Later, as president of the powerful Washington, D.C., branch of the National Association for the Advancement of Colored People (NAACP), a post he held for many years, he played an important role in efforts to influence action and opinion at the national level on racial questions. He was widely known during his time, remaining a visible personality almost until his death in 1930. He figures prominently, even now, in the accounts historians have written of racial thought and activism at the end of the nineteenth century and, indeed, through much of the decade of the 1920s.

But for all his relative prominence, Grimké remains a man unknown. As an activist, he has acquired a reputation for shifting allegiances that, ultimately, has little to do with either the role he sought to play or the role he did play in the difficult racial environment of post-Reconstruction and early twentieth-century America. As an intellectual and a writer, he produced an enormous amount of work—widely read biographies of Charles Sumner and William Lloyd Garrison as well as scores of pamphlets, magazine articles, and newspaper pieces—that was significant in its own time, however little noted it is in ours. As an individual, he experienced and confronted difficult and complicated social and cultural tendencies in a rapidly changing America, revealing much about the impact of those changes and their implications. His story represents an important chapter in the history of America; his life is one that deserves to be better known.

This is the first full-scale biography of Archibald Grimké, and it has involved the investigation of many different sources in many different places. The fundamental basis for this work was the large collection of Grimké family materials in the Moorland-Spingarn Research Center at Howard University, a finely organized and rich body of material that many scholars have consulted, with profit, on other topics. Additional research was done at other places, including the South Carolina Historical Society, the South Caroliniana Library, the William L. Clements Library of the University of Michigan, the Beinecke Rare Book and Manuscript Library at Yale University, the Houghton Library, the university archives, and the library of the Law School at Harvard University, the Library of Congress, the National Archives, the Boston University Library and the Boston Public Library, the Schomburg Center for Research in Black Culture of the New York Public Library, the University of California, San Diego, Library, and that of the University of California, Irvine. I am grateful to individuals at all those institutions for their assistance.

Completing this study was an expensive proposition, but financial help was provided to me by the National Endowment for the Humanities, the Academic Senate of the University of California, Irvine, along with the Division of Graduate Studies and Research, the Department of History, the Program in Comparative Culture, and the School of Social Sciences.

Special thanks should go, finally, to certain individuals. Among them are, particularly, Esme Bhan, of the Moorland-Spingarn Research Center, whose help with the Grimké family papers was enormous and whose encouragement of my work on the project was inestimable, and Michael Johnson, who lent not only his expertise but also a willing ear. I must also single out the efforts of three students who assisted me in the project at several points, Patricia Brooks, Kate Danaher, and Claire Joly, each of whom had to listen to far more about Archibald Grimké than, perhaps, anyone should. The patience, and fortitude, of my wife, Mary, and my daughter, Emily, have been beyond what anyone has a right to expect. I am grateful to all for their advice and assistance.

Archibald Grimké

1

Charleston

Archibald Grimké was born on August 17, 1849, at the Cane Acre plantation outside Charleston, the son of Henry Grimké, a planter and lawyer, and Nancy Weston, a slave of mixed ancestry who worked for the Grimké family. Nancy Weston had been the nurse for Henry's first wife, Selina, who died in 1843, and for their three children, Montague, Thomas, and Henrietta. Ultimately taking the name Grimké for herself, she was the mother of three sons by Henry. Archibald was the firstborn. A little over a year later, in 1850, his brother Francis was born; then, in 1852, the youngest brother, John.

The Grimké family into which Archibald was born was, on his father's side, one of the most famed and distinguished in Charleston and in South Carolina. Henry's father, John Faucheraud Grimké, was a colonel in the revolutionary war and, later, judge of the state supreme court. He was a man of wealth and substance, and, with his wife, Mary, the father of some fourteen children, eleven of whom survived to adulthood. Of these, several achieved distinction. There were, of course, the noted sisters Angelina and Sarah; but there was also Thomas Smith Grimké, one of the state's most original and independent thinkers at the time of his premature death in 1834, and Frederick Grimké, a scholarly attorney who removed to Ohio, where he served as a judge of that state's supreme court. The eldest son, John, distinguished himself as one of Charleston's most successful physicians.[1]

Henry could not claim such distinction. Born in January, 1801, the

1. Barnwell Rhett Heyward, "The Descendants of Col. William Rhett, of South Carolina," *South Carolina Historical and Genealogical Society Magazine,* IV (1903), 50–51.

ninth child and youngest son to reach adulthood, he was always a bit "indolent" and undisciplined, giving his family some trouble in his youth and never showing the drive his more famous siblings displayed. Like many other young white South Carolinians, he felt the call to be a planter and, at the death of his father in 1819, was given a family plantation in up-country Union County to manage. With his brother Thomas' encouragement, he studied law and ultimately abandoned up-country life to join his brother's Charleston firm in 1823, about a year before his marriage to the seventeen-year-old Selina Simmons. He was a good lawyer and built a successful practice in Charleston.[2]

Nancy Weston's background is obscure, and it is not known when she entered the Grimké household. Her father may have been white; she was clearly of mixed blood, although her mother was dark in complexion. In addition, she numbered among her kinspeople many free people of color; the name Weston was common in Charleston's free Negro community, including some of that community's wealthiest members, although she herself was not obviously connected with the more affluent Westons.

It is difficult to trace the course of the relationship between Henry and Nancy. She was a strong member of the Grimké household, taking much of the responsibility for raising the Grimkés' children and accepting little interference from either Henry or Selina as she went about her business. She had once thrown Henry to the floor when he threatened, on Selina's orders, to whip her, something he never attempted again. The relationship between the two began to take shape shortly after Selina's death, when Henry was in his mid-forties and Nancy about thirty-three. It blossomed after about 1847, when, following an unsuccessful run for a seat on the state supreme court, Henry decided to change his life and to abandon his urban, professional career for that of a planter. He acquired Cane Acre, a rice plantation in St. Paul's Parish, out from Charleston in Colleton County, with a work force of about thirty slaves. Nancy moved there with him. She did not live in the plantation house with Henry and his children but in a small house of her own across the yard. She continued to work in Henry's home but also did work for herself, raising chickens, pigs, and ducks that were considered her property. She remained

2. Adrienne Koch, ed., "A Family Crisis: Letters from John Faucheraud Grimké and Thomas Smith Grimké to Henry Grimké, 1818," *South Carolina Historical Magazine*, LXIX (1968), 171–92; John Belton O'Neall, *Biographical Sketches of the Bench and Bar of South Carolina* (2 vols., 1859; rpr. Spartanburg, 1975), II, 542.

close to Henry's children and played a prominent role in the business of the plantation generally. As she later told her son, she pretty much ran things on the Grimké estate.[3]

Certainly, she continued to influence Henry. She told her son of the time the plantation overseer got in a fit with the field hands, ordering them to work on the traditional day off for slaves, Sunday, as punishment. Nancy Weston objected and argued to Henry that such an action would be "disgraceful." Henry countermanded the order.[4]

Life on Cane Acre encouraged the relationship between Nancy Weston and Henry Grimké, and the possibilities for its realization grew stronger when the children left Henry's house for schooling, spending most of their time in Charleston and elsewhere while Henry and Nancy remained at home in Colleton County, managing the plantation and starting a family of their own. Nancy played an active role in the life of Henry's first family. Not only had she seen the children through their mother's death and taken charge of them thereafter, but she continued to participate in their lives, as in Henry's, while they were away at school. Although she could not read or write, she sent news to them through Henry's letters during their school years. She reported, especially, on the state of the ducks. She had been particularly fond of a parcel of Muscovies that died in an early freeze. And she prepared gifts for the boys, who were studying at the Citadel, giving them loving care and attention.[5]

In his letters to his sons, Henry always mentioned Nancy with affection. In one letter, he talked about an episode of fever that had put her in bed for over two weeks. Henry took her into his house and nursed her continuously during that time, using what he called his "practice, little physic and a plenty of starvation." By the time he wrote the letter, she had been free of fever for three days, but he still wanted her to rest and to wait until her own house got warm before he would let her return to it. Nancy, for her part, later told Archie that she had "believed absolutely" in Henry Grimké.[6]

3. Archibald H. Grimké, "Memoirs of Archibald H. Grimké," 88–89, in Archibald H. Grimké Papers, Box 2, Folder 47, Moorland-Spingarn Research Center, Howard University, Washington, D.C.; Koch, ed., "Family Crisis," 178; Henry Grimké, Broadside notice [ca. 1847], in South Caroliniana Library, University of South Carolina, Columbia.

4. Archibald Grimké, "Memoirs," 1–2.

5. Henry Grimké to E. Montague Grimké, October 1, 1850, July 21, 1851, in E. Montague Grimké Papers, South Caroliniana Library, University of South Carolina, Columbia.

6. Archibald Grimké, "Memoirs," 4; Henry Grimké to Dear Boys, n.d., in E. Montague Grimké Papers.

It would be a mistake, however, to assume that Henry shared his more famous abolitionist sisters' racial enlightenment. As a young man, he was a notably cruel master. One of the sharpest conflicts he ever had with his sister Angelina was over his treatment of a slave, and she confronted him during the late 1820s about his habitual cruelty toward his manservant, John. Examples of Henry's brutality proved especially useful to Angelina when she sought to lay bare slavery's cruel potentialities in her fight for its abolition. Both sisters felt better about him in later years, but he remained strongly attached to slavery and, whatever feelings he had for Nancy, to white supremacy. In a letter to Montague, for instance, he professed his faith in the doctrines of equality proclaimed in the American Declaration of Independence but concluded, "These remarks apply exclusively to the Caucasian race."[7]

Nevertheless, once Henry and Nancy had made their place at Cane Acre, they quickly created a family for themselves. Archie was born within a bit more than a year of the move, Frank and John soon thereafter. The relationship between Henry and the sons Nancy bore him was distant but affectionate. Certainly, Henry did not consider them slaves; he did not list them as such in the 1850 census of slaves on his plantation. Archie and Frank lived in the little house occupied by their mother, but Archie often went to the front door of his father's home, calling Henry out by making the sound of a horse's neigh and, after a little playful teasing, getting a reward. In an interesting reversal of one of the hoariest conventions of African-American autobiography, Archie recalled that his father named him. According to Archie, all the slave children on the plantation were automatically called James, and this applied to him as well. His father objected, however, and changed his son's name to Archibald, calling him Archie—a diminutive he kept for the rest of his life—from the beginning (the middle name, Henry, probably came later).[8]

Thus if Henry did not really treat his family like a family, he nevertheless showed affection for his sons and expressed hopes for them as well. After Frank's birth in November, 1850, Henry began to make plans to send Nancy and their children to Charleston so that the boys would not have to grow up on the plantation, a plan that accorded

7. Katharine Du Pre Lumpkin, *The Emancipation of Angelina Grimké* (Chapel Hill, 1974), 56–57; Henry Grimké to E. Montague Grimké, July 21, 1851, in E. Montague Grimké Papers.

8. Archibald Grimké, "Memoirs," 1.

well with what seem to have been Nancy's efforts, almost from the beginning, to live as independently as possible, though legally enslaved. The plan was credible. There were many such quasi-free slaves in Charleston during the late 1840s and early 1850s, who, though legally slaves, lived essentially free lives. This was particularly so because, since 1820, South Carolina law had been intended to make manumission impossible. Such was the status Henry proposed for his mulatto family, and Nancy had no reason to doubt him. She had a brother, Isaac, who seems to have occupied just such a position.[9]

The plan probably gained in credibility because of Nancy's easy entrée into the free and quasi-free black community that was so visible in Charleston in the decade before the Civil War. Having free relatives meant that she would not go wholly unprepared to live on her own in the city. Henry's intention was to leave the family in the care of Nancy's free relatives, providing money to ensure the comfort of her and her sons.[10]

These plans fell through, however, in September, 1852, shortly before the birth of Henry and Nancy's third son, when an epidemic of typhoid swept through the South Carolina low country and Henry was afflicted. He was ill for two weeks, nursed ceaselessly by Nancy, and died on September 28. The plantation did not survive his death for long. Within a few months, it and everything on it, including its slave work force—and Nancy's pigs, chickens, and ducks—was sold at auction.[11]

Nancy and her sons, however, were not sold in the auction. A few months after Archie's birth, Henry had added a codicil to his will providing for special treatment for them. Telling Nancy at the time that he could not free her because such an action was forbidden by South Carolina laws, which he approved, he proposed that, after his death, ownership of Nancy and any children should pass to his eldest son by Selina, Montague, in whom, he said, he had the greatest confidence. He also led Nancy to believe that he had made provision in his will for the protection of her family, confidentially binding Montague not to interfere with them. Archibald Grimké later remembered that Henry had assured Nancy of his "entire good faith" and appeared to have

9. *Ibid.*, 8–9; Michael P. Johnson and James L. Roark, *Black Masters: A Free Family of Color in the Old South* (New York: 1984), 35–36.

10. Archibald Grimké, "Memoirs," 4; Johnson and Roark, *Black Masters,* 50.

11. Koch, ed., "Family Crisis," 178; Heyward, "Descendants of Col. William Rhett," 50–51; Henry Justin Ferry, "Francis James Grimké: Portrait of a Black Puritan" (Ph.D. dissertation, Yale University, 1970), 19.

thought out the contingencies of their future life fairly fully. He told her that, though he would not free her, he would "leave you better than free, because I leave you to be taken care of." [12]

As it turned out, the will Henry left was remarkably general in its language, as Archibald Grimké was to learn when he saw it in 1906. But its general nature confirmed what Nancy felt was a "good faith" promise on Henry's part. Consistent with South Carolina law, it set no conditions on Montague, merely giving to him "and his heirs forever" the "Mulatto Servant girl named Nancy, with her present and future issue and increase." The lack of conditions is less striking than the singling out of Nancy and her children; nothing else in Henry's "property" received special notice. The will simply made one of his sisters, Eliza, executrix and gave her the authority to do with the estate as she saw fit, except for Henry's second family. [13]

That Eliza had some sense of the commitment her brother had made is indicated by her actions after the family became her responsibility. Whether she knew how close the relationship between Henry and Nancy had been is hard to say. Certainly, everyone knew that Nancy had worked diligently for Henry and, before, for Selina and her children. And, of course, there was the evidence of her two, and then three, mixed babies of whom Henry's fatherhood could not have been difficult to conjecture. In any case, she did arrange for them the quasi-free status Henry promised. She had them brought to Charleston, where they went to live, along with Montague, at this time not quite twenty years old, in the home Eliza shared with another sister, Mary. Eliza had set aside the proceeds from the sale of Nancy's livestock at auction and, a short time later, Nancy used those funds to pay for a cottage of her own, built by Samuel O'Hear, a free black drayman about Nancy's age who was a first cousin of her mother's and who owned the lot on which the cottage was built. There she and her sons were to live, occupying a status very like freedom, for the next eight years, the white Grimkés interfering with their lives not at all. [14]

12. Archibald Grimké to Angelina Grimké Weld, February 20, 1868, typed copy, in Archibald Grimké Papers, Box 1, Folder 9. On South Carolina law, see Johnson and Roark, *Black Masters,* 46.

13. Angelina Weld Grimké, Autobiographical sketch, in Angelina Weld Grimké Papers, Box 6, Folder 100, Moorland-Spingarn Research Center, Howard University, Washington, D.C.; Will of Henry Grimké, August 24, 1848, Codicil, December 15, 1849, Court of Probate, Will Book No. L, 1851–56, p. 103, Charleston, South Carolina.

14. Ferry, "Francis James Grimké," 12.

No one in Henry's white family did much to make good on his promise to provide the family with protection, however. As Archibald, at the age of eighteen, put it, Nancy was "thrown upon the uncharitable world to struggle with its foaming billows alone." Taking in washing and ironing from several Charleston hotels—work found with the help of Eliza—to support the family, Nancy found a quasi-freedom that meant more than a separation from white supervision; it was also a freedom to provide for her family, and the job was not easy. Archie later remembered these as years of grinding poverty, "bitter years." The family had little to eat, and at least some of that was furnished by two uncles—one of them Nancy's brother Isaac—who were butchers and who gave the family meat that would not sell readily.[15]

Despite the bitter poverty, Nancy worked hard to make what she saw as a proper life for her sons, not only materially but morally and culturally as well. Despite her constant struggle to support the family financially, she was able to give it a moral center. In his mid-thirties, when Archie gave a lecture based loosely on her life entitled, tellingly, "A Madonna of the South," it was this characteristic that he emphasized about her. An extremely religious woman, she trained her sons to stay away from tobacco, alcohol, and profanity, and she inculcated in them a background of piety that was to remain with Archibald and Francis, at least, all of their lives. In keeping with the domestic ethos of the nineteenth century, she did much to give her sons a sense that their home was a moral haven in a corrupt world and that her own virtue could give them the protection they needed.[16]

Nancy could provide such an influence because she was always willing to stand up for her children, just as she had always stood up for herself. One of his boyhood friends remembered her readiness "to face death in the defense and protection of her children," and Archibald concurred. She was certainly willing to confront white Charlestonians, as Archie remembered well. When, for example, one of the pigeons he kept for a youthful hobby got away, Nancy caught it for him, only to have a white family living next door try to claim it as their own. Nancy refused to give it up, and when the white woman hit her, Nancy threw the woman to the ground. Another white neighbor intervened, ordering the white woman out of Nancy's yard, and peace

15. Archibald Grimké to Angelina Grimké Weld, February 20, 1868; Archibald Grimké, "Memoirs," 8–9.
16. Boston *Hub,* May 31, 1884.

(along with the pigeon) was restored before any further damage was done. She would not always be so successful at protecting her children, but she would never shrink from the effort.[17]

Nancy had high hopes for her sons and encouraged them to develop ties not only with the Charleston free black community to which she was related but, as much as possible, with the elite portion of that very class- and color-conscious community. Coming Street, where they lived, was something of a center of free black life in Charleston; some of the city's most prominent families lived there, and Archie made most of his friends from among the children of free people on Coming and elsewhere in the city. Among them were Thomas Miller and T. McCants Stewart, both born free and both to achieve prominence in public affairs after the Civil War. Other friends and playmates included cousins Francis and John Weston, probably sons of his uncle Isaac, and Arthur O'Hear, one of the eight children of Samuel O'Hear and his wife, Julia, a dressmaker, who lived out on Line Street.[18]

Nancy encouraged strong ties to this community in a variety of ways. Poor as she was, she did what she could to ensure that her sons should receive an education and that they should go to school with the children of Charleston's free black elite. Although technically illegal, there were a number of schools for free blacks in antebellum Charleston, including some on Coming Street, and these schools provided opportunities for both education and social contact.[19]

Archie and Frank attended several schools, beginning at about the ages of five or six, the first offering little more than the rudiments of the alphabet and numbers, later ones a bit more. Nancy paid one dollar a month for her sons to stay in school, which they did until about 1862. Not only did she work to pay for their education, but, though unable to read herself, she listened patiently as her sons recited texts they had learned to read and sought to memorize. Like Frederick Douglass with the *Columbian Orator,* Archie learned from books of

17. Thomas C. Miller to Angelina Weld Grimké, March 26, 1925, in Angelina Weld Grimké Papers; Box 1, Folder 12; Archibald Grimké, "Memoirs," 46–48.

18. See, for example, T. McCants Stewart to Francis J. Grimké, July 18, 1920, in Francis J. Grimké Papers, Box 5, Folder 224, Moorland-Spingarn Research Center, Howard University, Washington, D.C.

19. Angelina W. Grimké, "A Biographical Sketch of Archibald H. Grimké," *Opportunity,* III (February, 1925), 45; C. W. Birnie, "Education of the Negro in Charleston, South Carolina, Prior to the Civil War," *Journal of Negro History,* XII (1927), 19–20; William C. Hine, "Frustration, Factionalism, and Failure: Black Political Leadership and the Republican Party in Reconstruction Charleston, 1865–1877" (Ph.D. dissertation, Kent State University, 1979), 12.

speeches, called "Speakers," given heavily to patriotic themes and thus to the doctrines of freedom and liberty which were so contrary to the orthodoxies of the slave South. In retrospect, he gave those speeches much credit for his own intellectual emancipation from slave society.[20]

He also cemented his ties to his childhood friends as they went to school together. Archie and his brothers, despite their nominal slave status, met no barriers from their free kinsmen and companions. Their mixed origins and light complexions probably helped balance out their legal status within the group. They played together, and they fought together, too, even confronting gangs of white boys on the street as they made their way to school. Archie later recalled having been quite a fighter, with skills to complement those of his brothers: John was the leading "butter," Frank, the "champion 'biter.'" Archie was known for his ability as a "kicker," and together they made a fairly invincible team, especially when they were joined by their mates from school.[21]

Nancy also helped to firm the boys' religious connections in free black society. Though Nancy was a Baptist, an organization that appealed most strongly to slaves and the free lower class, by the end of the decade she had enrolled her sons in a Presbyterian Sunday school and church, the Zion Church, that catered to the city's black elite. The Sunday school was conducted by some of the more aristocratic young ladies in Charleston's free society, and it provided a place where, as Archie later remembered, he and his brothers found a congenial environment in company with their friends from school.[22]

Nancy obviously wanted her sons to find a niche compatible with what she had fought for in her own life and with the promises Henry had expressed, despite their legal status. She had never been accommodating to slavery, and she raised her sons in a way that distanced them from the institution as much as possible, given the realities of Charleston life.

At the same time, she had no illusions about the world her sons were entering. She worried, for example, about their fights with white boys on the way to school. Despite her own willingness to stand

20. Archibald Grimké, "Memoirs," 14–15.

21. Angelina W. Grimké, "Biographical Sketch," 45; Thomas Miller to Angelina Weld Grimké, March 26, 1925, in Angelina Weld Grimké Papers; Archibald Grimké, "Memoirs," 17.

22. Ferry, "Francis James Grimké," 24; Luther P. Jackson, "Religious Instruction of Negroes, 1830–1860, with Special Reference to South Carolina," *Journal of Negro History,* XV (1930), 100–102, 104–105; Archibald Grimké, "Memoirs," 13.

up to anyone, she did what she could to prevent her boys from fighting and thus to minimize the still greater danger that could arise. They tried to follow her advice, Archie later recalled, and suffered for it. Finally, a friend persuaded her that the boys had to be allowed to defend themselves against the white boys who were bothering them, and she had to relent, though she was not comfortable doing so.[23]

Archibald Grimké remembered that, young as he was, he had a good idea of his place in the world of late antebellum Charleston. Although he lived primarily among free people, he never forgot that he was a member of a society in which race was the ultimate reality, in which every black person, regardless of status, was vulnerable to the demands of a dominant white ruling structure, in which every black person, free or not, had to adjust to the power of that structure. In a memorial to his childhood friend Joseph Lee, written later in life, Archie recalled the vulnerability that he had already learned to feel after the death of his father. Paraphrasing the awful words of Justice Roger Taney in the *Dred Scott* decision by saying that in slave society, "the colored boy and girl, the colored man and woman, whether bond or free, had no rights which the white boy and girl, the white man and woman were bound by law or public opinion to respect," he described black life as a battle for "self-preservation" and asserted that "they learned early to pass much of their lives in an underworld—in an underworld, far removed from the white man's eyes and ears."[24]

Clearly, whatever privileges he may have enjoyed, Archie had no illusions that his being a child of Henry Grimké gave him an immunity from the conditions that faced anyone who was not white in antebellum Charleston. For him, white Charleston was a distinct and mostly hostile community; he knew that relief came only by avoiding that community as much as possible.

Archie's understanding of race was to be powerfully enhanced while he was still a child with the coming of the Civil War. As sectional tensions heightened at the close of the 1850s, so, too, did the difficulties facing Charleston's blacks, both free and slave. These difficulties have been fully documented by historians. Race relations became more tense as all blacks became objects of increasing suspicion. As Michael Johnson and James Roark have shown, these suspicions led to a wave of arrests of blacks unable to prove their right to indepen-

23. Archibald Grimké, "Memoirs," 17.
24. Archibald H. Grimké, "Joseph Lee," in Archibald Grimké Papers, Box 18, Folder 349.

dence; they culminated, by August of 1860, in the reenslavement of many people who had lived free for years and a threat to enslave even those who had been wholly free for generations. Though only ten or eleven years old at this time, Archie, as well as his brothers and their companions, were aware of the tensions that were developing in Charleston. With the coming of secession at the end of 1860, when he was eleven, the tension became especially strong and, soon enough, especially personal.[25]

Although Nancy and her sons appear to have lived a fairly stable life during the 1850s, that stability ceased abruptly in 1860, when Montague decided to put an end to the independence the family had known and to bring Archie into his home as a house servant. Whether he was influenced by the general crisis facing Charleston's black community is not known. Montague was strongly aware of the changes taking place because he served, from the beginning of the crisis, as a member of a commission appointed to deal with the removal of blacks "and other property" from Charleston in the event of an invasion. Archie later remembered that Montague's behavior toward him worsened along with conditions in Charleston.[26]

But conditions in Montague's own life had changed as well. In 1855, at the age of twenty-two, he had married Julia Hibben, but she died in 1857. Then, in September, 1860, he married Julia Catherine Bridges of Alabama. It quickly became apparent that her housekeeping requirements differed from those of her predecessor.[27]

Thus it was not long after Montague's marriage to Julia Bridges that Archie and Frank were called to his home by their elderly aunts Mary and Eliza, who lived with him, and told that when they met her they were to say, "How do you do mistress and how glad we are to meet you." They refused, but they did respond to the new bride with a simple bow. She gave the distinct impression of being pleased with them, an impression that, especially in the context of the time, worried them and, later, their mother. They were right to feel concerned because it was only shortly thereafter that Montague made his decision known and Archie, over Nancy's protests, became a family servant. Soon after, Frank, too, was taken in, leaving only young John to enjoy

25. Johnson and Roark, *Black Masters,* chaps. 6–7; Archibald Grimké, "Memoirs," 53–54.

26. Documents related to Montague Grimké's work on the commission are in Grimké Family Papers, Folders 42–47, South Carolina Historical Society, Charleston; Archibald Grimké, "Memoirs," 53.

27. Heyward, "Descendants of Col. William Rhett," 69.

the freedom all had previously shared. He, too, would be taken before the war's end.[28]

There was little to separate Archie's life in Montague's household from that of other slaves. His duties were not difficult, chiefly consisting of running errands and waiting table. Montague did compromise with their father's intent a bit, allowing the two boys to continue living with their mother, only working days in their half-brother's household (a pattern not unusual within the city of Charleston). They were even permitted to continue attending school throughout their time in his service. Nevertheless, there was little else to differentiate their experiences from those of others trapped in Charleston's most prominent institution. They were subjected to the white Grimkés' total discipline and authority.[29]

Archie did not take easily to his enslavement. Montague's aunt Eliza was Archie's chief supervisor, and Archie—showing early signs of a stubbornness that was never to leave—consistently resisted her instruction, feigning stupidity and refusing to learn his duties with any quickness. One of his jobs was to set the table, and he almost always did it incorrectly, forcing Eliza to rearrange everything after he had finished. Frank was even less amenable to his new role and showed it not simply by doing his work poorly but by leaving whenever he felt like it. As was the case earlier in their lives, when they habitually fought with white boys, Nancy worried about the situations her sons were putting themselves in and, though a fighter herself, knew the limitations that had to be observed. Despite her efforts to prevent their being enslaved, she counseled them to patience and returned Frank, apologetically, when he absconded. She urged Archie to work conscientiously. In neither case were her efforts very successful.[30]

Archie, however, soon learned the problems with which his mother was already familiar and became powerfully aware of the extreme vulnerability of anyone held in slavery and of the arbitrary violence of slaveholders. On one occasion, on his way home from work, he stepped on a piece of glass and badly cut his foot. The next morning, he was unable to get to work; the injury kept him at home for several days. Finally, Montague and his wife, becoming impatient, went to Nancy's home for him. Despite the compromises Nancy had

28. Archibald Grimké, "Memoirs," 27–28; Archibald Grimké to Angelina Grimké Weld, February 20, 1868.

29. Richard C. Wade, *Slavery in the Cities: The South, 1820–1860* (New York, 1964), 32.

30. Archibald Grimké, "Memoirs," 29–30.

earlier been forced to make, she had not lost her fire, and she turned on Montague, reminding him that Archie was Henry's child and therefore Montague's brother and of his agreement to take care of the family after Henry's death. Montague called her a liar—though surely he must have known better—and flew into a rage. He did not strike her, but he went to the police. She was arrested and taken to the workhouse, a Charleston facility for the punishment of slaves, where she was confined in a cell for about a week. Eating nothing while there, she finally became so ill that the family physician urged Montague to have her released, which he did.[31]

Neither Archie nor Montague, however, was chastened by the experience. The conflict between the two continued until Archie had worked in Montague's house for almost two years, well into 1862, when an episode occurred that brought things to a head. Archie had been asked to build a fire to warm the dining room for breakfast but was unable to get it to burn to Montague's satisfaction. For this failure, he suffered a severe beating, Montague flogging the boy with his slipper. Archie screamed, but Montague continued the beating until he was out of breath. Montague's wife, Julia, who had often expressed a fondness for Archie, only cautioned her husband, lest the Grimkés get a reputation for cruelty. To protect their reputation, they decided to have the punishment administered at the workhouse, and Archie was taken there at once.[32]

Charleston's workhouse was not a place where Archie could have expected leniency, and he received none. Although he was only thirteen years old, he was the victim of a flogging, the severity of which Montague demanded. The boy's feet were put in stocks and his hands tied to a sort of pulley. A dirty cap was put over his head, and his bare back was tightly stretched. Each blow of the leather strap drew blood, and the flogging lasted so long that he lost count of the strokes. He knew, however, that he had received at least thirty, a severe punishment even by the standards of the time. Archie remained defiant. He told the man with the strap that Montague had done this "to his own brother." The anger on his face when he returned to Montague's house led the "sympathetic" Julia to suggest that Montague had not "given him half enough." Later, the equally recalcitrant Frank was sent for a dose of the same slaveholder's medicine.[33]

31. *Ibid.*, 71–75; Archibald Grimké to Angelina Grimké Weld, February 20, 1868.
32. Archibald Grimké, "Memoirs," 53–54.
33. *Ibid.;* on the Charleston workhouse, see Wade, *Slavery in the Cities,* 96–97.

Archie was sent home to his mother's care. He decided to run away, a decision in which his younger brother concurred. This was not a safe course of action. Charleston authorities were always on the lookout for runaways, and anyone known to be harboring an escaped slave could be in real trouble. Free Negroes who did so could be enslaved. Thus Archie did not tell his mother about his plan, not wanting to place her in jeopardy as a suspected accomplice. Until Montague came looking for him, she thought he had resumed his duties in Montague's home.[34]

What he had done was to go to the house next door, the home of another black family, seeking refuge. There was already another escaped slave in the house, a woman, and her presence led to a narrow escape for Archie within a short time. The authorities had learned about her and came to retake her. She tried to flee and even sought help from Nancy, but she was captured after a brief struggle. Archie knew he could not remain where he was, nor could he go home, so, under cover of darkness, he found refuge in the home of another free black family, who took him in after seeing how badly he had been beaten. He stayed only a few weeks, however, before the woman of the house, worried about her own vulnerability, begged him to leave. He then hid in a little house in the yard.

By this time, his mother knew what he had done and, although she had avoided contact with him for several weeks, now came for him and brought him back to his own home. But she had also reached her own limits and, despite her earlier feeling of a need to compromise with Montague's authority, now determined to help her son escape.

It was impossible, of course, for Archie to stay with his mother. He was too vulnerable there to Montague's searches. But now wartime conditions seemed to offer better opportunities. His mother contacted a free black man and distant relative, Thomas Cole, a drayman, who lived on Line Street, for assistance. Cole, who had bought his own freedom and that of his family, followed the war closely in the newspapers, and his whole family favored the Union cause. Cole offered to take Archie, along with a group of other runaways, to join the flood of slaves seizing freedom by fleeing to the Union lines. Archie was not to make it that far, but he did leave for the Coles' home.

Simply getting to the Coles' was not easy because he had to go from Coming to Line without being seen. The solution was to dress him as a girl, and in that disguise, he made his way under cover of

34. Archibald Grimké, "Memoirs," 58.

darkness to the Coles. The escape was successful, and Archie entered the house he was not to leave for over two years, until the fall of Charleston in February, 1865.

Montague continued to look for him during this time, although he apparently learned his lesson in dealing with Archie's mother and did not use her to try to get at her sons. Even white family members had taken him to task for sending her to the workhouse, and he was stymied in any attempt to get her to reveal Archie's whereabouts.[35]

Nevertheless, Archie felt his life at the Coles' to be precarious. He was afraid to go outside the house, at least in daytime, and the blinds were kept closed lest anyone passing by see him inside. He recalled being so frightened of being seen that he was reluctant to pass before a window, closed blinds or no. The gate to the house was kept locked, and the family devised a warning system to signal Archie to run upstairs in the event of any apparent danger. Archie was so skittish that one member of the household, with more than a touch of politically tinged sarcasm, nicknamed him "Morgan," after the Confederate guerrilla leader John Hunt Morgan, "because like Morgan I was always retreating."[36]

Nevertheless, he tried to maintain something of a life while in hiding. The Coles had children of their own, and Archie mixed in with them, even disguised as a girl, attending their sessions with Alrek Francis, a free black man who went from house to house as a teacher during the war. And he put his education to use by serving as the family's designated reader. He read newspapers, focusing on the war news, especially the fortunes of the Union troops. He also read books, including Harriet Beecher Stowe's *Uncle Tom's Cabin,* Hinton Rowan Helper's *Impending Crisis*—books almost as dangerous for the Coles to harbor in wartime Charleston as a runaway slave—and a not entirely irrelevant pair of novels about love and noble action across class lines, Charles Reade's comedy of manners, *"Love Me Little, Love Me Long,"* and Wilkie Collins' *Dead Secret.* He later remembered being powerfully moved by Stowe's work, in particular, weeping over the deaths of Eva St. Clair and Uncle Tom and following Eliza's escape with great excitement. But Archie's life in hiding was not always easy. Not only did he fear being captured—a fear that increased when he once saw Montague riding by the house—but he had other difficulties. Once, when desperately ill, he knew he could not risk seeking

35. *Ibid.,* 76.
36. *Ibid.,* 72.

medical attention and even had to endure a discussion of what should be done with his body should he die so that it would not be discovered that the Coles had harbored him.[37]

But he survived, and when the city fell, was able to emerge from hiding. In the immediate postwar period he was reunited with his family. Frank, too, had known adventure during the war. He, too, had resisted Montague's efforts to make him a slave. Archie recalled that "when they took my brother Frank, they soon found out they had caught a Tartar." And he, too, had run away. First, he went to the Confederate army, where he served as a valet for about two years. On a brief visit to Charleston, however, he was recognized, arrested, and taken to the workhouse, where he was held for several months. He fell seriously ill during that time and was finally sent back to Montague for care. By this time, Montague had apparently learned his lesson about Frank and, rather than try to keep the youngster at home, sold him. His new owner was an officer in the Confederate army, and young Frank finished out the war in the officer's service, returning to his mother with the end of the war and the coming of freedom.[38]

The fall of Charleston was the beginning of a time of excitement and change for the Grimké family. Archie and Frank entered into the excitement with a spirit of adventure. Almost as soon as the city fell, they, along with cousins Arthur O'Hear and Francis Weston, offered themselves as officers' boys to the Union soldiers and were immediately taken on. They witnessed skirmishes between the occupying forces and a few rebel holdouts and were put to work scavenging for food for the officers from the surrounding countryside. Archie remembered that as a particular adventure, especially when six or more of the officers' boys were all chasing after the same chicken, each hoping to please his employer. But not everything about their new lives was fun; Archie later remembered the hardship of accompanying the troops on marches in the rain and mud of wintertime Charleston, and, ultimately, he and all his companions were invalided home with chills and fever. Frank went first, Archie, last.[39]

The end of the war brought an end to any contact between the two different Grimké families. Frank threatened to whip Montague after the war ended, and Montague, perhaps aware of the spirit of his father's other family, kept out of sight. But other events were taking place

37. *Ibid.,* 77–80.
38. *Ibid.,* 80; Francis J. Grimké to "Dear Bro," January 24, 1887, in Francis Grimké Papers, Box 1, Folder 1.
39. Archibald Grimké, "Memoirs," 98–101.

in the city and in the family that were to have major effects on the lives of Archie and his brother Frank.

Among the first institutions and opportunities to take shape for blacks in postwar Charleston concerned education. Immediately after the occupation of Charleston, the military seized the schools and established a Bureau of Education, which moved to provide public education for blacks. Among those created soon after the war was the Morris Street School. Nancy was employed as a housekeeper for the school and was thus able to find places for her sons to study there. The school was under the leadership of Frances Pillsbury, who had been a school principal in Massachusetts before coming to Charleston with her husband, Gilbert—abolitionist, Freedmen's Bureau agent, and, later, Republican mayor of the city—at the close of the war.[40]

Although it is not known what subjects the Grimké boys studied in Pillsbury's school, the curriculum was probably similar to that of other freedmen's schools led by northern teachers that offered students a mixture of basic education, moral uplift, and antislavery ideas, none of which Archie would have found unfamiliar.[41]

But more significant than the curricula they studied was that coming into contact with Pillsbury ensured that their stay in Reconstruction Charleston would be brief. Frances Pillsbury was well-connected in abolitionist circles. Archibald and Francis Grimké quickly caught her attention, in part because of their obvious ability as students but also because of their last name. She, of course, knew of the Grimké sisters in Massachusetts, and she was intrigued that three of her brightest pupils shared the same last name, although, apparently, she did not pursue the connection. Nevertheless, she asked Archie if his mother would permit him and Frank to go to the North to continue their education, and Nancy, who was ambitious for them, readily agreed. By the fall of 1865 Pillsbury had corresponded with people in the North and made arrangements for them with Samuel E. Sewall, an abolitionist and a friend of the Grimké sisters. Toward the end of the year, when Archie was sixteen and Frank fifteen, they left Charleston to begin the next phase of their lives.

40. Joel Williamson, *After Slavery: The Negro in South Carolina During Reconstruction, 1861–1877* (Chapel Hill, 1965), 211; Angelina W. Grimké, "Biographical Sketch," 45. On Gilbert Pillsbury, see Hine, "Frustration, Factionalism, and Failure," 63–65, 128–33, 167.

41. Robert Morris, *Reading, 'Riting, and Reconstruction: The Education of Freedmen in the South, 1861–1870* (Chicago, 1981), 174–80, 208; Leon F. Litwack, *Been in the Storm So Long: The Aftermath of Slavery* (New York, 1979), 481, 500.

2

Lincoln

Archibald Grimké and his brother Francis left Charleston filled with hopes and expectations. They went first to Hilton Head Island, south of the city, where they were put under the care of Major Martin R. Delany, the outspoken former abolitionist and pan-Africanist who had been a physician in the Union army and was serving at that time as a subassistant commissioner of the Freedmen's Bureau at Hilton Head. He put the young men on a boat to New York, where they went first to the office of the bureau and then by train to Springfield, Massachusetts. In Springfield, they stayed briefly at the home of Dr. Jefferson Church, who treated them to what Archie later remembered as a powerful experience, a performance of Shakespeare's *King Lear,* featuring the great actor Edwin Forrest.[1]

After their visit with Dr. Church, the brothers made their way to Boston, where they stopped in at the New England office of the Freedmen's Aid Society—seeing, among others, the illustrious young black abolitionist Charlotte Forten—and received assistance in reaching their new homes. Frank was settled with a family in Stoneham, Massachusetts, a few miles north of Boston. Archie went to live with a family in Peacedale, Rhode Island, near the coast. The boys were expected to work, in return for which the families were to provide them with room, board, and education.[2]

The situation was not, however, entirely what they expected, and

1. Archibald H. Grimké, "Memoirs of Archibald H. Grimké," 103–106, in Archibald H. Grimké Papers, Box 2, Folder 47, Moorland-Spingarn Research Center, Howard University, Washington, D.C.
   2. *Ibid.,* 107–109.

Archie soon began to feel that the stay in the North was not giving him the opportunities he had hoped for. His mother was aware of this, and, deeply concerned, went to Frances Pillsbury for help. In April, 1866, Pillsbury arranged an interview for the brothers with Isaac Rendall, president of Lincoln University in Pennsylvania, with a view to their admission there. Rendall worried about their relative youth and lack of education, but, ultimately, he was sufficiently impressed with them to be persuaded that, despite their ages, they were prepared to enter the school. They began their studies there almost immediately, Archie supported by a church in New York, Frank by a Squire Hotchkiss, also of New York.[3]

Lincoln University, located near Chester, Pennsylvania, was almost a decade old when the Grimké brothers arrived in 1866. Founded by the Presbyterian minister John M. Dickey after he had difficulty finding a spot for a black student in any Pennsylvania seminary, the school had initially been known as Ashmun Institute, named for Jehudi Ashmun, a colonizationist and "conductor" in the early effort to settle Liberia.[4]

At the time Archie and Frank Grimké entered Lincoln—its name changed in 1866 to honor the great emancipator—it was a small but growing institution. There were 88 students in 1867, the brothers' first full year there. Some were young, like Archie and Frank and like their boyhood friend Thomas Miller, who was among their classmates, but at least 30 were veterans of the Civil War. The student body had grown rapidly by the time the Grimkés graduated in 1870, when there were 174 students. The faculty was small—two professors and two tutors in 1867, with a third added during the period Archie and Frank were there.[5]

The university consisted of two main departments. The Preparatory Department was designed to prepare young men for collegiate work, and in the years immediately following emancipation, it en-

3. Francis J. Grimké to "Dear Bro," January 24, 1887, in Francis J. Grimké Papers, Box 1, Folder 1, Moorland-Spingarn Research Center, Howard University, Washington, D.C.; Angelina W. Grimké, "A Biographical Sketch of Archibald H. Grimké," *Opportunity*, III (February, 1925), 45; Katherine Du Pre Lumpkin, *The Emancipation of Angelina Grimké* (Chapel Hill, 1974), 226.

4. Horace Mann Bond, *Education for Freedom: A History of Lincoln University, Pennsylvania* ([Lincoln University, Pa.], 1976), 153, 210–11, 235.

5. Bond, *Education for Freedom,* 276; William D. Johnson, *Lincoln University: or, The Nation's First Pledge of Emancipation* (Philadelphia, 1867), 12–13; Thomas Miller to Francis J. Grimké, January 22, 1936, in Francis Grimké Papers, Box 4, Folder 188.

rolled the vast majority of the school's students. The Collegiate Department had just added a third-year curriculum in 1866–1867, and in the following year, a fourth, degree-year was added. Lincoln awarded its first bachelor's degrees in 1868. Archie and Frank first entered the Preparatory Department, spending their first spring and then their first full academic year there, before going on to their college-level studies in the fall of 1867.[6]

In keeping with Dickey's original purposes, the main focus of the curriculum at all levels was classical and theological. Every year included a course on the Bible and religion, with emphasis on the Presbyterian faith, as well as courses in rhetoric, history, mathematics (algebra, geometry, and trigonometry), the natural sciences, and Latin and Greek. Readings included a strong dose of the great classical writers—Caesar, Homer, Cicero, Virgil, Tacitus, and Herodotus—as well as more recent works of stature and Presbyterian orthodoxy such as Charles Hodge's *Way of Life,* despite its author's proslavery past. There were also courses in psychology and economics and, for seniors, a course in English literature and literary criticism. Archie remembered that all of the students were eager to learn, enthusiastic, and wanted to get as much education as they could. Conditions, however, were not always the best. The students were housed in a barrackslike dormitory sleeping twenty to a room. Because of their obvious ability, Archie and Frank were soon singled out for special attention. Both did remarkably well in their courses, although Archie was weak in chemistry, finishing first or second in their class every term. President Rendall considered them the school's "foremost students."[7]

The four years at Lincoln were active ones for both boys in ways that went beyond their formal studies. Although Archie always made much of the strong religious background his mother had provided him, it was, according to his brother, while at Lincoln that he made his public profession of faith. Archie and Frank had a falling-out over religion during their first months at Lincoln. Shortly after their en-

6. Bond, *Education for Freedom,* 281.

7. *Ibid.,* 274–82; on Hodge, see Larry E. Tise, *Proslavery: A History of the Defense of Slavery in America, 1701–1840* (Athens, Ga., 1987), 277–78; Archibald Grimké, "Memoirs," 107–109; "Transcript Record for Archibald Henry Grimké," in Archibald Grimké Papers, Box 2, Folder 43; Francis James Grimké, Academic record, Lincoln University, in Francis Grimké Papers, Box 1, Folder 5; Isaac N. Rendall to Angelina Grimké Weld, January 15, 1870, in Weld-Grimké Papers, Box 14, William L. Clements Library, University of Michigan, Ann Arbor.

trance, a religious revival broke out among the students, and Archie was among the first to be affected. He earnestly sought to save his own soul and, with typical enthusiasm, that of his brother as well. Frank, however, was less interested than Archie in religion, and there was no end of argument between them, Frank adopting a skeptical position for the only time in his life. Archie later remembered that "my earnestness was so great to save myself and him also from the burning fires of Hell that I determined to take what I could peaceably from him, otherwise to take it any how, convinced he must be per-suaded to enter the fold of the meek and lowly Jesus." Events then took a turn that revealed the volatility and quickness to anger that were part of Archie's character all his life. Frank finally got fed up with Archie's preaching and became abusive. Archie quickly lost his temper and "what little Christianity" he had, later remembering that, thus provoked, "the youthful follower of the meek and lowly Jesus became very belligerent and from hot words we finally came to blows," which neither converted Frank nor made Archie feel good about his own ability to live up to the teachings about which he felt so enthusiastic. It would not be the last time that meekness and lowliness would be significant by their absence in his life.[8]

Still, despite his failure with Frank and with himself, Archie re-mained devoted to the church at Lincoln. His character and devotion were such that he was elected to "the high and responsible position as ruling elder of the Ashmun Church," a Presbyterian church, a post he occupied through his college career.[9]

Archie was also active in the university's literary academic societies, including the Philosophian Society, a group organized to discuss ma-jor political and philosophical issues, and the Garnet Lyceum—named for the black abolitionist and minister Henry Highland Garnet—which included all the university's students and was devoted to "de-bating, reading, composition, and speaking." In 1870, Archie's first published writing appeared in Frederick Douglass' Washington, D.C., newspaper the *New Era*, in a letter recounting the anniversary festivities of the "Garnet Literary Association."[10]

Perhaps the only real difficulty the brothers encountered while at Lincoln was financial. Although each had support for the four years

8. Archibald Grimké, "Memoirs," 110–11.
9. Angelina W. Grimké, "Biographical Sketch," 46.
10. *Ibid.;* Francis J. Grimké, undated MS., in Archibald Grimké Papers, Box 2, Folder 53; Johnson, *Lincoln University,* 13; Washington *New Era,* May 12, 1870.

there, it was never enough to allow them any comfort. During the summers, they joined many of their fellow students in going back to the South to teach in freedmen's schools or to wait tables. President Rendall helped them find jobs and worried about the pressure they felt from "ungratified wants." After graduation, he continued to provide them with assistance and a place, encouraging them to attend the university's Law Department, which had been established in 1870, and hiring both as instructors in the Preparatory Department—Archie in English grammar and Frank in arithmetic. Frank also served for a brief period as financial agent of the school and Archie as the school's first (and for some decades last) black librarian. Both remained at the school at least through the 1871–1872 academic year, Frank a year beyond, Archie earning a master's degree in 1872.[11]

Still, the major event in the lives of the brothers during their time at Lincoln was their meeting with their aunts in 1868. The story of that meeting has often been told. In February, 1868, Angelina Grimké Weld was reading an issue of the *National Anti-Slavery Standard* when she came upon an article reprinted from the Boston *Commonwealth,* "Negroes and the Higher Studies," quoting Lincoln professor Edwin R. Bower. Seeking to disprove black inferiority, Bower referred to his own experiences teaching black students at Lincoln, comparing them favorably with "any class I have ever heard." He concluded by singling out one of the participants, "by the name of Grimkie, who came here two years ago, just out of slavery."[12]

Despite the misspelling, Angelina could not miss the similarity of the name to her own. According to her biographer, Katherine Lumpkin, Angelina, after reading the article, took to her room for some time; then, after several hours of discussion with her sister Sarah and her husband, the great abolitionist orator Theodore Dwight Weld, she decided to write to "Mr. Grimké" at Lincoln. Identifying herself as "the youngest sister of Dr. John Grimké," she told him about herself, her family, and the careers she and Sarah had made in the antislavery cause. Noting the name, she suggested, innocently, that perhaps the young man to whom her letter was addressed might have been the slave of one of her brothers. Could he tell her more about himself?[13]

11. Bond, *Education for Freedom,* 322, 434; Angelina W. Grimké, "Biographical Sketch," 46; Henry Justin Ferry, "Francis James Grimké: Portrait of a Black Puritan" (Ph.D. dissertation, Yale University, 1970), 62–63.

12. *National Anti-Slavery Standard,* XXVIII (February 8, 1868), [2].

13. Lumpkin, *Emancipation of Angelina Grimké,* 220; Angelina Grimké Weld to Mr. Grimké, February 15, 1868, in Archibald Grimké Papers, Box 1, Folder 10.

Archie wrote her a long letter in reply. He knew who she was, both from hearing family members talk about her and Sarah and from his own knowledge of the antislavery cause acquired in his childhood, and said he was pleased, if surprised, to hear from her. He told her that he was the son of her brother Henry Grimké. He told her about his mother and about Francis and John, about Henry's promises to Nancy and their hard lives in Charleston, and about their brother Montague's cruel efforts to enslave them during the war. Demonstrating his familiarity with antislavery rhetoric, Archie wrote that at the war's beginning, "we were still struggling in the mighty grasp of the hideous monster, slavery. At last it received its death blow, it was buried in the grave of dishonor never more to smite the land with a curse & *Freedom* was proclaimed to *all men*." Then he told her how Frances Pillsbury had helped them come to the North and to Lincoln. He also brought her up-to-date on her Charleston relatives and enclosed pictures of himself and Frank.[14]

Archie's letter had a devastating effect on Angelina. As her subsequent actions proved, this was not so much because of learning she had black relations—she had long refused to acknowledge racial distinctions in public or private life—as because of what Archie's letter said about her brother and her own family's culpability in the system she abhorred. She had long been troubled by the vulnerability of female slaves in a system based on brutal physical power. And she could only assume that the evidence of Archie and his brothers pointed to Henry's having succumbed to the temptations slave ownership created. After reading Archie's letter, she was prostrated for several days. Then, in a decision that would have surprised no one who knew her, she recovered with a determination to acknowledge the boys as her nephews and to take them under her care. Her husband and sister readily concurred. Given her views, the choice was inevitable. As her daughter Sarah Weld later wrote, "Her brother had wronged these children; his sisters must right them."[15]

She made her decision known in letters to Frank and Archie. In her first reply, written soon after she learned their identity, she made clear

14. Archibald H. Grimké to Angelina Grimké Weld, February 20, 1868, in Archibald Grimké Papers, Box 1, Folder 9.
15. Sarah Weld Hamilton, "Memories of Theodore Dwight Weld, the St. John of the Abolitionists," 367–68, in Weld-Grimké Papers, Box 18; Catherine H. Birney, *The Grimké Sisters: Sarah and Angelina Grimké, the First American Women Advocates of Abolition and Woman's Rights* (1885; rpr. Westport, Conn., 1969), 287; Gerda Lerner, *The Grimké Sisters from South Carolina: Rebels Against Slavery* (Boston, 1967), 361–62.

her willingness to help them and their youngest brother, John. But she spent much of her time discussing the Grimké family of which she considered them members. With some irony, she told them, "I am glad you have taken the name of Grimké—it was *once,* one of the noblest names in Carolina," and then went on to an account of her feeling that her adored brother Thomas "would have become an abolitionist, & that he would have declared his convictions on this subject, as boldly as he did his unpopular opinions on Nullification, at the time of the intense excitement on this subject in Charleston." Thomas had been a strong Unionist (he was also an educational reformer and an ardent pacifist), and Angelina recommended his writings on the subject to her nephews as "very useful & instructive, & may possibly help to mould your characters & shape your course in life." She apparently sent those writings to them because some of his works, as well as those by another brother, Frederick, became a permanent part of Francis Grimké's library. She told them more about Thomas, sent them a picture of him, and later, when Archie was studying law at Lincoln, said she hoped the picture would keep the example and inspiration of that much-loved brother before him.[16]

This family connection meant much to Angelina, and she was determined to make the most she could out of her nephews. Admitting that "it was the grief of my heart that during the last war, not one of the name of Grimké—neither man nor woman—was found on the side of loyalty & freedom all bow'd down to gether & worship'd Slavery—'the Mother of *all* abominations,'" she urged them, "now bear this *once* honor'd name—I charge you most solemnly by your upright conduct, & your life-long devotion to the eternal principles of justice & humanity & Religion to lift *this name* out of the dust, where it now lies, & set it once more among the princes of our land." She continued to write in a similar vein for several weeks and then resolved to visit her two new nephews at Lincoln's June commencement.[17]

Along with her son Charles Stuart Weld, Angelina stayed at Lincoln for a week. There, in the presence of President Rendall and the brothers' childhood friend and fellow student Tom Miller, she met her nephews. She spoke with them more about their lives in Charleston and about making arrangements for John to travel north once he had

16. Angelina Grimké Weld to Archibald and Francis Grimké, February 29, 1868, in Archibald Grimké Papers, Box 1, Folder 11; Angelina Grimké Weld to Archibald H. Grimké, January 9, [?], *ibid.,* Box 1, Folder 22; Anna Julia Cooper, *Personal Recollections of the Grimké Family* (2 vols.; N.p., 1951), I, 25.

17. Angelina Grimké Weld to Archibald and Francis Grimké, February 29, 1868.

received all the education he could in Charleston. She discussed her nephews' progress at Lincoln with their professors. And she invited Archie and Frank to visit her home in Hyde Park, near Boston, when they were able. Angelina was in poor health when she made the visit, and it must have been exhausting for her, but she was happy to meet her nephews, proud of them, and still more eager to take an active role in their further education.[18]

It is hard to determine Archie's and Frank's immediate reactions to their aunts. Historian Gerda Lerner has commented that from the tone of his letters, Archie seems to have expected little beyond a polite exchange of letters and a maintenance of racial barriers. Certainly his Charleston experiences would not have prepared him for the openness and, as Lerner says, genuine love his newly found relatives were to show. He was receiving a dramatic introduction to a very new world, one in which hostility and dissimulation did not play the role they had in Archie's previous dealings with whites. The adjustments he had to make would have been enormous.[19]

But the relationship was on the whole positive for both Archie and his brother. They needed financial help, and Angelina did what she could to provide it. They wrote when they needed help, and she sent small amounts of money—twenty dollars here and there—even when, as on one occasion, she had to borrow it. She and Sarah also collected money for John, who joined Archie and Frank for a while but, unhappy in the North and apparently not so apt a student as his brothers, returned to the South. He was to have virtually no contact with his two brothers thereafter.[20]

Sarah Grimké and the Welds also began to assert themselves as new parents to the young men and were determined to mold Archie and Frank into the kind of individuals they admired. Although much that the brothers learned reinforced the teachings of their mother, the lessons were taught firmly and consistently over the next several years. They were impressed, for example, with the importance of achieving both financial and moral independence and were told by Angelina to avoid "leaning on others for support in any way, mentally or bodily," and to cultivate "conscious dignity of character & oneness

18. Birney, *Grimké Sisters,* 295; Sarah Moore Grimké to Sarah [Douglass], December 1, 1868, in Weld-Grimké Papers, Box 14.

19. Lerner, *Grimké Sisters,* 361–62.

20. Angelina Grimké Weld to "Dear Boys," January 23, 1869[?], in Archibald Grimké Papers, Box 1, Folder 15; Sarah Moore Grimké to Sarah [Douglass], December 1, 1869.

of purpose." Failure in this regard, she fretted, was a "great defect of Southern character," and she had no wish for them to succumb to it—although, as Nancy's children, they were in little danger.[21]

The virtues of moderation were also to be learned. These had long been important to Sarah and, notably, to the Welds (whose courtship thirty years before has been nicely described by historian Ronald Walters as "an orgy of restraint"). Archie and Frank were to learn that lesson forcefully when, returning Angelina's visit to Lincoln, they went to Hyde Park. Archie remembered the visit fondly in later life, for the Welds had received him and Frank warmly. But Archie also remembered that they had looked a little ridiculous. The Welds thrived on plainness in food, in dress, and in living. Archie and Frank, despite their poverty, showed up in Boston carrying canes and wearing high silk hats and custom-made boots, perhaps not making the impression they had desired. Whether they were rebuked for their ostentation we do not know, but Archie was to remember the gaffe for the rest of his life.[22]

As their undergraduate careers at Lincoln came to a close in 1870, Frank and Archie showed that they had learned some of their lessons well, perhaps too well, at least from their aunts' point of view, especially the lesson of independence. They never indicated any resentment toward their aunts' efforts to mold their characters, but both Archie and Frank continued to follow their own leads and with the stubbornness that had always characterized them.

Throughout the second half of their senior year at Lincoln, there were frequent visits between the Grimké brothers and their aunts. When Archie and Frank had earlier proposed to spend one summer working as waiters, both aunts approved of their desire to do manual labor. But as they approached graduation, Sarah encouraged them to take a year off before continuing their studies, writing, "We *all* hope you will take a year of rest from study & by outdoor labor put yourselves in brain working trim. . . . You have had years of brain sweat, now try the sweat of the brow." This had long been a favored idea in the Grimké family—indeed, brother Thomas had been a champion of manual labor as a part of education during the 1820s and 1830s, as had Weld. They believed that overworking the brain uses energy meant for other parts of the body and that doses of manual labor could restore the proper balance.[23]

21. Angelina Grimké Weld to "Dear Boys," January 23, 1869[?].

22. Ronald G. Walters, *The Antislavery Appeal: American Abolitionism After 1830* (Baltimore, 1976), 79–80; Angelina W. Grimké, "Biographical Sketch," 46.

23. Sarah Moore Grimké to Archibald and Francis Grimké, February 3, 1870, in

But Archie and Frank did not take their aunts' advice, making it clear that they would plan their own lives for the immediate future. It was apparently during their last year as Lincoln undergraduates that both Archie and Frank decided to go on to law school and, with Rendall's encouragement, to do so at the about-to-be-established school at Lincoln. Angelina and Sarah were ambivalent about the decision. At first, after having advised their nephews to engage in manual labor for a year, they tried to get them at least to look for an alternative to Lincoln. Concerned about the cost, Angelina suggested in April that Archie consider going into an attorney's office where he could learn the rudiments of law and be paid, then spend a year in law school before going into the office of a "Counsellor at Law" to complete his training. She offered to look out for a place for him in Boston.[24]

Both aunts continued to suggest alternatives. During the summer, Angelina wrote to them enthusiastically about Cornell University. In part she was enthusiastic because Cornell paid particular attention to "physical culture" so that the body as well as the mind was attended to, and she thought this was especially important for Archie, who, she said, was "more delicate" than his brothers. She also hoped that he and Frank could get out of Lincoln's segregated environment and go to an institution "where a majority of the students are white." In urging her nephews to leave Lincoln, Angelina was less concerned that they would suffer from contact with black peers than hostile to racial separation, however benign the intent, and wanted to see her nephews in an integrated community. Even while they were at Lincoln, she had tried to encourage them to think about Oberlin, "where scores of color'd young men & women have been educated in the *same* classes with white men & women—*no* distinction of color or race ever has been recognized there." She was, of course, aware that Cornell could "command many more advantages than Lincoln possibly can just now."[25]

But both Archie and Frank, perhaps not yet comfortable with the thought of leaving a black world, decided to remain at Lincoln, where they could support themselves financially with their postgraduate

Archibald Grimké Papers, Box 1, Folder 2; Robert H. Abzug, *Passionate Liberator: Theodore Dwight Weld and the Dilemma of Reform* (New York, 1980), 59–61.

24. Angelina Grimké Weld to Archibald H. Grimké, April 30, [?], in Archibald Grimké Papers, Box 1, Folder 21.

25. Angelina Grimké Weld to Archibald Grimké, July 24, [?], in Archibald Grimké Papers, Box 1, Folder 27; Angelina Weld to Archibald and Francis Grimké, February 29, 1868.

jobs. The law program they entered in 1870, in the first year of its existence, was not strong. There was only one other student besides themselves (in the second year there were only two others), and the program apparently involved little more than the students' reading law on their own and then meeting with a lawyer for recitations.[26]

Neither Sarah nor Angelina seems to have been disappointed in them despite the show of resistance. The young men had accomplished a great deal, and both sisters admired what they had done. If Henry had proved corrupt beyond their fears, they had come to admire Nancy and saw in her sons—their nephews—the potential for improving the family name. Sarah Grimké gave them great praise when, in a letter to Garrison, she wrote, "Is it not remarkable that these young men should far exceed in talents any of my other Grimké nephews, even their half brothers bear no comparison with them & my brother Thomas' sons, distinguished as he was, are far inferior to them in intellectual power." But perhaps her ultimate accolade was when she told Archie how much he reminded her of Thomas.[27]

Thus Sarah and Angelina easily became reconciled to the desires of both to take up the law and to remain at Lincoln, for which they were willing to provide still further support. The stay, however, was to be fairly brief. Frank seems to have continued on into the 1872–1873 academic year, the law program's final one, before going to Howard University's law school the following year and then, changing his career plans, entering Princeton Theological Seminary in 1875. Archie, finally acceding to Sarah's advice, went to Boston in 1872 to enter Harvard Law School.[28]

When Archibald Grimké entered Harvard Law School, it was small and undergoing change. In response to stinging criticisms, the curriculum had been tightened and a system of examinations added, under the supervision of Christopher C. Langdell, who had been appointed dean in 1870.[29]

26. Bond, *Education for Freedom,* 434.

27. Sarah Moore Grimké to William Lloyd Garrison, February 13, 1871, in William Lloyd Garrison Papers, Boston Public Library; Sarah Moore Grimké to "My young friends," November 10, 1870, in Archibald Grimké Papers, Box 1, Folder 2.

28. Bond, *Education for Freedom,* 434; Angelina Grimké Weld to Archibald H. Grimké, January 9, [?], in Archibald Grimké Papers, Box 1, Folder 22; Francis Grimké to "Dear Bro," January 24, 1887, in Francis Grimké Papers; Angelina W. Grimké, "Biographical Sketch," 46.

29. Charles Warren, *History of the Harvard Law School and of Early Legal Conditions in America* (3 vols.; New York, 1908), II, 366, 372, 379–84; Arthur E. Sutherland, *The Law at Harvard: A History of Ideas and Men, 1817–1967* (Cambridge, Mass., 1967), 177.

Archibald entered the class of 1874 as one of about half the ninety-two men with college degrees, thus bypassing a newly instituted entrance examination, and as a classmate of Henry Cabot Lodge, with whom he later worked in Boston Republican politics. During both his years at Harvard, he took courses from Dean Langdell, as well as Emory Washburn, then Bussey Professor, who taught real property and constitutional law, and James Barr Ames, hired during Grimké's second year, who taught civil procedure with Langdell. It is difficult to know how he did in his courses because no transcript has survived, but he won one of four Bussey scholarships—awarded "to meritorious students standing in need of such assistance"—to help provide financial support for his second year in the school. And he was one of about half the students in his class to finish the two-year course with an LL.B.[30]

Archibald Grimké was not the Harvard Law School's first black student, but he was among the first. George Ruffin, with whom he later became well acquainted, had preceded him by a few years, finishing in 1869. While Grimké was there, James H. Wolff, later to be a partner of his, entered the school as a member of the class of 1875. Despite his visibility, Grimké seems to have encountered few racial problems (unlike Ruffin, who had faced some discrimination during his time at the school). At least once, a white student from the South refused to sit with him in the room where the students dined in common. Grimké was quickly joined, however, by two other white students, one of whom, Cyrus W. Heizer, was to become a life-long friend, in an ostentatious rejection of their southern colleague's bigotry.[31]

More important than the problem of color in Grimké's law studies was the perennial problem of money. His first year at Harvard cost about $450, which the Welds and Sarah were pledged to support but which cost them dearly. Sarah took on much of the burden of providing support up to the time of her death in December, 1873. Angelina wrote him that Sarah was "living a life of constant self denial" to

30. Warren, *History*, II, 520; *The Harvard University Catalogue, 1872–73* (Cambridge, Mass., 1873), 96–99; *The Harvard University Catalogue, 1873–74* (Cambridge, Mass., 1874), 108–13, 115; *Quinquennial Catalogue of the Law School of Harvard University, 1817–1934* (Cambridge, Mass., 1935), 99–101; Corporation Records, Harvard University, Vol. XII, 1873–80, p. 8, Harvard University Archives, Cambridge, Mass.

31. Warren, *History*, II, 292–93, III, 125, 146; Ellen Stebbins to Angelina Weld Grimké, January 20, 1936, in Angelina Weld Grimké Papers, Box 2, Folder 18, Moorland-Spingarn Research Center, Howard University, Washington, D.C.

support him fully—both sisters wanted him to graduate without en-
cumbering any debt—and urged him to cut back on his expenses as
much as possible. Sarah also sought to interest publisher Francis Garrison, son of the abolitionist, in her first work of fiction, any proceeds
from it to go toward helping Archie. Both sisters also went to the
wealthy and generous abolitionist Gerrit Smith to get additional help
toward meeting his expenses. Archie lived much of the time in Di-
vinity Hall, in one of the less expensive rooms on the Harvard cam-
pus, at other times with Maria Walling, a member of Boston's abolitionist community and a friend of the Welds. His expenses were very
close to the minimum estimated in the Harvard catalog for a first-year
law student. Undoubtedly the Bussey scholarship, which covered
his second-year fee but left him still to pay for his room and board
and books, was helpful, but his education strained the Weld-Grimké
resources.[32]

But supporting him through Harvard was not all his aunts did for
him during these early years in Boston. They also introduced him to
some of the men and women who had made up the "Boston clique,"
centered around Garrison, from the days of abolition. Although the
Welds were not, properly, Bostonians, having moved to the area in
1863, they had long been close to many of those whose careers had
been based in the city—to Garrison himself, to the Pillsburys (Gilbert's very radical brother Parker), to Lucy Stone, and others. They
introduced young Archie to these old friends and others, including
Charles Sumner, Wendell Phillips, Lewis Hayden, and Frederick
Douglass.[33] They also introduced him to their longtime black friend
and correspondent Sarah Douglass of Philadelphia.

These introductions had a substantial impact on Archie. His daughter wrote that these new acquaintances did much to make him "a liberal in religion, a radical in the Woman Suffrage Movement, in politics
and on the race question" (the first of these not only a drastic change
from Lincoln days but destined to cause his brother Frank much cha-
grin later in their lives). More than that, the social life he assumed
through his aunts put him into the truly integrated world they had
created for themselves and more deeply than had been possible for
him before. Here was a world in which white and black men and

32. Angelina Grimké Weld to Archibald Grimké, April 28, [?], in Archibald Grimké
Papers, Box 1, Folder 25; Sarah Grimké to Gerrit Smith, October 19, 1873, Weld-
Grimké Papers, Box 15; *Harvard Catalogue, 1872–73,* 88, 96, 100.
33. Angelina W. Grimké, "Biographical Sketch," 46.

women interacted, on the surface at least, as equals and friends. It was, moreover, a community in which black and white men and women had long worked together in the cause of racial justice. Many of those whom Grimké met had been deeply involved in the effort. White champions of racial justice, including Garrison, Phillips, and Sumner, had worked closely with such prominent black figures as Hayden, William C. Nell, and Douglass for the passage of nondiscriminatory legislation covering everything from intermarriage to public accommodations. They succeeded in creating in Boston, despite the continuing presence of discrimination, undoubtedly the best environment for blacks in America at the time Grimké arrived even as they initiated and maintained a tradition of interracial cooperation in political and social action.[34]

This change in his situation, including the social contacts he made through his aunts, was to be important to Archibald Grimké. To be sure, some of the acquaintances were never to go beyond a friendly acknowledgment on the street—more than he could expect in Charleston from whites—but others evolved into enduring friendships. Moreover, from the support he received from white colleagues during the dining hall incident to the openness with which he was accepted by so many white Bostonians, not to mention the acceptance he saw accorded to such black men and women as Hayden, Frederick Douglass, and Sarah Douglass, especially within the Weld-Grimké circle, he was made aware of possibilities for contact and relationships across racial lines far different from anything he had known before. This new knowledge created a major shift in perspective in his own life, public and private, toward a thoroughgoing integrationism he was never to give up that became increasingly evident as he entered adulthood and began his professional life.

But no less important, these introductions around Boston helped provide the bases for much that would happen later in Archibald Grimké's life, not only because some of these acquaintanceships were long-lasting, blossoming into friendships that would be sustained for years, but also because some were of great professional significance to him, not only in the earliest days of his career but later in life.

Perhaps meeting such people influenced Archibald Grimké's deci-

34. *Ibid.*; James Oliver Horton and Lois C. Horton, *Black Bostonians: Family Life and Community Struggle in the Antebellum North* (New York, 1979), chap. 6; John Daniels, *In Freedom's Birthplace: A Study of the Boston Negroes* (1914; rpr. New York, 1968), 85–94; Willard B. Gatewood, *Aristocrats of Color: The Black Elite, 1880–1920* (Bloomington, 1991), 110.

sion after graduation in 1874, to remain in Boston. His aunt Angelina was not entirely pleased. She felt that his chances would be better in the South and had hoped from the beginning that one way in which Archie would redeem the family name would be by trying to bring racial equality to his, and her, home state. But Archibald had come to feel too much at home in the North, particularly in Boston. Its "new world" was far more appealing to him than anything in Charleston. With help, especially from his sometime landlady, Maria Walling, he was able to get a position with one of Boston's leading attorneys, William I. Bowditch, himself a Harvard Law School graduate, who had been active in both abolition and civil rights in Boston, and began a fairly brief career as a Boston lawyer.[35]

35. Angelina W. Grimké, "Biographical Sketch," 46.

3

Boston

In 1874, twenty-four years old and armed with his Harvard degree, Archibald Grimké joined the office of William Bowditch, one of Boston's most prominent attorneys. Not yet admitted to the bar, Archie seems to have been very much a student in Bowditch's office. He worked in Boston but boarded in Hyde Park, where the Welds lived. In 1875, he was admitted to the Suffolk County Bar and went into partnership with James Wolff, who had been a year behind him at Harvard. From an office on Washington Street near the Old Corner Bookshop they practiced together for about three years, until Wolff took a position in the government.[1]

Grimké does not seem to have played an active role in Boston's public life during these early years of his career. He did some writing and lecturing, activities that within a few years would occupy the central place in his life. In 1878, he was appointed justice of the peace. But much of his attention seems to have focused on his struggling practice, which mainly involved securing pensions for black Civil War veterans.[2]

1. Angelina W. Grimké, "A Biographical Sketch of Archibald H. Grimké," *Opportunity*, III (February, 1925), 46; Charles Warren, *History of the Harvard Law School and of Early Legal Conditions in America* (3 vols.; New York, 1908), III, 20, 146; *Boston City Directories*, 1875–80.

2. Appointment certificates in Archibald H. Grimké Papers, Box 2, Folder 45, Moorland-Spingarn Research Center, Howard University, Washington, D.C.; Ellen Stebbins to Angelina Weld Grimké, January 20, 1936, in Angelina Weld Grimké Papers, Box 2, Folder 18, Moorland-Spingarn Research Center, Howard University, Washington, D.C. Stebbins' letter is a major source for details about Archibald Grimké's early social life.

Still, if he was not yet active in Boston's public affairs, Grimké seems to have led a very active social life during this period of young adulthood, particularly in the circle of friends he met through the Welds. Of the more prominent former abolitionists, he was especially close to the Garrisons and to Wendell Phillips, for whom he felt strong admiration. Grimké and Phillips were often together when Archie was a young man, the two of them frequently seen walking hand in hand along the streets. Archie also accompanied Phillips home some evenings to make sure the older man got there safely. He also continued his contact with the Pillsburys, beginning a friendship with Albert E. Pillsbury, Parker Pillsbury's nephew, that continued for over half a century. His friendship with Lillie Buffum Chace Wyman, two years his senior and daughter of a prominent abolitionist family, led to a lifelong correspondence and visits that ended only with his death.[3]

He was especially close to Ellen Bradford—Nelly—about two years younger than he and descended from a long line of antislavery and social reform activists, as well as from the Mayflower colonist William Bradford. They met in about 1876 or 1877 through their mutual friend Cyrus Heizer and corresponded regularly throughout their lives. After Grimké's death in 1930, she corresponded with his daughter. One of those letters, written in 1936, provides an excellent portrait of Archibald Grimké as a young man about society. He was, she wrote, "rather slender, erect, and I should say of medium height, with a clear direct look of great intelligence." She also remembered that he had "manners so exactly right there was nothing to remark about them." As young people, they talked together, discovered that they had similar tastes in literature, and found that they "*laughed* a great deal together on slight provocation."[4]

Over the next couple of years, they saw each other often. In the summer of 1877, she recalled, they traveled with the women's suffragist speaker Hulda Lord and with Cyrus Heizer to Lord's father's farm in Rockland for a weekend in the country. Archie and Heizer had to avoid "old Mr. Lord, 'stripped to the buff'" in his bath, a sight that so convulsed them that, later, laughter made Archie, "brushing his teeth with powdered charcoal, splutter it 'all over him'" Nelly later wrote, "I can see his eyes dance now." She also remembered a boat trip up the Charles River with Francis Grimké and one of her aunts,

---

3. Archibald Grimké, "Memoirs of Archibald H. Grimké," 113, in Archibald Grimké Papers, Box 2, Folder 47.
4. Stebbins to Angelina Grimké, January 20, 1936.

when she and Archie laughed as the breeze blew her hat's ribbon stream-
ers into his eyes. It was a memory Archie saved as well. During their
time together, Nelly apparently had strong feelings for Archie. She
joked with him, and as she learned more about his early life, she was
so moved she found herself unable to talk with him about it. They
exchanged notes regularly, and she visited him often at his Washington Street office. If their later correspondence is any indication, she
was an important part of his life. He looked to her as a valued source
of approval for his ideas and activities; she felt for him both admiration
and affection. How far their relationship might have gone is difficult
to say. Shortly after the intimacy had begun to strengthen, Nelly's
father received a position that took the family out of Boston, and,
though she later returned, Archie by then was engaged to Sarah Stanley. Nelly attended the wedding with Heizer, and as she was saying
her good-byes, she and Archie found themselves alone together at the
end of a long sitting room. They looked in each other's eyes and, to
their mutual astonishment, exchanged "a swift kiss." A short time
later, she married Solomon B. Stebbins, a prominent Boston Republican politician who was to do much to aid Archibald Grimké's entrance into public life a short time thereafter.[5]

Grimké also remained close to the Welds. He visited them often,
met people in their home, and brought his friends—including Nelly—
to meet them. His aunt Angelina died in October, 1879, after years of
poor health and a series of strokes. Her death did not, however, cut
him off from Theodore Weld or from the couple's children. Weld always referred to Archie and Frank as his nephews, and Archie, living
nearby, maintained a good relationship with Weld. After Archie's
daughter Angelina's birth in 1880, she, too, became a part of the Weld
circle. She stayed in the Weld home when Archibald had to be away,
and she presented a poem she wrote for Weld at his ninetieth birthday
celebration in 1893. In 1895, when Weld died, he left Archie eighty-
seven shares of stock in an insurance company, worth five dollars a
share, to help provide for Angelina's future needs.[6]

5. *Ibid.*
6. *Ibid.;* Gerda Lerner, *The Grimké Sisters from South Carolina: Rebels Against Slavery* (Boston, 1967), 367; Robert H. Abzug, *Passionate Liberator: Theodore Dwight Weld
and the Dilemma of Reform* (New York, 1980), 296; Benjamin P. Thomas, *Theodore Weld:
Crusader for Freedom* (New Brunswick, 1950), 259; Norfolk County *Gazette,* November 25, 1893; Archibald H. Grimké to "Dear Home Ones," July 12, 1895, in Francis J.
Grimké Papers, Box 3, Folder 119, Moorland-Spingarn Research Center, Howard University, Washington, D.C.

Beginning with his entering Harvard, most of Grimké's social life was among whites. Outside his law practice with Wolff, which involved a largely black clientele, he seems to have known only a few black Bostonians, spending his time either with his white relatives or friends. There is no evidence that he consciously rejected black society, although he later recalled getting on much better with white than with black Bostonians. He remained on good terms with some members of Boston's black elite, including the Ruffins and Lewis Hayden, who were as cultured and sophisticated as any among the white company he tended to keep. Nor did he then or later sharply draw a color line in his choice of African-American friends, favoring those who were light in complexion like himself. But, perhaps in the exuberance of finding himself in a new world, one that had been closed to him in Charleston and at Lincoln, he decided to be as much a part of that world as he could.[7]

He was undoubtedly encouraged by his contacts with whites in Boston and earlier. There seem to have been few if any tensions in these relationships. In light of his Charleston background and the impatience he had shown in the face of anything resembling abuse, he probably would have reacted strongly had there been. But he was in a hospitable environment, and it is not surprising that his relationships were comfortable. Nor do there appear to have been any tensions in his relationships with such young white women as Lillie Buffum Chace Wyman and Nelly Bradford, despite the usual white hostility to intimacy across racial lines.

Archie's social life differed from that of his brother Francis almost from the time they left Lincoln. At Princeton, Frank Grimké had enjoyed the company of several black fellow students, including Matthew Anderson, Hugh Browne, and Daniel Culp. After finishing at Princeton, Frank had gone to Washington, D.C., where, in 1878, he had become assistant pastor of the Fifteenth Street Presbyterian Church, a center for elite black life in the city. From that point on, he was to have little or no social contact with white people, a fact he never regretted. Perhaps because he did not share Archie's Boston experience and close contact with the Welds, Frank's Charleston background guided him more than it did his older brother.[8]

7. Angelina W. Grimké, "Biographical Sketch," 47; Archibald Grimké, "Memoirs," 112; Willard B. Gatewood, *Aristocrats of Color: The Black Elite, 1880–1920* (Bloomington, 1991), 109–11.
8. Henry Justin Ferry, "Francis James Grimké: Portrait of a Black Puritan" (Ph.D.

This difference was most significant in their marriages, which oc-curred less than half a year apart. Francis, having assumed his duties at the Fifteenth Street Church and making his way into Washington's black society, had cemented his place by marrying Charlotte Forten, member of a wealthy Philadelphia black family. Their wedding was attended by such black figures as the Purvises, Frederick Douglass, and Richard Greener, a Harvard-educated South Carolinian.[9]

Archie, however, married across racial lines. Sarah Stanley, a young woman about Archie's age, came from an antislavery background. She was a student at Boston University when Archie met her, and they had known each other for more than two years when, in early 1879 and with the apparent blessing of his Boston family and their friends, he asked Sarah's father for her hand in marriage.[10]

Archie's language in asking for Sarah's hand displayed the restraint and good manners he could bring to such a serious situation. He told her father, an Episcopal priest in Michigan: "I cannot do what I now intend without first seeking to secure your approval. Such approval sir would give me great pleasure." And he certainly knew the rules of courtship, for he told the man of his long friendship with Sarah, which "has developed a mutual & high regard which have in time grown to what we both concurrently believe a deep & abiding affection."[11]

He received a prompt reply, and it may not have been what his Boston experiences might have led him to expect. Stanley was polite, but he clearly did not like the idea of the proposed marriage. In writing to Archie, he said only that he had "some misgivings in this case" and wished that he and Sarah's mother had been "consulted" earlier. In a letter to Sarah, written the following day, he did not conceal his anger. Accusing her of falling in with the Boston "unitarians," he wrote that her plans had "filled our hearts with mourning," and he

dissertation, Yale University, 1970), 93; Francis J. Grimké, *The Works of Francis J. Grimké,* ed. Carter G. Woodson (4 vols.; Washington, D.C., 1942), III, 344; Gatewood, *Aristocrats of Color,* 46, 286–87.

9. Francis J. Grimké to "Dear Bro," January 24, 1887, in Francis Grimké Papers, Box 1, Folder 1; Janice Sumler Lewis, "The Fortens of Philadelphia: An Afro-American Family and Nineteenth-Century Reform" (Ph.D. dissertation, Georgetown University, 1978), 228–29.

10. Angelina Weld Grimké, notes on father, in Archibald Grimké Papers, Box 2, Folder 51; Archibald Grimké to M. C. Stanley, February 9, 1879, *ibid.,* Box 3, Folder 82.

11. Archibald H. Grimké to M. C. Stanley, February 9, 1879.

asked her how she thought those same "unitarian" friends might feel should it be one of their own daughters. "We look upon it as a sad day," he wrote, "when you went to Boston and especially when you associated yourself with the deniers of Christ and the insane theorisers of that infidel city." Antislavery was one thing; "amalgamation," something else.[12]

Still, the marriage plans continued. Sarah disparaged her father's objections and even ignored the advice of her and Archie's old friend Lucy Stone, a women's rights advocate and former abolitionist, to postpone the marriage. On April 19, a few months short of Archie's thirtieth birthday, the wedding was held at the Beacon Hill home of Mrs. Charles C. Curtis, a friend of the Welds, officiated by the Reverend C. A. Bartol, a radical Unitarian minister whom Archie had met through the Welds. The number of guests was fairly small and the ceremony simple.[13]

At first, the marriage was happy. Archie maintained his office on Washington Street, and the newlywed couple moved into a house on nearby Temple. Their love was strong. When Archie had to be away from Boston about a month after the ceremony, Sarah wrote to him: "I no longer have a separate being. My soul has gone and only a dull machine moves about these rooms or the streets and Commons of Boston, all is unmeaning haze until my prince return and revivify with his breath and magic touch." A little over ten months after their wedding, on February 27, 1880, they were blessed by the birth of their daughter. They named her Angelina Weld Grimké after the aunt who had been so important in Archie's life.[14]

But the happiness did not last long. By the summer of 1882, when Sarah went with Angelina—"Nana"—for a visit to her home on Mackinaw Island, problems had begun to appear. It was at this time that the family moved out of their home on Temple, though Archie maintained his office on Washington, and into an apartment in the home of James Leverett on Milton Avenue in Hyde Park. Archie remained behind to arrange for the move while Sarah and Nana were in

12. M. C. Stanley to Archibald H. Grimké, February 20, 1879, in Archibald Grimké Papers, Box 3, Folder 74; M. C. Stanley to Sarah Stanley, February 21, 1879, *ibid.,* Box 1, Folder 5.
13. Sarah Stanley to Archibald H. Grimké, March 1, 1879, in Archibald Grimké Papers, Box 3, Folder 76; Lucy Stone to Sarah Stanley, March 8, 1879, *ibid.,* Box 1, Folder 7; Ellen Stebbins to Angelina Grimké, January 20, February 26, 1936, in Angelina Grimké Papers, Box 2, Folder 18; New York *Times,* April 28, 1879.
14. Sarah Stanley Grimké to Archibald H. Grimké, May 29, 1879, in Archibald Grimké Papers, Box 3, Folder 76; *Boston City Directory,* 1879.

Michigan. Sarah returned to Hyde Park after her visit, but by May, 1883, she and Nana were back in Michigan with her parents. This time, she did not return.[15]

It is not clear what caused the marriage to fail; the surviving letters tell only Archie's side of the story. He did worry, at least once, that what he called "the unusual character of our union" had caused his wife to be tense and irritable; he worried whenever Sarah became angry that "perhaps she regretted our marriage, if not the marriage exactly the unusual circumstances of our union." This made him overly sensitive, which could hardly have lessened whatever tensions had arisen between them. He also noted that Sarah's health was never very good, which he felt had exacerbated their problems.[16]

A major difficulty seems to have been a charge or set of charges made against him by one of Sarah's good friends, a Mrs. Stuart. The charge is not spelled out in any of the correspondence that grew out of the breaking up of the marriage. That he may have been accused of seeing another woman is indicated in a letter Sarah wrote to him about a year and a half later, warning him "that the one you call your good fairly is your evil genius, in that she prompts you to seek *fame & power* instead of *Peace* and *Good-will*." He was about to become heavily involved in Boston Republican politics when Sarah left him and was spending a good deal of time with Solomon Stebbins, secretary of the party's state committee and husband of Ellen Bradford. He was spending time with Nelly, as well. Whether there was more to the relationship between Archie and Nelly is only a matter for speculation.[17]

Sarah's leaving was, as their daughter later described it, "a terrible blow" for Archie, and it appeared for a while "as if he might lose his mind." By this time, Sarah's father had become fully reconciled to the marriage—he addressed Archie as "my dear son," and Archie called him "father Stanley"—and tried to serve as a mediator for the couple, a role Archie hoped he could play effectively.[18]

15. Sarah Stanley Grimké to Archibald H. Grimké, June 29, 1882, in Archibald Grimké Papers, Box 3, Folder 77; Sarah Stanley Grimké to Archibald Grimké, May 5, 1883, *ibid.*, Box 3, Folder 78; Angelina W. Grimké, "Biographical Sketch," 47; *List of Assessed Polls, Town of Hyde Park, 1890–1902* (12 vols. in 1; Hyde Park, 1890–1902), 1890, pp. 10, 14.

16. Archibald H. Grimké to M. C. Stanley, May 18, 1883, in Archibald Grimké Papers, Box 3, Folder 82.

17. Sarah Stanley Grimké to Archibald H. Grimké, January 11, 1885, *ibid.*, Box 3, Folder 79; A. E. Pillsbury to Archibald H. Grimké, October 8, 1883, *ibid.*, Box 5, Folder 100; Archibald H. Grimké to Sarah Stanley Grimké, n.d., *ibid.*, Box 3, Folder 81.

18. Angelina Grimké, notes on father; M. C. Stanley to Archibald H. Grimké, May 14, 1883, *ibid.*, Box 3, Folder 74; Archibald Grimké to M. C. Stanley, May 18, 1883.

Archie turned to others for assistance as well. His friend Albert Pillsbury heard from both sides in the dispute, as did his brother Frank. And, not surprisingly, Archie spoke long with his "uncle Theodore," whose advice he seems to have respected more than anyone else's. Indeed, when he wrote to Sarah, hoping to bring about a reconciliation, he first showed his letters to his uncle to ensure that they expressed the right tone. Such care, however, did not keep Archie's characteristically volatile temper from coming through. In some of his letters, he addressed her as "My Dear Wife," pointedly crossing out the word "dear." Perhaps it is not surprising, therefore, that none of this effort succeeded in changing Sarah's mind to leave him.[19]

Whatever the cause, the marriage was beyond repair. The only real uncertainty, once Sarah had gone, had to do with Nana. Archie had some sense, encouraged by Pillsbury, that part of Sarah's motivation in leaving him was a desire, prompted by Mrs. Stuart, to take Nana away from him. Sarah did wish to have custody of their daughter and asked Archie to assure her that he would assert no legal claim for Nana's custody. Archie did not want to give up his daughter. Nevertheless, he reluctantly agreed to Sarah's terms, still trying to reassure her, and Angelina remained in her mother's and grandparents' care for about four years, the object of affection.

Nevertheless, there were problems. Sarah had been in poor health throughout the marriage and did not improve after the separation. It was hard for her to give Nana the attention she deserved. And by 1884, Sarah had begun a career of her own. Perhaps reflecting her own problems and concerns, she began to teach correspondence courses on the theory that physical illnesses and personal difficulties were susceptible to psychological solutions and published her first book on the subject, *Personified Unthinkables: An Argument Against Physical Causation*. In the fall of 1886, she published her second book, *First Lessons in Reality, or, The Psychical Basis of Physical Health*. In the tradition of American occultism, these works drew on ancient Egyptian religions and traditions of alchemy, mysticism, and astrology to formulate an approach to personal health and well-being. She became well-known in her field and began to travel fairly extensively.[20]

19. A. E. Pillsbury to Archibald H. Grimké, May 24, 1883, *ibid.,* Box 5, Folder 100; Archibald H. Grimké to Sarah Stanley Grimké, n.d., Sarah Stanley Grimké to Francis J. Grimké, September 5, 1884, *ibid.,* Box 3, Folder 78.

20. Sarah Stanley Grimké, *Personified Unthinkables: An Argument Against Physical Causation* (Ann Arbor, 1884); Sarah Stanley Grimké, *First Lessons in Reality, or, The Psychical Basis of Physical Health* (Detroit, 1886).

But the issue of race was more significant than pressures of health and career. In the spring of 1887, Sarah wrote to Archie saying that Angelina was "getting old enough to see and feel the *thoughts* of others, which the difference of race and color naturally engender regarding her." Sarah did not mention any specific incidents, leading one to suspect that Archie may have been right in his initial feelings about their problems together. A few days after writing to Archie of her concerns, Sarah put the seven-year-old Nana on a train from California to Boston. Sarah and Nana continued to write to each other— Sarah missed her daughter terribly, and there is no evidence that Angelina ever thought of her mother with anything but fondness— but they never saw each other again.[21]

Sarah pursued her career. In 1888 she wrote to Archie that she had decided to go abroad on the basis of "very favorable offers of literary work," and she did. After leaving California, she went to New Zealand, but her health remained poor, and while there, she suffered a heart attack. She returned to Michigan, then went to San Diego. She died there, having taken poison, at the end of August, 1898. She had continued to write—her works were collected in a posthumous volume, *Esoteric Lessons,* published in 1900—and upon her death, as she had promised Archie years earlier, her estate went to Nana. The amount, after medical and funeral expenses were deducted, was $32.70. Archie returned the money to her father.[22]

Angelina entered Archie's world and apparently was happy there, although it was not the nonwhite world her mother had decided she should have. She also made something of a scholarly and literary mark on Hyde Park. In her first year in school, as a seven-year-old, she followed in her father's academic footsteps by compiling an average of 88 percent. By 1893–1894, when she was a teenager, she had about the same average and ranked third in her class. She was a particularly good student in such subjects as grammar, history, and spelling. And she took part in some school activities. For the May Day children's program, she participated in one of the dance numbers. Coincidentally, one of Theodore Weld's grandchildren, Louis, was the leader of

21. Sarah Stanley Grimké to Archibald H. Grimké, April 25, 1887, and Sarah Stanley Grimké to Archibald H. Grimké, telegram, April 27, 1887, in Archibald Grimké Papers, Box 3, Folder 79.

22. Sarah Stanley Grimké to Archibald H. Grimké, May 11, 1888, *ibid.,* Box 3, Folder 79; M. C. Stanley to Archibald H. Grimké, 74; M. C. Stanley to Butler Wilson, November 3, 1989, *ibid.,* Box 1, Folder 6; Sarah Stanley Grimké estate documents, *ibid.,* Box 15, Folder 279; Sarah Stanley Grimké, *Esoteric Lessons* (Denver, 1900).

another. In 1894, the local Norfolk County *Gazette* described her as "well known" in the community.[23]

She also began a literary career that was to blossom when she reached adulthood and was a source of pride and interest to Archie. She was writing poetry when she was no older than eleven, and her tribute to Weld, delivered in 1893, was written when she was twelve. Her first published poem, "The Grave in the Corner," a sentimental saga of a young girl's mourning for the young soldier she had loved, appeared in the Norfolk County *Gazette* in May, 1893, when she was thirteen.[24]

Archie was disturbed for some time about the breakup of his marriage, but it did not cause him to withdraw from society or from contact with the white world. The circumstances of the separation may have prevented him from doing so because he was supported by such white friends as Albert Pillsbury and his once-hostile father-in-law, M. C. Stanley. But more important, during the time he underwent the agony of separation from his wife and, temporarily, from his daughter he entered public life, assuming a role he was to occupy for over ten years until, in 1894, he was appointed and confirmed as the American consul to Santo Domingo.

23. Angelina Weld Grimké, Grade cards, Fairmount School, Hyde Park, in Angelina Grimké Papers, Box 6, Folder 102; Norfolk County *Gazette,* April 29, 1893, July 28, 1894.
24. Norfolk County *Gazette,* May 27, 1893.

4

The Politician

Archibald Grimké's public career began when, in 1883, as he entered his mid-thirties, he enthusiastically jumped into the volatile world of Boston party politics as editor of a Republican-sponsored newspaper for black Bostonians, the *Hub,* and as a spokesman for the Republican party in one of the hottest elections in years, the campaign to elect George Robinson over the incumbent Democrat Benjamin F. Butler for the governorship of Massachusetts. It is not clear how or why Grimké came to be associated with the *Hub*. In June, 1883, a black Boston Republican newspaper, the *Leader,* underwent a shake-up. Its editor, Howard L. Smith, had broken with the party and was fired, and the paper was renamed the *New Leader* and given to William W. Bryant and Butler R. Wilson, then a Boston University law student. By early July, the paper had been renamed again, as the *Hub,* its mission to support the Republican party in the upcoming elections. By the August 4 issue, Archibald Grimké had joined Wilson as co-editor.

Most likely, he had been brought into the picture by Ellen Bradford's husband, Solomon Stebbins, and encouraged by Ellen Stebbins herself. But there were other reasons for Grimké to become involved with the *Hub* and with politics in general. He had already begun to speak out on social issues, giving occasional talks as early as the late 1870s, and the times were such as to encourage anyone with even a speck of social—and racial—concern to speak out. Reconstruction had officially ended in 1877 with the withdrawal of federal troops from the South by President Rutherford B. Hayes. A Democratic resurgence followed, promising a steady erosion of the rights of black citizens in the South and a renewed outburst of white violence against southern blacks aimed at cementing white supremacy. Grimké was aware of these events, as he showed immediately upon assuming his editorship, and that position provided an ideal opportunity for him to give voice to his views. Before long he was the main figure associated with the *Hub*.[1]

The campaign of 1883, the initial focus for the *Hub,* was particularly important for Massachusetts politics and Republicans. Butler had aroused great passion in Massachusetts, especially among some of Boston's more prominent Republicans. These leaders constituted a strong and vocal reform wing that had developed in the party during the scandal-ridden final years of the Grant administration. Butler, then a Radical Republican congressman, had been associated with some of the more corrupt elements in that administration. The *Hub's* effort to hold black Boston voters in line with the Republicans and in opposition to Butler was both important and difficult. Butler had significant black support.

Blacks constituted a notable political force in Boston in the early 1880s, as they had since the end of the Civil War. Such important men as Lewis Hayden, George L. Ruffin, and Edwin Walker had held offices at both the state and local levels, testifying to the strength of the black vote in Boston and Massachusetts politics. Although, as elsewhere in the nation, Boston and Massachusetts black voters were overwhelmingly Republican, there was much to attract them to Butler. He had a good record of supporting black people during the Civil War and Reconstruction. Moreover, in the 1883 campaign, he also had strong support from such leading black figures as James M. Trotter, Edwin Walker, and Rhode Islander George Temple Downing and from the white abolitionist and close friend of Grimké, Wendell Phillips.[2]

Grimké ran the *Hub* in a way that accorded well with his volatile disposition, while putting it squarely in the militant abolitionist tradition of his aunts and their friends. Promising in an early issue of the paper to write "without fear or favor" on the questions of the day, neither to "give nor accept quarter," Grimké set about the job of defeating Butler with enthusiasm—and a torrent of invective. He waved the bloody shirt, describing Butler as the candidate of the party that

1. New York *Globe,* June 23, 1883; Boston *Morning Journal,* July 12, August 11, 1883; Ellen B. Stebbins to Angelina Weld Grimké, January 20, 1936, in Angelina Weld Grimké Papers, Box 2, Folder 18, Moorland-Spingarn Research Center, Howard University, Washington, D.C.

2. New York *Globe,* November 17, 1883; John Daniels, *In Freedom's Birthplace: A Study of the Boston Negroes* (1914; rpr. New York, 1968), 101–102.

was the "protector of the Ku-Klux Klan and the parent of lawless-ness." Referring to Butler's heavy Irish-American support, he said one of Butler's strongholds was "the bar-room" and likened Butler's sup-porters to the mob that had attacked Garrison almost a half-century before. And he vilified those black Butler partisans who, seeking to soften any Democratic identity, called themselves Independents, by connecting the label to the compromises of 1877, writing that "Inde-pendent has too much negrophobia clinging to it to be very grateful to our olfactories," adding, "there is too much political hasheesh in the dressing; too much Paris-green in the gravy."[3]

To be sure, Grimké was not the only journalist to write in this tone. Newspapers of his time were notorious for their strident language and strong partisanship. But it was a style he learned quickly, and it ex-pressed his own predispositions and some of the key influences on him. He would use similar tactics the rest of his life.

Strong words were needed in the fight against Butler. As the cam-paign progressed, it became obvious that Butler was willing to work hard for black votes, as was indicated in mid-September, when he nominated Edwin Walker, son of the militant abolitionist David Wal-ker and longtime community leader, to fill a vacancy as judge of pro-bate for Plymouth County.[4]

It is difficult to tell whether Butler really believed Walker to be the best man for the job or whether he used the nomination in hope of breaking the Republican hold on black voters. Walker certainly had the support of black Bostonians. A Conference of Colored Men, led by Butler Wilson and Grimké's onetime partner James Wolff, and with Grimké in attendance, passed a resolution in late September urging the county council to confirm Walker's nomination. The *Hub,* seeking to minimize the damage, editorially claimed credit for Walker's nomi-nation, saying it had put pressure on Butler.[5]

Butler was helped even more when the Republican-dominated council rejected Walker in early October. Grimké, keeping the faith, declared that color had nothing to do with Walker's rejection, al-though he urged the Republicans to follow Butler's lead—actually, to improve on it—by nominating a black man of ability to some impor-

3. Boston *Hub,* August 18, 25, September 1, 1883.

4. New York *Globe,* November 17, 1883; Boston *Globe,* September 13, 22, Octo-ber 31, 1883; James Oliver Horton and Lois E. Horton, *Black Bostonians: Family Life and Community Struggle in the Antebellum North* (New York, 1979), 57.

5. Boston *Morning Journal,* September 18, 1883; New York *Globe,* September 22, 29, 1883; Boston *Hub,* September 22, 1883.

tant position. The council sought to make up for any damage its re-jection might have done by urging the nomination of George L. Ruf-fin to the post—a nomination Butler made and the council confirmed after the election.[6]

Ultimately, Butler was defeated, despite a fairly good showing among black voters. Nevertheless, such figures as Ruffin and the old-time abolitionist Lewis Hayden felt that the *Hub,* and Grimké in par-ticular, had been very effective. They urged that the party continue to support Grimké and the paper, a sentiment endorsed by such influen-tial Republicans as Grimké's former classmate Henry Cabot Lodge, J. M. Forbes, and John F. Andrew, as well as by the party papers the *Herald* and the *Morning Journal.*[7]

The *Hub* had made Grimké a visible figure. Though he had long confined his social life and other activities mainly to his circle of white friends and associates, by 1883 he began to gain prominence among Boston's black elite. In January of that year, in a survey of elite black Bostonians by the New York *Globe*'s editor Thomas Fortune, there was no mention of Grimké. By September, he had not only become known through the *Hub* but had taken a leading role in the Conference of Colored Men which had sought to persuade the Republican-dominated council to confirm Walker.[8]

How much all of this affected his social life is hard to say. Living in Hyde Park, where the population was mostly white, he was away from the main areas of black population in the city, although his foe in the Butler election, James Trotter, also lived there, and the two men apparently had some contact (a contact that increased when, in 1887, Angelina came to live with her father; although Trotter's eldest child, William Monroe, was somewhat older than Angelina, he had two daughters, Maude and Bessie, who were closer to her in age, and the three became good friends). At the same time, much of Grimké's so-cial life in Hyde Park remained centered around his uncle Theodore,

6. Boston *Morning Journal,* October 6, 8, 1883; New York *Globe,* November 17, 1883; Boston *Hub,* October 13, 1883.

7. New York *Globe,* November 17, 1883; Lewis Hayden and George L. Ruffin to John D. Long, December 26, 1883, in John D. Long Papers, Massachusetts Historical Society, Boston; E. D. Barbour to John F. Andrew, November 30, 1883, in John F. Andrew Papers, Massachusetts Historical Society; Subscription book, *The Hub,* No-vember 10, 1883, in Archibald H. Grimké Papers, Box 10, Folder 190, Moorland-Spingarn Research Center, Howard University, Washington, D.C.; Boston *Hub,* No-vember 17, December 8, 1883.

8. New York *Globe,* January 6, 1883; Boston *Hub,* September 22, 1883.

Weld's children, and the Welds' friends. Even in his religious life, to the extent that he had one, Grimké had little to do with the predominantly black churches that were becoming increasingly visible in Boston, joining the Welds in attending the Hyde Park Unitarian Church.[9]

But Grimké did more than maintain his place in Boston's black society as editor of the *Hub*. He also used his position to speak out on a range of matters of importance not only to black Bostonians but to black Americans generally and began to take a leading role in public affairs. In response to the Danville, Virginia, massacre, for instance, he wrote a pair of columns using militant language in the best tradition of Garrisonian abolitionism, as well as his own volatile disposition, urging black citizens to demand their rights "until the chivalrous assassins of the South are made to respect law and order." He repeated this language a few weeks later at an indignation meeting at which he gave the major address.[10]

The *Hub* served him well by giving him the opportunity to be an articulate public figure, making his views known on a range of issues. When, in early 1884, in a ceremony performed by Francis Grimké, Frederick Douglass married across racial lines, Archibald, acutely sensitive because of the condition of his own marriage, used his columns to defend Douglass against black critics who accused him of abandoning his race. Grimké also promoted causes that had been important to his aunts by championing temperance and urging the general reform and uplift of the race. And his paper published works by his friends, including the young John Cromwell, who wrote a series of letters for him, and Albert Pillsbury, for whom he published a sentimental little poem.[11]

He also found the paper a useful place to ensure that his public lectures received a wide audience. In late May, 1884, for example, he gave the main address before the annual meeting of the Moral Education Association, in which he reflected back, in a semifictional way, on his mother's moral strength and influence. In the address he called "A Madonna of the South," he spoke only of two of her sons, omitting the less successful John.[12]

His writings for the *Hub* revealed the breadth and depth of the intellectual influences he had encountered, not just in the abolitionist

9. Stephen R. Fox, *The Guardian of Boston: William Monroe Trotter* (New York, 1970), 8, 14.

10. Boston *Hub*, November 10, 17, 1883.

11. *Ibid.*, February 2, April 19, 1884.

12. *Ibid.*, May 31, 1884.

tradition, which had helped form his taste for bellicose words and the bloody shirt, but from the cultured world of Boston in which he had moved from the time of his arrival. In particular, Emersonian Transcendentalism influenced his thinking. He applied it to contemporary affairs, urging his readers to recognize that the world is governed by moral law, "by mind," in a way that could reinforce continuing action and optimism in the most difficult times.[13]

The pattern he established in the early years of the *Hub* continued to operate in his career for the rest of his life. This was evident, on one hand, in his strong language and dedication to militancy in pressing the case for equal justice, and, on the other, attempting to put that case in a more general framework of moral ideas and original thought. Grimké was never simply an orator or agitator, though both these activities took up a fair amount of his time throughout his long career. He was also a thinker and scholar, who sought constantly to develop new perspectives on the old problem of racial injustice and oppression in the postemancipation United States.

When he used the columns of his paper to reflect, somewhat self-consciously, on the question of race, his thoughts were not entirely clear and were bound up in both his political concerns and his personal life. He wrote that one cannot reject what he called "one's racehood," for it is inseparable from one's manhood. But he argued in a way his integrationist aunts would have understood that "our manhood must increase; our racehood decrease—i.e. the consciousness of it." Directly attacking his contemporaries who argued the importance of racial identity and unity, even to the point of self-segregation, he asked, "How often are we reminded by American prejudice, by proscription laws, that we are negroes?" Must this be done "by our own people also? Shall we allow our racehood to limit our expanding powers and destiny? Shall we not rather say, 'Know ye not, all ye, that *we are men?*'" Grimké was not about to deny his "racehood," but he was concerned about the limits it could place on him and about the need to move both thought and action outside the constraints defined by clichéd approaches to racial issues.[14]

The *Hub* thus became Grimké's forum for many issues and his main base of support. But the *Hub* was not a firm base. The Republican party, having accomplished the immediate aim of defeating Butler,

13. See S. P. Fullinwider, *The Mind and Mood of Black America: 20th Century Thought* (Homewood, Ill., 1969), 18–19.
14. Boston *Hub,* March 1, 1884.

pretty much left Grimké on his own to support the paper. Party leaders saw some use in continuing the paper. One local Republican wrote to state senator and Boston leader John F. Andrew that the paper could have great effect in maintaining the loyalty of southern voters to the party in the upcoming presidential campaign, urging Andrew to take a hand in "guiding our colored brother aright." But although Lodge and Forbes, among others, solicited subscriptions for it and promised him a contribution of $1,000, this was never paid. Grimké continued to request it as late as 1886, over a year after the *Hub* ceased publication in January, 1885. He finally had to secure whatever limited contributions he could to enhance his own financial support for the paper.[15]

Still, Grimké continued to work for the party and to make a name for himself, not only as an editor but also as a speaker. He used the latter talent to try to raise money for the *Hub,* most notably in a remarkably even-handed but critical lecture he delivered at his brother's Washington church in February, 1884, on the career of John C. Calhoun. He was assisted in this effort by the prominent Massachusetts Republican and former governor John D. Long, who provided the introduction. It was also as a speaker that he took one of the most important early steps of his career in a lecture delivered in early April, 1884. Wendell Phillips, his longtime friend despite their recent political differences, had died the preceding February. In appreciation of Phillips' antislavery role and postwar efforts on behalf of racial equality, leading members of Boston's black community met in February to organize a tribute to him. The attendees represented the cream of the black elite, including W. H. Dupree, who chaired the meeting, James Wolff, Lewis Hayden, and Julius Chappelle. Grimké was nominated by Wolff and chosen over both Thomas Fortune and the historian George Washington Williams to deliver the main speech. The tribute was to be held on April 9 at Tremont Temple.[16]

The tribute was attended by the city's leading black citizens. Hayden, Wolff, Chappelle, Butler Wilson and Ruffin were there; Ruffin, having been chosen over Edwin Walker, presided. So, too, were the most distinguished white veterans of abolition or their children: Weld,

15. Barbour to Andrew, November 30, 1883, in Andrew Papers; Subscription book, the *Hub,* November 10, 1883, Archibald H. Grimké to Henry Cabot Lodge, April 17, 20, 1886, in Archibald Grimké Papers, Box 10, Folder 190.

16. Clipping, n.d., in Archibald Grimké Papers, Box 36, Folder 734; Archibald Grimké, "John C. Calhoun," *ibid.,* Box 18, Folder 334; New York *Globe,* February 24, March 8, 1884; Boston *Hub,* March 8, 1884.

C. A. Bartol, Elizur Wright, Samuel Sewall, Samuel May, Thomas Wentworth Higginson, Grimké's friend Albert E. Pillsbury, the sons of William Lloyd Garrison, and Grimké's first patron in the legal profession, William I. Bowditch.

Grimké's speech showed his familiarity with the main themes of the abolitionist tradition and the strength of that tradition in his own thinking. He was beginning to work with those themes in ways that were to have continuing implications for his later approaches to social and racial questions. Framing his lecture in terms of the "irrepressible conflict" model of the Civil War's causation—a view that had been extremely important in abolitionist rhetoric (and also in Calhounian southern nationalism—a few years later, Grimké described Calhoun as among the first to understand the causes of disunion)—he traced the birth of Garrisonian abolitionism and Phillips' emergence as a leader. He declared that from that time there had been a virtual state of war between "two belligerent governments, two hostile social systems," which must end in armed conflict.[17]

The rest of the speech was devoted to an account of Phillips' life and, above all, a celebration of his character. Especially notable in Grimké's treatment of Phillips' heroism was his presentation of Phillips as an outcast, devoted to truth regardless of who it offended, of a man whose words were weapons in the battle for justice. It was a model he had already adopted for himself in editing the *Hub*, and the speech became a justification for that model in times when truth and right were in peril. A time of crisis requires brutal, sublime language in response, he said, and, echoing his pledge in the *Hub* to speak without fear or favor, such conditions require a willingness to stand alone, even as, "at moments of supreme passion," Phillips willingly "trampled upon the sentiments of his best friends." Grimké said Phillips was "an army in himself," devoted to "truth, justice, righteousness," which Grimké, recalling his Transcendentalist ideas expressed in the *Hub,* called "the only permanent forces in the universe." Taken with Grimké's earlier comments about his own purposes and with his own approach to political action, the Phillips speech represented a good picture of what, to Grimké, was heroic action, of what, to him, was a character to aspire to.[18]

17. Archibald H. Grimké, *A Eulogy on Wendell Phillips, Delivered in Tremont Temple, Boston, April 9, 1884, Together with the Proceedings Incident Thereto, Letters, etc.* (Boston, 1884), 28; Archibald Grimké, *The Life of Charles Sumner: The Scholar in Politics* (New York, 1892), 155.

18. Grimké, *Eulogy on Phillips,* 24, 26, 29.

Grimké's celebration of abolitionism and its values was well received. The speech was often interrupted by applause and was praised by the local papers for its eloquence. It was also noticed, with favor, by those elite white Bostonians who had been in the audience. Shortly after the speech, Grimké received a letter of congratulations from former governor John D. Long. He also received an endorsement of his "sentiments" and an appreciation of his eloquence signed by some of the most important Bostonians: Bowditch, Bartol, Sewall, John F. Andrew, Higginson, George A. Flagg, Forbes, Henry Parkman, Wright, Oliver Ames, Weld, and Henry Cabot Lodge. Some of those signers were also among the leaders of Republicanism in Massachusetts. Lodge, of course, was one. Henry Parkman had been secretary of the party's city committee in Boston during the 1883 election; Oliver Ames had been the party's candidate for lieutenant governor. John F. Andrew was a Republican state senator. George Flagg was secretary of the state Republican convention that met at the end of the month (Long was the president). The speech seems to have confirmed Grimké as a man of talent among Massachusetts Republicans.[19]

His talents were not long in being rewarded. Although they seem to have brought little if anything to the *Hub,* they gave Grimké more visibility, first at the party's state convention and later at its national convention in Chicago.

Massachusetts had a divided Republican party in 1884, the year that saw the rise of a group known as the Mugwumps in party politics. The Mugwumps were the elite of Massachusetts Republicanism: educated, wealthy, independent-minded, and eager for political reform. At the state convention that met at Tremont Temple on April 30, 1884, the Mugwumps were far from a dominant voice. The convention seems to have been dominated by party regulars, its main function to choose delegates to the national convention scheduled for the following June. Those chosen were generally outside the Mugwump camp, though they were not hostile to reform, and included George F. Hoar, William Crapo, Lodge, and Long. Among the alternates, there was only one prominent Mugwump, Higginson. But also among the alternates was Archibald Grimké, and there had been much popular support for his selection.[20]

19. Archibald H. Grimké to John D. Long, April 17, 1884, in Long Papers; "Endorsement of Sentiments in Address in Memory of Wendell Phillips," in Archibald Grimké Papers, Box 39, Folder 759.
20. Boston *Evening Transcript,* April 30, 1884; Norfolk County *Gazette,* May 3, 10, 1884.

The June convention in Chicago, which Grimké attended and at which he was given a small role, was deeply divided, a contest between Chester Arthur, the incumbent, who was not well liked by reform-minded Republicans, and James G. Blaine, the Maine senator, whom they detested. Blaine won on the fourth ballot, to the great disappointment of the reformers, and became the party's nominee.[21]

Grimké's job in the convention had been to help hold southern delegates for Arthur in opposition to Blaine. He seems to have done his job well, basing his approach on Arthur's sectionalist strategy, of which many Mugwumps heartily disapproved. Black southern delegates, he asserted, could not back a man who did not have the confidence of the united North or who was willing to appeal to southern whites. He placed his faith in the good sense of the black southern delegates, who, he said, could not be "purchased" and would, therefore, remain solid for Arthur.[22]

Although Blaine's nomination precipitated a major defection of Massachusetts reformers from the Republican party—including Higginson and Forbes, Moorfield Storey, John F. Andrew, and Charles R. Codman, all of whom, as "bolters," gave their support to the Democratic nominee, Grover Cleveland—Grimké remained loyal to the party and continued to work for it in the *Hub*. With an anger that was almost personal, he attacked what he accurately saw as the Mugwump's indifference to black Americans (though he acknowledged that the regular party was hardly above reproach), aiming invective at the Mugwumps and their policies, especially free trade and "sound money," which he felt were based on an immoral greed that took attention away from the real issues of human rights. Giving his paper's support to Blaine, Grimké declared his optimism about a Republican victory, "the Boston *Advertiser,* the Adams family, the kid glove aristocracy, and the blue blood money bags and reformers to the contrary notwithstanding." When he described one Mugwump rally, he condemned the remarks of such distinguished bolters as Higginson and Codman as "eloquent cant and twaddle." His angry words may not have made him another Wendell Phillips, but he made a conscientious effort. And he continued to aim invective, especially at the Republican bolters, for several months, working actively—if in vain—for Blaine's election through the 1884 campaign.[23]

21. John M. Dobson, *Politics in the Gilded Age: A New Perspective on Reform* (New York, 1972), 102–106; Stanley P. Hirshson, *Farewell to the Bloody Shirt: Northern Republicans and the Southern Negro, 1877–1893* (Bloomington, 1962), 120–22.

22. Clipping, n.d., in Archibald Grimké Papers, Box 36, Folder 719.

23. Geoffrey Blodgett, *The Gentle Reformers: Massachusetts Democrats in the Cleveland

Politics so occupied Grimké's time during that important election year that it is astonishing he had time for much else. His law practice continued, although it is uncertain how much time he devoted to it. His *Hub* co-editor Butler Wilson graduated from Boston University Law School in June, and Grimké took him in as a partner, a professional association that lasted for about two years. But he also engaged in diverse activities, some of which were at least significant to his career as the Blaine campaign. Of perhaps the greatest long-term importance was his appointment by Governor Robinson in September, 1884, to the board of trustees of the Westborough State Hospital, a homeopathic hospital for the insane, which the legislature had established the preceding June. He was elected secretary at the first meeting, a post he held for the next ten years.[24]

The appointment was important because it gave Grimké an association with Charles Codman, one of the bolters and chairman of the hospital board. Codman, whom the *Hub* had singled out for scorn during the campaign, had long been a distinguished participant in Massachusetts politics. In 1883, when Grimké entered politics, Codman was president of the state Republican convention and an ardent foe of Benjamin Butler. His bolting the party not only drew Grimké's fire but ended his political career, although after the 1884 election, he became a frequent and trusted correspondent of Grover Cleveland, advising him on Massachusetts appointments and urging him, contrary to the Mugwump stereotype, to show fairness to black Americans. In 1887, for example, Codman was successful in advising the president to appoint Grimké's fellow Hyde Park resident James M. Trotter as recorder of deeds in Washington. As Westborough trustees, he and Grimké met together regularly, and the relationship that developed between them led to Grimké being described as Codman's protégé. This relationship was to have important if not immediate effects on Grimké's public career.[25]

Era (Cambridge, Mass., 1966), 20–24; Dobson, *Politics in the Gilded Age,* 116–17; Boston *Hub,* June 14, 21, 1884.

24. Norfolk County *Gazette,* July 26, 1884, July 28, 1894; Boston *Herald,* September 24, 1886.

25. Boston *Globe,* September 19, 1883; Charles Warren, *History of the Harvard Law School and of Early Legal Conditions in America* (3 vols.; New York, 1908), III, 57; Blodgett, *Gentle Reformers,* 22; Annette Cartwright to Archibald H. Grimké, October 7, 1918, in Archibald Grimké Papers, Box 4, Folder 89. Evidence of Codman's relationship with President Cleveland comes, for example, from Charles Codman to Grover Cleveland, May 30, September 12, 19, 1885, February 9, 1887, in Grover Cleveland Papers, Library of Congress.

Grimké also remained active with Boston's black leadership, though he was a somewhat controversial figure. During the latter part of 1884, he was named one of Massachusetts' "colored commissioners" for the giant New Orleans world's fair, scheduled to open at the end of that year. Within a short time, however, he resigned, verbally blasting both the exhibition and the national commissioner for the "colored department," former senator Blanche K. Bruce, over an issue involving the allocation of funds. Grimké felt that exhibition policy gave black commissioners less authority than others over funds and was a deliberate insult to the commissioners and that Bruce had submitted too willingly to the insult. Although many people, white as well as black, agreed with Grimké that the exhibition policy was unconscionable, his action, particularly his attack on Bruce, caused some consternation within Boston's black leadership. Still, it did him no permanent harm—as historian William McFeely has remarked, antagonisms among black politicians at this time tended not to last. Within a short time, Grimké was selected to provide leadership in two local problems involving discrimination at city skating rinks and at the New England Conservatory of Music, situations in which he involved himself thoroughly and with some success.[26]

At about this same time, Grimké became more active in the movement for women's rights and women's suffrage, an issue that had been important to his aunts. They had done much to combine the cause of women's rights with that of abolition and to fight for an important place for women within the abolition movement.

As editor of the *Hub,* Grimké had taken up the women's cause, supporting it editorially and urging that his readers consult the works of such important leaders of the movement as Lucy Stone. In November, 1884, after the election, he was invited to address a local meeting of the National Woman Suffrage Association, a pioneering organization of black women devoted to the cause. Attendance at the meeting was small, but Grimké, by all accounts, was eloquent, taking as his topic "Fundamental Justice Our Best Medicine." Identifying the equality of the sexes with racial equality, he claimed that "the advent of inequality was the advent of evil in the world" and that the realization of democracy, including equality of race and gender, was the tendency of history, despite the resistance it might encounter.[27]

26. An account of the New Orleans problems is in the New York *Globe,* November 8, 1884; William S. McFeely, *Frederick Douglass* (New York, 1991), 314.
27. Boston *Hub,* December 22, 1883.

The speech marked the beginning of his dedication to the cause of women's suffrage. In February, 1885, he was the only male to speak at the third annual meeting of the National Woman Suffrage Association of Massachusetts. He repeated his talk "Fundamental Justice Our Best Medicine" and was followed on the program by Susan B. Anthony. Accounts in the local papers were strongly favorable, and none noted Grimké's race. He became president of the Massachusetts Woman's Suffrage Association, a black organization engaged in suffrage agitation, and in September he spoke at a meeting before a largely black audience called to denounce his old associate state legislator Julius Chappelle for a questionable record on the issue. During the following year, Grimké served as a marshal at two major suffrage meetings held in Boston, joining his uncle Theodore Weld to listen to and applaud the speeches of Lucy Stone and others.[28]

Grimké's mention of the inevitability of democracy was significant. It was an idea he may have gotten initially from his aunts, who had taught him that "progress eternal developemental [sic] is the universal law of Being." It could also be found in the writings of many contemporary historians, including George Bancroft, whose work Grimké knew and admired. It joined political concerns with that more general view of a world governed by moral force and "mind" that Grimké had stressed before.[29]

But even more important and a harbinger of a thoroughgoing reorientation in his thought that was to become increasingly important over the next decade or so was that, in discussing the historical necessity of democracy and describing the forces arrayed against it, Grimké paid special attention to what he saw as the chief force for inequality in American life: "Corporate wealth has become the motive force behind government. Monopoly and money are constantly growing to be the power behind elections, behind legislatures, behind the multifarious forces of our American Democracy." This money power, he declared, penetrated every aspect of daily life and created a "network of oppression" arrayed against every virtue of American democracy. In an analogy of more than historical interest, he asserted that corporate despotism, "like the Slave Power . . . has become aggressive and

28. Program of the Third Annual Meeting of the National Woman Suffrage Association of Massachusetts, in Archibald Grimké Papers, Box 39, Folder 772; Miscellaneous clippings, n.d., *ibid.,* Box 36, Folder 719; Marshal's badge, *ibid.,* Box 39, Folder 764; New York *Freeman,* November 7, 14, 1885; Boston *Herald,* March 17, 1886.

29. Angelina Grimké Weld to Archibald Grimké, May 30, [?], in Archibald Grimké Papers, Box 1, Folder 26; Grimké, *Life of Sumner,* 98.

national," continually giving proof of its power and creating a world in which the rich get richer and the poor, poorer. The chief goal of democratic forces should be, he said, the extinction of "the mastodons of corporate despotism and money power," a goal which woman suffrage would help those forces to achieve."[30]

This reasoning was not without antecedents in his thinking. The attacks on the Mugwumps for putting economics over principle in embracing the South anticipated this evocation of the dangers of wealth. Moreover, there was much in the rhetoric of abolitionism as stated by Weld, as well as in the rhetoric of Bancroftian democratic history, that anticipated Grimké's words. But new influences were affecting Grimké's thinking at about this time. Almost certainly the main source of these influences was a book published in 1884 by the black journalist Thomas Fortune, *Black and White,* in which Fortune asserted that the race problem in the South had an economic foundation. Grimké had read the book shortly before his woman suffrage speech and, describing it as an argument that "the Southern problem is more a question of labor and capital, landlord and tenant, than one of a conflict of race," found it wholly convincing.[31]

Fortune's book covered a range of issues but drew heavily on Henry George's 1879 *Progress and Poverty.* Like George, Fortune attacked the "money power," which he and Grimké compared to the antebellum slave power. Urging the unity of black and white workers, he elaborated on George's view that a chief problem in the postwar South was that the master class held its power as a result of having maintained its monopoly on land, leaving the freedmen no less at its mercy than the slaves had been before emancipation. Fortune and George were not, of course, the only voices decrying monopoly and corporate wealth in American life. But Fortune's book and, through it, Henry George's were clearly identifiable sources for Grimké.[32]

This new direction in Grimké's thought was to add a new twist to his politics. At about the time he began to show the influence of For-

30. Boston *Hub,* November 22, 1884.

31. On Weld and others see Herbert Aptheker, *Abolitionism: A Revolutionary Movement* (Boston, 1989), 15, 33; Boston *Hub,* October 4, 1884.

32. Henry George, *Progress and Poverty: An Inquiry into the Cause of Industrial Depressions and of Increase of Want with Increase of Wealth* (1879; rpr. New York, 1962), 354–55; T. Thomas Fortune, *Black and White: Land, Labor, and Politics in the South* (1884; rpr. New York, 1968), 36; see Leon Fink, *Workingmen's Democracy: The Knights of Labor and American Politics* (Urbana, 1983), 4; Bernard K. Johnpoll with Lillian Johnpoll, *The Impossible Dream: The Rise and Demise of the American Left* (Westport, Conn., 1981), 118–19.

tune and George, he was also beginning to reevaluate his connection with the Republican party, moving toward bolting himself. Although a decade later he would date his move out of the party to 1886, his disenchantment with the Republicans may have occurred as early as the Blaine nomination, as he noted in his comments on black support for the Republican ticket at the time.[33]

By 1885, that disenchantment had become strong. In an address that seems to have been made shortly after Cleveland's inauguration, he accused the Republicans of having "dropped" the Negro in 1876 and noted how, beginning in 1884, some northern Democrats had begun to "cultivate Africa." In 1886, he broke his Republican tie, joining the Independent movement he had earlier condemned and with a completeness that contradicted much that he had said before. The reasons for his switch were probably complex. Looking back in 1894, Grimké remembered that the chief reason for his defection from the Republicans was the tariff issue, and, although he said little about it at the time, by 1888 he had become an ardent free trader, a position advocated by both George and Fortune, rejecting his earlier party-line loyalty to protection. His increasing orientation toward economic issues may well have played a part in his decision, but the situation was yet more complicated.[34]

There were several factors, in addition to economic ideas, that probably led Grimké to leave the Republican party. The change was not inconsistent with much in Grimké's background. As his brother Francis later observed, party loyalty could hardly have come easily for Archibald Grimké, imbued as he was with the ideal of independence. Moreover, the reference to the tariff issue, like Grimké's turn to economic concerns generally at about this time, was subtly consistent with the ideas of racial identity presented in the earlier *Hub* editorial on "racehood" and "manhood." In that piece, Grimké had demanded the need for both, and by talking about economics as much as race, he demonstrated both an independence and a breadth that defied stereotypes and political proscriptions, which after 1877 had become increasingly problematic. Personal ties may also have been important. Charles Codman was certainly one influence, as both men later acknowledged. Solomon Stebbins, too, had shown Mugwump leanings and was believed to be moving away from the Republican party as early as January, 1886.[35]

33. For the 1886 date, see Norfolk County *Gazette,* July 28, 1894.
34. *Ibid.*
35. Charles R. Codman to Grover Cleveland, January 11, 1889, in Cleveland Pa-

But perhaps key was Grimké's anger, hardly out of character for him, toward the Republican leadership, particularly over the financing of the *Hub*. In April, 1886, Grimké wrote a series of letters to Henry Cabot Lodge, reminding him of the promised $1,000 for support of the paper. While acknowledging that he had no legal claim to that money, he pointed out that legal title in the paper was vested in the state committee and that its continuation through the 1884 election had been urged by Lodge and the committee despite any financial difficulties. He ascribed much of the paper's financial difficulty to the Mugwump defection and noted that he probably could have received better support by going along with the defectors. There is no doubt that Grimké felt he had been deceived by the Republicans and that the deception had cost him a good deal of money.[36]

Once the election of 1886 was in full swing, Grimké left no doubt about his change of view, moving into the Independent camp with all the enthusiasm and high spirits that had marked other shifts in his life. John F. Andrew, one of the bolters, was the Democratic nominee to run against the Republican Oliver Ames, and he brought the large Mugwump contingent with him to the Democratic party. In mid-October, Charles Codman declared himself to be wholly a Democrat, and toward the end of the month Grimké wrote a long letter to the Mugwump Boston *Herald,* declaring his admiration for that Independent movement he had earlier condemned and urging black voters to reject their Republican ties and support Andrew. A few days later he sent an equally long letter on the same subject to Thomas Fortune's New York *Freeman,* which itself had come out for Andrew over Ames.[37]

He worked hard for Andrew throughout the campaign, writing to all the Boston papers on the Democrat's behalf. As might be expected, he was roundly attacked by Republican loyalists, white as well as black, although, as usual, any divisions were not permanent. It was not long after the election (which Ames won) before some of his erstwhile antagonists endorsed him to replace George Ruffin, who had died at the close of the campaign, in a judgeship, though nothing came

pers; New York *Age,* January 26, 1889; Boston *Herald,* January 13, 1886; see also Hirshson, *Bloody Shirt,* 132–33; James M. McPherson, *The Abolitionist Legacy: From Reconstruction to the NAACP* (Princeton, 1975), 126–27.

36. Archibald Grimké to Lodge, April 17, 20, 1886.

37. Norfolk County *Gazette,* October 2, 1886; Boston *Globe,* October 14, 1886; Boston *Herald,* October 25, 1886; New York *Freeman,* October 9, 30, 1886.

of the endorsement. Governor Ames, whom he had worked so hard
to defeat, appointed him to a place on the committee to erect a monu-
ment to Crispus Attucks in Boston Common.[38]

His shifting political allegiance had little effect on his stature as a
public man. Over the next couple of years Grimké continued to be in
demand, speaking, writing, and involving himself in an array of matters. But he moved increasingly into the camp identified with the economic views he had begun to express in both the women's suffrage
address and his political activity. He became something of a partisan
in the city's burgeoning labor movement, affiliating with the educational arm of the movement—the Central Labor Union—and championing the eight-hour law as a check on rampant capitalism.

Partisan politics, however, remained his main focus of public interest, and at the end of 1887 and early 1888, with an approaching
presidential election, Grimké soon turned his attention back in that
direction, retaining his Independent label but devoting himself to the
cause of the Democratic party. In early September, he became a vice-
president of the Hyde Park Democratic Club, and he devoted the next
two months to the reelection of the Democratic incumbent, Cleveland, over his Republic opponent, Benjamin Harrison.[39]

Two issues occupied most of Grimké's attention during the 1888
election campaign. One concerned local politics. The old abolitionist
Thomas Wentworth Higginson was the Democratic nominee for Massachusetts' fifth congressional district seat, and Grimké supported his
candidacy. This could not have been easy for him. Since the Mugwump bolt, Higginson's stand on racial questions had not been clearly
on the side of black Americans. He had, for example, defended southern efforts to disfranchise blacks during the mid-1880s and even suggested that blacks had voluntarily refrained from political activity, despite the evidence of violence intended to discourage them from it, a
stand that inspired great black opposition to him.[40]

Nevertheless, Grimké strongly supported Higginson through the
campaign, focusing chiefly on his abolitionist past—a strategy Higginson himself relied on—while ignoring Higginson's less fortunate,
more embarrassing ideas about sectionalism and black suffrage. And
he was not above attacking one of the candidate's more vocal black

38. Boston *Advocate,* November 27, 1886; New York *Freeman,* September 22, 1888.

39. Norfolk County *Gazette,* September 8, 1888.

40. Tilden G. Edelstein, *Strange Enthusiasm: A Life of Thomas Wentworth Higginson*
(New Haven, 1968), 377–78.

critics, Frederick Douglass, who had widely publicized his opposition to the former abolitionist. At one gathering, which Higginson supporter Samuel Sewall also attended, Grimké spoke of his pride at being present with "one of the original abolitionists at a time when Mr. Douglass had not escaped from slavery." And he chided Douglass for claiming to represent blacks, saying that he, too, represented "between 1,000,000 and 2,000,000 laboring men of this country." He also accused Douglass of "intermeddling" in Massachusetts affairs.[41]

Higginson lost the election. Despite Grimké's efforts and his own, he failed to garner much support from black voters. Even Grimké's former co-worker Butler Wilson remained firmly in the Republican camp, exchanging a public correspondence with Douglass to bolster the efforts of Higginson's Republican opponent.[42]

Grimké did no better with the election of Cleveland. He spoke about the president's record, which had not been hostile to black Americans, but he focused more on the question he would later claim brought him to the Democrats, the tariff. On this issue, he joined Charles Codman, who had become a strong free trade Democrat. The two of them spoke—along with such other notables as Josiah Quincy, William Everett, and Sherman Hoar—at Tremont Temple on October 19, 1888, at a gathering sponsored by the Harvard Tariff Reform Club. This was one of the most fully covered meetings of the campaign. Among those in attendance—all vice-presidents of the club—were James Barr Ames, Charles Eliot Norton, John F. Andrew, Francis James Child, John Fiske, William Lloyd Garrison, Jr., Higginson, William James, Robert Treat Paine, Francis Parkman, Leverett Saltonstall, Nathan S. Shaler, Moorfield Storey, and John B. Thayer, to mention only a few. Grimké was greeted with enthusiasm, and his remarks were well received, as he urged black voters "to take hold of this tariff question, which concerns them as much as it does the white man, and with the Democrats and that noble man, Grover Cleveland." Grimké had, by now, become fully convinced of the positions he had begun to explore only about three years before.[43]

Grimké did not go unrewarded for his efforts on the Democratic party's behalf. On November 2, 1888, four days before the election, he received his party's nomination for state representative from Hyde

41. Boston *Globe,* October 20, 1888; Edelstein, *Strange Enthusiasm,* 377.
42. Edelstein, *Strange Enthusiasm,* 378–79; Boston *Evening Transcript,* October 16, 29, 1888.
43. Boston *Evening Transcript,* October 5, 20, 1888; Boston *Herald,* October 20, 1888.

Park, running against the Republican Ferdinand Wyman. He lost. There could not have been much of a campaign, and it was not bitter. After the election, the Republican but always friendly Norfolk County *Gazette* of Hyde Park editorialized, "Mr. Grimké is a man of strong convictions and high personal honor, and it was this opinion of his fellow townsmen that took away somewhat the sting of political ingratitude which they felt, and softened the asperities which might have been expressed." In any case, Grimké lost by 360 votes out of about 1,500 votes cast. It was not a bad showing, but he ran about 50 votes behind the national ticket, which gave the *Gazette* the opportunity to crow "that the Democracy did not fully appreciate their opportunity and that their prejudice against the race was much stronger than their party fealty."[44]

Codman tried to reward Grimké further about two months later. On January 11, 1889, apparently at Grimké's request, he wrote to the outgoing President Cleveland suggesting Grimké for the just vacated post of consul to Santo Domingo in the Dominican Republic. The post had become vacant when the previous consul, H. C. C. Astwood, a minister in the African Methodist Episcopal church, was fired under a cloud of suspicion. Codman gave Grimké a glowing recommendation, including an account of Grimké's history from slavery to freedom, and wrote that over the past five years, as a result of their work on the hospital board, he had "seen a great deal of him" and had "a thorough knowledge of his character, abilities and attainments." Needless to say, he cited Grimké's dedication to the Cleveland campaign in the preceding election. He also suggested that James Trotter, whom he had sponsored earlier, could support the recommendation.[45]

Codman's recommendation was accepted. On January 23, Cleveland submitted the nomination to the Senate, where it appeared to be well received. The Hyde Park *Times* commended the president for the choice, adding that it was "generally believed that Mr. Grimké will be confirmed." The Mugwump Boston *Transcript* also commended the selection, saying, inaccurately, that Grimké had "for some time taken no active part in politics" but concluding that "the country needs a man of sterling character and level head as its representative at the Dominican capital, and should the present nomination be confirmed, its requirements will be fully and thoroughly met." Grimké

44. Boston *Globe,* November 2, 1888; Norfolk County *Gazette,* November 10, 1888.
45. Codman to Cleveland, January 11, 1889.

also had the endorsement of such prominent black Bostonians as Lewis Hayden, Edward Everett Brown, and Julius C. Chappelle.[46]

The commendations and endorsements were not, however, enough. Cleveland was a lame-duck president, and though many of his final nominations went through, Grimké's was allowed to die, unacted upon before the Congress adjourned preceding the inauguration of President Harrison. Astwood remained in place on temporary duty. There is no doubt that Grimké's nomination was denied intentionally. Massachusetts senator George F. Hoar, a strong Republican, had opposed the nomination because of Grimké's ties to the Mugwumps, whom Hoar wanted to punish. According to one account, Hoar was especially indignant because of Grimké's being a black Mugwump, making the sin all the greater. In the words of the writer of this account: "Mr. Grimké is a scholarly gentleman, of rare refinement and purity of character also. This makes the case all the worse. He is all the more dangerous example to set before the people." Grimké was to wait five years, until Cleveland was back in the White House, before he got the post he wanted.[47]

Despite the failure, and with Cleveland out of the presidency, Grimké remained fairly active in public affairs, if not, perhaps, to the extent that he had been for the previous five or six years. In 1889, for example, following up on his interest in Henry George, he became president of the Hyde Park Single Tax Club, using it chiefly to espouse his free trade views. In that same year, he was one of the officers of a Hyde Park committee formed to support a constitutional amendment to prohibit the manufacture and sale of alcoholic beverages in Massachusetts (an issue on which he disagreed with Codman). He was joined in this effort by Theodore Weld and by Ferdinand Wyman, who had defeated him for office in the 1888 election. The amendment was defeated statewide but did carry Hyde Park.[48]

Even though he was at least once mentioned as a possibility for a job in the Harrison administration, he remained, though still calling himself an Independent, with the Democrats. During the 1890 election, he again took to the stump with Codman in support of the Democratic party, speaking against the Republicans in regard to tariff policy and to Henry Cabot Lodge's so-called Force Bill, designed to

46. *Congressional Record,* 50th Cong., 2nd Sess., 1137; Hyde Park *Times,* January 25, 1889; Boston *Evening Transcript,* January 30, 1889; Springfield *Republican,* January 24, 1889.

47. Clipping, n.d., in Archibald Grimké Papers, Box 36, Folder 719.

48. Norfolk County *Gazette,* February 23, 1889; Boston *Herald,* April 9, 1890.

protect black suffrage in the South by providing for federal supervisors, empowered to pass on the qualifications of any voter challenged in a federal election and to receive ballots wrongfully refused by local officials. Though the bill was ultimately defeated, in early 1891, it was a hot issue in the 1890 campaign, including that in Massachusetts, where it had the support of virtually every leading black political figure.[49]

Democrats, knowing that the bill would protect southern Republican votes, were strongly opposed to it, and among the opposition was Archibald Grimké. In a speech delivered at New Bedford about a week before the election, he linked the Lodge bill with Republican partisanship and denied that there were nobler motives. Saving black votes, he noted, saved the party, and this, in turn, saved Republican policies, including a high tariff.[50]

Grimké never said anything about his stance on the Force Bill beyond what he offered in his speeches, and it was a stance he would reverse when similar legislation was proposed in the future. He probably saw his position as more than self-serving, and it probably was an indication of his view, developed over the preceding six or seven years, that partisan politics and economics presented the best approach to racial questions. It may also have had something to do with his grudge against Lodge for failing to support the *Hub*. That his position was somewhat strained is clear, but he had become a politician and, having adopted that course, was prepared to pursue it consistently and with dedication.

Such partisanship makes all the more interesting the turn his life was to take over the next decade.

49. Rayford Logan, *The Betrayal of the Negro, from Rutherford B. Hayes to Woodrow Wilson* (Rev. ed.; London, 1965), 70–81.
50. Boston *Herald*, October 30, 1890.

5

Scholar and Diplomat

The election of 1890 began a political hiatus for Archibald Grimké. Perhaps still disappointed over the failure of his Santo Domingo appointment and faced, at about the same time, with a long and difficult illness on the part of his daughter, he was less and less conspicuous in partisan politics for the next several years. He did not, however, remove himself entirely. As late as 1892, he lent his name to the local committee for the election of Grover Cleveland to the presidency, writing letters to Boston newspapers on behalf of the cause. He also supported his old friend Tom Miller in a disputed South Carolina race for the United States Congress, contacting his friends in the Massachusetts delegation and garnering support from his colleague Charles Codman. But such activity did not compare with the level he had engaged in earlier.

Apart from personal reasons that might have led him to reduce his political involvement, no doubt a prime reason for his doing so lay in the increasing attention he was giving to other things, especially his literary work. During his years as a political figure, Archibald Grimké had become fairly well-known as a speaker and writer. As early as 1887, his local newspaper, the Norfolk County *Gazette,* described him as a speaker with "a national reputation." Even so august and noted a figure as the white southern racial liberal George W. Cable called him, in 1888, one of the leading spokesmen for racial justice.[1]

After about 1890, however, as he became much more ambitious

1. Norfolk County *Gazette,* October 29, 1887; George W. Cable, *The Negro Question: A Selection of Writings on Civil Rights in the South,* ed. Arlin Turner (Garden City, N.Y., 1958), 173.

about his literary work and his political activity lessened noticeably, Grimké's reputation began to grow. He broadened the range of topics on which he wrote and the audiences he addressed. In April, 1890, for example, he drew on his experiences as a member of the board of the Westborough Hospital to do a piece for the Boston *Herald* on mental illness and treatment techniques. In June, 1891, he did an essay, published in the Boston *Comment,* on the expulsion of Jews from Russia, which he decried as a crime of international proportions. He also drew parallels between the fate of the Jews in Russia and the vulnerability of blacks in the South, although he did not dwell on the analogy.[2]

And, of course, he continued to write on essentially racial topics, developing his ideas, elaborating on them, applying them to new situations. In May, 1890, he delivered an address at Tremont Temple titled "The Opening Up of Africa," describing both the industrial potential of the continent and the danger posed by its possible exploitation at the hands of monopoly power. He also became involved in a debate in a major intellectual journal of the period, the *Open Court,* initiated by a series of communications to the magazine from the paleontologist Professor Edward D. Cope, arguing from Lamarckian principles that racial characteristics made "American-Africans" wholly unassimilable into American society and its institutions. Grimké responded to Cope's ideas with a long letter to the *Open Court,* ridiculing Cope's view that the "Indo-European race," which had engaged in the worst exploitation imaginable, not only of blacks but of other "races," should be celebrated for its purity of character.[3]

During this time he also completed the two major works of his literary career, full-length biographies of two men whom he had met early in his adult years and revered all his life, William Lloyd Garrison and Charles Sumner. These books—published in 1891 and 1892—were part of the American Reformer Series published by Funk and Wagnalls and had been commissioned by Francis Garrison, son of William Lloyd and a Funk and Wagnalls executive. The books were com-

2. Boston *Herald,* April 24, 1890; Clipping, n.d., in Archibald H. Grimké Papers, Box 36, Folder 734, Moorland-Spingarn Research Center, Howard University, Washington, D.C.

3. New York *Age,* May 31, 1890; Archibald H. Grimké, "The Opening Up of Africa," *New Ideal,* III (1890), 351, 355; George W. Stocking, Jr., *Race, Culture, and Evolution: Essays in the History of Anthropology* (New York, 1968), 239, 246–47; E. D. Cope, "The Perils of the Indo-European," *Open Court,* III (1890), 2053–54; Cope, "The Return of the Negroes to Africa," *Open Court,* III (1890), 2110–11; Archibald H. Grimké, "The Indo-European and the Negro," *Open Court,* IV (1890), 2149.

missioned in May, 1890, which almost certainly explains Grimké's decreasing public activity at that time.[4]

There is, unfortunately, no information about the commissioning of these books. Grimké had known the Garrisons, including Francis, since his early days in Boston. Francis Garrison was involved in the Independent movement at the same time Grimké was, encouraging a close relationship between the two men. In addition, Garrison and his brother Wendell Phillips Garrison had just produced a four-volume biography of their father, which appeared between 1885 and 1889, and Grimké had written a favorable review of the first volume for the *Christian Register*. But Grimké had also been thinking about the antislavery movement at about the time he received the commission. He had recently developed addresses on the life of Sumner and on the Civil War hero Robert Gould Shaw. He had also produced a brief article for the *New England Magazine* on landmark antislavery buildings in Boston in which he commented on the movement itself.[5]

Thus the offer must have been highly attractive. The books, with the imprint of a major American publisher, promised him a larger audience than he had ever had. They were widely and favorably reviewed and contributed to his reputation as a writer and scholar. Not only were the subjects dear to him as friends and as admirable men, but writing their biographies helped him fulfill a goal he had set early in his days with the *Hub,* to address issues that were racially important but to go beyond "racehood" and to show himself as a "man" as well. After the books appeared, Grimké was praised by Thomas Fortune for showing "that we can do something in literature besides dwell on race grievances and do it well."[6]

The two books were an important step in Grimké's career. They broke little new substantive ground—the Garrison volume was based almost entirely on the earlier work by the abolitionist's sons—but they did give Grimké the opportunity to summarize and reflect on many of the disparate themes he had addressed in the lecture hall or on the stump, going back to the Phillips speech and in less readily available

4. New York *Age,* May 31, 1890.

5. A. H. Grimké, "William Lloyd Garrison," *Christian Register* (December 3, 1895), 776; Archibald H. Grimké, "Charles Sumner," in Archibald Grimké Papers, Box 19, Folder 355; Grimké, "Anti-Slavery in Boston," *New England Magazine* (December, 1890), 441–59, offprint in Spingarn Collection, Moorland-Spingarn Research Center, Howard University, Washington, D.C.; Archibald H. Grimké, "Colonel Shaw and His Black Regiment," *New England Magazine,* n.s., I (1890), 675, 679.

6. New York *Age,* November 19, 1892.

essays. Taking as his central theme in both the operation of the "moral law" in history, he tried to show how each man, by courageous action and heroic persistence, helped to further the fulfillment of the law. He traced Garrison's development into a public man and his single-minded dedication to the cause of antislavery. Focusing on the side of his subject that was, like himself, petulant and reproachful, he showed how Garrison used his philippic to create a tidal wave of reform and revolution. If Grimké recognized some problems with Garrison's obsessive and stern approach to his cause—especially his difficulty in working with others—he nevertheless tried to show how the nature of the times made possible the efficacy of such a man as Garrison and how Garrison responded to that demand to become a creator as well as a figure of history. Grimké used Garrison's life as an example of moral heroism in a complex world in ways that had obvious parallels to his own recent career as a journalist, turned activist, turned man of letters.

The Sumner book had similar personal implications for him. It was subtitled *The Scholar in Politics* and again explored the question of moral efficacy in the world of politics. Grimké contrasted the political Sumner with the antipolitical Garrison, making clear his preference for the former. He focused on the parts of Sumner that represented his own predilections, devoting much of the book to accounts of Sumner's more stirring addresses and singling out for attention those passages in which Sumner's invective reached heights to which Archie himself could only stand in awe. Even more than in the Garrison book, he drew obvious parallels with his own career. At one point he described Sumner, anachronistically, as "the first great Mugwump of Massachusetts." Thus even more than the Garrison volume, the Sumner biography allowed him to think about the work he had been doing as a public man for the preceding decade, as well as the more general issues of heroism in history.[7]

With the appearance of these books he seemed well on his way to creating a significant and visible literary career. Over the next couple of years, he spoke and wrote frequently on the topics covered in the books. His literary career, however, was soon interrupted when Grimké was named to the consulship to Santo Domingo, in the Dominican Republic. Toward the end of January, 1894, the American consul to Santo Domingo died. John R. Meade was white, and Presi-

7. Archibald H. Grimké, *The Life of Charles Sumner: The Scholar in Politics* (New York, 1892), 398.

dent Cleveland's inclination was to fill the vacancy with another white man. Nevertheless, Codman again urged the president to nominate Grimké to the post. Cleveland delayed for some time but ultimately decided to take Codman's advice, submitting Grimké's name to the Senate.[8]

As had been the case five years earlier, Grimké's nomination got a favorable public response. As had not been the case five years earlier, however, his nomination was presented to a Democratic Senate, and in a week, on July 30, 1894, his appointment was confirmed.[9]

Grimké joined a growing company of black Americans appointed to such posts. Since the Reconstruction era, Santo Domingo, along with neighboring Haiti, had usually been given to black appointees. Although Grimké's immediate predecessor was white, his appointment followed by only a few years that of H. C. C. Astwood. Another black man, University of Pennsylvania graduate John S. Durham, had served in the same post in 1890 before moving on in 1891 to Haiti. There, he succeeded Grimké's most illustrious black predecessor in the foreign service, Frederick Douglass, who himself had succeeded the notable lawyer and political figure John Mercer Langston. Grimké was joining distinguished company by assuming a diplomatic post and a relatively small one as well; only about a dozen black Americans had reached the consular level. He was still fairly young, just turning forty-four, and could view his appointment as exceptional recognition.[10]

The next several weeks were spent preparing for his new assignment, receiving his instructions from the State Department, and arranging to leave Angelina in the care of Francis and Charlotte Grimké. He also used the occasion to give an interview to the Washington *Star* in which he reiterated his support for Cleveland and the Democratic party, though he claimed to be "so much taken up with my literary work that I have not given much attention to political affairs." The *Star*'s reporter went a bit too far in further describing Grimké as one who had "never taken an active part in politics." (A few years later,

8. Grover Cleveland to Charles Codman, July 17, 1894, in Charles R. Codman Papers, Massachusetts Historical Society, Boston.

9. Boston *Globe,* July 27, 1894; Norfolk County *Gazette,* July 28, 1894; *Congressional Record,* 53rd Cong., 2nd Sess., 7812, 7990.

10. Allison Blakely, "Black U.S. Consuls and Diplomats and Black Leadership, 1880–1920," *Umoja,* I (1977), 4–5; U.S. National Archives and Records Service, *Black Studies: A Select Catalogue of National Archives Microfilm Publications* (Washington, D.C., 1984), 6–7.

the Boston *Evening Transcript* compared Grimké's appointment to those of William Dean Howells, Bret Harte, and Albion Tourgée as being "due to his literary character.") In mid-October, he departed for his new post.[11]

The ship on which Grimké traveled to Santo Domingo got caught in a severe storm; after calm returned, it was run onto reefs bordering the narrow channel into the port of Grand Turk, where it was scheduled to stop. Grimké used the enforced break to enjoy what he saw as complete political and civil equality across racial lines in the Caribbean world he was visiting for the first time. After a voyage of almost a month, he reached Santo Domingo on November 16, 1894, and moved into a large house in what he called "the best part of the city"—a house owned by an American sugar planter named Alexander Bass. He soon initiated friendships with consular representatives of the other powers, with members of the Dominican government, and with the American community on the island. Except for a brief leave during 1896, Grimké was to make this his home for most of the next four years, until the summer of 1898, when he was replaced, virtually removing himself from the political, social, and economic concerns that had occupied so much of his time and effort for the preceding ten years.[12]

The Dominican Republic had long had a tumultuous history and was not the most stable of countries in the mid-1890s. Variously under Spanish and Haitian rule, the country had been independent since 1844, although it had known few years of peace and prosperity. Since about 1882, it had been under the dictatorship of General Ulises Heureaux, a black man who had risen through the ranks of the Dominican army, making a distinguished career for himself as a military commander. Facing constant threats of revolution and chronic economic crises, he exercised the presidency with an iron fist.[13]

11. Archibald Grimké to W. W. Rockhill, September 1, 1894, Grimké to Edwin F. Uhl, October 29, 1894, both in Despatches from U.S. Consuls in Santo Domingo, 1837–1906, National Archives; Washington *Evening Star,* September 24, 1894; Boston *Evening Transcript,* October 2, 1897.

12. Archibald H. Grimké, "A Voyage to Santo Domingo," *Southern Workman,* XXIX (1900), 512–13; Archibald Grimké to Edwin F. Uhl, November 19, 26, 1894, in Despatches from U.S. Consuls; Archibald Grimké to Angelina Weld Grimké, November 25, 1894, in Angelina Weld Grimké Papers, Box 4, Folder 65, Moorland-Spingarn Research Center, Howard University, Washington, D.C.

13. Selden Rodman, *Quisqueya: A History of the Dominican Republic* (Seattle, 1964), 92; Sumner Welles, *Naboth's Vineyard: The Dominican Republic, 1844–1924* (2 vols., 1926; rpr. Mamoroneck, N.Y., 1966), I, 448, 450, 458–60.

As consul, Grimké was to be involved in some of the issues of intrigue and particularly finance affecting the Heureaux government in its relations with the United States. Much of the agricultural and industrial improvement for which Heureaux could claim credit was financed by American investment. Because he was the highest-ranking American official resident in the republic—reporting to the American ambassador in neighboring Haiti, who also served as chargé d'affaires to Santo Domingo—he had much to do during his stay on the island.[14] Early in his term, he was called on to mediate a dispute, which almost came to war, between Heureaux and the French government over state finances, cooperating with the Spanish consul, and, as he saw it, defining a significant place for himself in the diplomatic community and in the eyes of the Dominican dictator. He also had to address matters of less international significance. While he was dealing with the French tensions, he also had to solve the problems posed when the entire crew of an American steamer was arrested for disorderly conduct. He was able to gain their release and, as he noted with satisfaction, to give the ship's American captain, a man "full of Southern prejudice," a "sharp lesson on the impudence of coming to the American Consul on such an errand."[15]

Such experiences must have enhanced his pleasure with the post. Having lived with American racism for so much of his life, now as a diplomat, he was dealt with as an equal and on the basis of his abilities rather than his color. Other black diplomats in the Caribbean, notably Frederick Douglass in Haiti a few years before, had had a similar experience. Grimké even seemed to have cordial relations with American businessmen, who often were at loggerheads with the Dominican government over contractual matters and were forced to come to him for aid. He usually served them well. Even Boston, with all its virtues, had never been like this.[16]

Grimké was generally a good diplomat. On only one issue did he find himself in what might have been an untenable situation. This came toward the end of his term, in 1898, and involved the American acquisition of a coaling station at Samaná Bay. American

14. Rodman, *Quisqueya*, 104–105; Welles, *Naboth's Vineyard*, I, 476, 495; Melvin M. Knight, *The Americans in Santo Domingo* (New York, 1928), 17; New York *Times*, June 1, 1894.

15. Archibald Grimké to "Dear Home Ones," February 1, 1895, in Francis J. Grimké Papers, Box 3, Folder 111, Moorland-Spingarn Research Center, Howard University, Washington, D.C.

16. William S. McFeely, *Frederick Douglass* (New York, 1991), 340.

interest in the bay as a depot went back at least to 1849, in the early years of Dominican independence, and had been revived from time to time. In January, 1895, when Dominican troubles with the French were reaching a tense stage, Grimké wrote to the State Department that the United States might be able to use the situation to create relations that would improve the possibility of acquiring Samaná. In late 1897, Grimké wrote that the chances of acquiring a lease were good, although internal opposition remained "formidable," if not "insurmountable."[17]

The matter came to a head in early 1898. In the days just preceding the outbreak of the Spanish-American War, coinciding with the end of Grimké's term (in the neutral republic, he was little affected by the war), Heureaux, as always needing money, concocted a plot to speed the process, suggesting to Grimké that, though constrained by popular opinion from ceding Samaná, "he wishes our Government to aid him by taking the initiative, by seizing the Bay for instance to satisfy some claim of American citizens against his Government, in the payment of which his Government may have defaulted." Heureaux would then claim compensation for the American action, consummating the purchase.[18]

The plan was a dangerous one, and it was probably fortunate for Grimké that before it was accomplished he left Santo Domingo. William McKinley, a Republican, had been elected president in 1896, and Grimké, as a political appointee, was unsure of retaining the position. He was not eager to leave, and he had help in his efforts to keep the position. As early as May, 1897, his brother Francis wrote to Archibald Grimké's onetime political companion—and McKinley's secretary of the navy—John D. Long, to urge his help in keeping Grimké on, which Long agreed to give. A concerted effort in Grimké's behalf was also made by some of the Americans whose interests he had represented in Santo Domingo, a measure of his effectiveness.[19]

The effort seemed to have some effect; as late as January, 1898,

17. Welles, *Naboth's Vineyard*, I, 92, 325, 481; Archibald Grimké to Edwin F. Uhl, February 3, 1895, Grimké to William Day, November 18, 1897, both in Despatches from U.S. Consuls.

18. Archibald Grimké to William Day, April 7, 1898, in Despatches from U.S. Consuls; Thomas W. Cridlen [?] to Archibald Grimké, April 25, 1898, in Archibald Grimké Papers, Box 24, Folder 486; Welles, *Naboth's Vineyard,* II, 529.

19. Francis J. Grimké to John D. Long, May 3, 1897, William Clyde to William Day, June 2, 1897, H. M. Hanna to Nathaniel McKay, June 11, 1897, all in Records of the Department of State, National Archives.

Grimké thought the prospects were good for his retaining the post. But in March, McKinley appointed Campbell G. Maxwell to the consulship. By the middle of July, Grimké was back in the United States.[20]

Grimké's unhappiness at being replaced led him to make an effort before he left for home to create a working relationship with Heureaux, to be pursued upon his return to the United States. Grimké proposed to represent Heureaux as a "secret agent" in the United States in the continuing effort to arrange an American purchase of Samaná. From the tone of his letters it was clear that Grimké hoped to represent Heureaux's interests, rather than those of the United States, even as he did something for his own. As he told Heureaux, he alone was to be employed in such a capacity, and Heureaux was to put him "in such circumstances that I may devote my whole attention to it until it is finished." Heureaux was not in any position to pursue the matter. His government was broke, and his own authority was weakening. Still, Grimké made a few inquiries, and the two men corresponded for the next several months, until Heureaux's assassination in mid-1899 put an end to any formal contact Grimké had with the island and its government.[21]

Grimké's willingness to work for Heureaux probably represented more than a fit of pique against the United States. Grimké obviously enjoyed his experience in Santo Domingo, as his lack of eagerness to leave and his unwillingness to break his connections even after his return to the United States make clear. Undoubtedly, much of his enjoyment was owing to his consular activities and the place they gave him in an international community.

No less important, this professional status was the mark, he believed, of the more general atmosphere of racial equality in the international and Caribbean community. In writing to his family about a ball he attended, he said, "There is not the slightest hint on such an occasion of the existence of such a thing as prejudice against color, not even among the Americans." He added, "You will hardly credit it that

20. Scott Frias to President William McKinley, May 2, 1898, Charles R. Codman to John D. Long, June 5, 1898, both in Records of the Department of State; U.S. Citizens Group to William McKinley, May 13, 1898, in Archibald Grimké Papers, Box 24, Folder 484; John D. Long to Charles R. Codman, June 7, 1898, in Archibald Grimké Papers, Box 10, Folder 208; Archibald Grimké to Angelina Grimké, July 15, 1898, in Angelina Grimké Papers, Box 4, Folder 68.
21. Archibald Grimké to President Ulises Heureaux, July 14, August 22, 1898, in Archibald Grimké Papers, Box 24, Folder 479.

after they live here a while they (the Americans) seem to lose their diabolic ability of detecting the presence of a drop of black blood in one of us. The gift seems to be reversed for they seem to have a marvellous faculty for finding in one of us a drop of white blood. And a few drops of this blood here have a wonderfully whitening effect." Again, nothing in his past had been like this.[22]

Perhaps he was most impressed that Heureaux, a black man, was governing a multiracial republic. Heureaux actually posed a dilemma for Grimké. The relationship between the two men was strong and remained so even after Grimké returned to the United States. He was aware, however, that Heureaux had crushed his opposition "by a system of despotism as minute and absolute as that which exists to-day in Russia." Still, Grimké ultimately came down on Heureaux's side. He felt that the Dominican situation required a strong man such as Heureaux. As he noted in 1904, Heureaux's reign was followed by a succession of revolutions. Grimké worried that, unless these revolutions were stopped, the United States was likely to step in, reducing the republic to an American protectorate—as did happen in a little over a decade. Grimké predicted a result that agreed with the observation of some other black leaders upon the triumph of American expansionism following the Spanish-American War. American rule, Grimké predicted, would bring "American colorphobia." He wrote, "Then will there be order and stable government in Santo Domingo, but there will appear for the first time there also cruel caste distinction, race contempt and insolence and plenty of them, race rule, inequality and oppression and no end of them, such as curse to-day the colored people of the United States." There was, he believed, only one alternative to a segregated society dominated by racist white Americans: an effective tyrant-president like Heureaux.[23]

Grimké's Santo Domingo experiences showed him that an alternative to the segregated society of the United States was possible. His own vision was perhaps idyllic. It is a sad irony that even as he was expressing his fears in 1904 of the introduction of American "colorphobia" into the island, the still independent republic, now under white rule, was expressing its desire that only a white man be sent to

22. Archibald Grimké to "Dear Home Ones," February 27, 1895, in Francis Grimké Papers, Box 3, Folder 112; Blakeley, "Black U.S. Consuls," 9.

23. Archibald Grimké to "Dear Home Ones," April 7, 1895, in Francis Grimké Papers, Box 3, Folder 113; Archibald H. Grimké, "The Dominican Republic and Her Revolutions," *Voice of the Negro,* I (1904), 136, 137, 138.

represent the United States in Santo Domingo. But what he saw strengthened his view that prejudice was arbitrary and, all too often, as his sarcastic letter home makes clear, a product of cynicism on the part of white Americans.[24]

But Dominican and diplomatic affairs were not the only things on Grimké's mind during his almost four years outside the United States. Matters at home also took some of his attention. These did not include any of the events taking place in politics and race relations during his time abroad, which is interesting because the mid-1890s was one of the most volatile points in the history of American racism, marking the consolidation of Jim Crow and disfranchisement, especially in the South. These were also the years that saw the emergence of Booker T. Washington as a major force in black American politics and thought; Washington delivered his notorious Atlanta Compromise address in 1895.

Grimké had some contact with Washington during this time, although it did not involve ideology. In 1895, while in Santo Domingo, he was named along with William I. Bowditch as co-executor of the estate of Emmeline Cushing, who had wanted to set up a school for colored children—at least, for Protestant colored children. Bowditch and Grimké set up a fund for that purpose, but feeling there was not enough money to set up a school, they decided to give donations to existing institutions, including Washington's Tuskegee. They may have been encouraged by Francis Grimké, who was friendly with Washington. In the late summer of 1896, during a brief leave from Santo Domingo, Grimké met with Washington to discuss the donation and later wrote to him from Santo Domingo on the same subject.[25]

But the matters at home that concerned him most during the time he was in Santo Domingo had mainly to do with his family. In February, 1895, his uncle Theodore Weld died in Massachusetts, and, less than three weeks later, so did his mother, Nancy Weston Grimké, who has been living in Washington with Francis. Her death hurt him, although he wrote that he felt "strangely near" her, even in death. This was one of the few times that either Archibald or Francis heard

24. Louis R. Harlan and Raymond W. Smock, eds., *The Booker T. Washington Papers* (14 vols.; Urbana, 1972–89), VII, 490.

25. Archibald Grimké to Booker T. Washington, October 1, 1896, June 5, 1897, in Booker T. Washington Papers, Library of Congress; Cushing estate documents, in Archibald Grimké Papers, Box 15, Folders 281–83.

from their brother John, who wrote to say that he could not attend the funeral.[26]

Grimké also had a daughter to raise. Angelina was fourteen years old at the time of his departure, and these were difficult years in her life—and, as a result, in his. Living together in Hyde Park, after her mother had sent her back to him, Angelina and her father had grown close, and, although he could not take her with him, he worried a great deal about her and tried as best he could to raise her by long distance. It was not easy.

When Archibald Grimké first began his term in Santo Domingo, Angelina moved in with her uncle and aunt, Francis and Charlotte Forten Grimké, in Washington, Archie nevertheless felt responsible for Angelina, and he wrote to her often to ask about her doings and to give her fatherly advice. He worried about her education and wanted her to take advantage of the opportunities available to her. In an early letter, he urged her to learn French and German, noting that Charlotte Grimké not only was fluent in French but had translated French works for publication. He continued to stress Angelina's education as the years passed. He also worried about her ability to get along with others. At the outset, he urged her to be "a great comfort & satisfaction" to the family in Washington, and he expressed his concerns about this during the time he was in Santo Domingo. Both her education and relationships were tied in with other virtues he felt were important for her to cultivate.[27]

Archie was right to worry about his daughter. Angelina was headstrong as a youngster, and she did not mellow with time. Thus her time in her Uncle Frank's household proved to be fairly short. In June, 1895, her aunt Charlotte wrote to Archibald to say that she could not care for Angelina for another year. Washington, she said, had been a bad influence on Angelina, and she thought her niece should go somewhere else. Archie was greatly upset. He wrote: "I had hoped against hope that you would disappoint this dread of mine & prove your self in every respect worthy to live in such a city as Washington, that you

26. Archibald Grimké to "Dear Home Ones," March 16, 1895, in Francis Grimké Papers, Box 3, Folder 112; John Grimké to Francis Grimké, March 16, 1895, *ibid.,* Box 3, Folder 126; Henry Justin Ferry, "Francis James Grimké: Portrait of a Black Puritan" (Ph.D. dissertation, Yale University, 1970), 109–11.

27. Archibald Grimké to Angelina Grimké, November 20, 1894, in Angelina Grimké Papers, Box 4, Folder 65; Archibald Grimké to Angelina Grimké, February 7, 1895, *ibid.,* Box 4, Folder 66.

would try to be a comfort & joy in the home of your uncle & aunt. I
know now that you have been neither, my dear child." He urged her
to be "brave, & true, & good, & do what you must do henceforth like
a little woman" and told her that she could only blame herself for the
decision he had to make, namely, to send her away. Then he told her
the ideals she must make her goal: "All I want you to do now is to
turn over a new leaf in your dear young life & begin a noble chapter
of achievement in every good thing & work, & of conquest of *self.*"[28]

Angelina did not immediately take his advice to heart. They undoubtedly had much to talk about during his brief visit to the United
States. For much of the time he was away, she was a lackadaisical
student. Grimké worried about her seriousness. While she was staying
with Frank and Charlotte, he wrote to her about her choice of reading.
She had written to him of her pleasure at reading *The Last Days of
Pompeii.* He replied: "I knew that you would like Pompeii. It is indeed
a great historical novel. But you must not allow yourself to read nothing but novels & such literature. The stomach of your mind can't stand
nothing but candy in the way of food." And he added, "You don't
want to be like every Tom, Dick & Harry of a shopgirl of the mentally
weak & empty pated simpletons of the feminine world, I know well."
Typically, he took her failings personally, once scolding her for failing
to write regularly and questioning why she "should care so little for
him & his feelings."[29]

The problems remained throughout his time away. Grimké arranged for her to go to Carleton Academy in Northfield, Minnesota.
She did well enough in her studies that Grimké could write to her,
during the fall term, of the pleasure she was giving him and of his
certainty that she would succeed in making herself "a lovable young
girl & a noble woman." But his happiness was short-lived; her dili-
gence began to weaken, and she failed to continue her studies beyond
a year. Leaving Carleton, she moved back to Boston, where she went
first to Cushing Academy and then to Boston Normal School of
Gymnastics, later to become Wellesley College.[30]

As late as 1899, after his return and when she was almost nineteen

28. Archibald Grimké to Angelina Grimké, June 19, 1895, *ibid.,* Box 4, Folder 66.
29. Archibald Grimké to Angelina Grimké, April 25, 1895, *ibid.,* Box 4, Folder 66;
Archibald Grimké to Angelina Grimké, August 23, 1897, *ibid.,* Box 4, Folder 67.
30. Archibald Grimké to Angelina Grimké, October 29, 1895, *ibid.,* Box 4, Folder
66; Mama Day to Angelina Grimké, August 4, 1898, *ibid.,* Box 1, Folder 4; Archibald
Grimké to Frank and Lottie, February 20, 1896, in Francis Grimké Papers, Box 3,
Folder 121.

years old, his patience showed its limits. He threatened to withdraw her from school and to "put you to learn some trade instead."
Whether as a result of the threat or for some other reason, Angelina's
work improved, ultimately satisfying her father, and she graduated
in 1902.[31]

Archie was a nag, and he sometimes let his temper get the best of
him, but he obviously loved his daughter. As the letters show, he
remained devoted to the values of independence and achievement he
had learned to prize in his own life, and he had the same sense of their
precariousness in hers that he had learned to feel about them in himself
and others.

His concern about Angelina was probably enhanced by his absence.
There is no correspondence to indicate how he felt about leaving her
for almost four years and how she felt about his going. It would be
mere speculation to see guilt in his nagging letters or anger in her
tendencies toward willfulness. But his feelings for her had always been
strong, even when he reluctantly gave up her custody at the time of
his divorce, and he continued to display them when he was away,
worrying about her growing up, wanting to hear from her regularly,
and telling her about his experiences. This strong relationship between
father and daughter was to play an important part in his activities for
the rest of his life.

By the time Grimké returned from the Dominican Republic, he had
seen and experienced a lot. He was almost fifty years old. He had gone
from slavery to freedom and to a place of accomplishment in letters,
politics, and statesmanship. Nevertheless, the eight to ten years following his return were to be the most eventful—and, in some ways,
the most ambiguous—of his life. America was changing rapidly, culturally, socially, and politically. The American system of race relations was changing even more rapidly and more radically. Archibald
Grimké was to occupy a complex and problematic place in it.

31. Archibald Grimké to Angelina Grimké, December 1, 1898, in Angelina Grimké
Papers, Box 4, Folder 68; Archibald Grimké to Angelina Grimké, January 29, 1899,
ibid., Box 4, Folder 69; Archibald Grimké to Angelina Grimké, May 6, 1900, *ibid.,* Box
4, Folder 70.

6

Washington

The next five years of Archibald Grimké's life were filled with mounting tensions and increasing activism. Returning to the United States in 1898, he divided his time between Washington, D.C., where he boarded with his brother Francis, and Boston, entering rapidly into the life of each city. He did not try to revive his legal practice. His daughter later noted that after his return, he engaged in no "paying occupation" other than his public work in racial activism and literary pursuits. He probably had some money left over from Santo Domingo, along with a small legacy from Weld, and this, with an occasional legal fee, provided a base for his support. Shortly after his return, advised by Whitefield McKinlay—a younger Charleston cousin and leading figure in the capital—Grimké began investing in Washington real estate, which provided him with a fairly good income over the rest of his life. Never a wealthy man, he was comfortably fixed.[1]

But he devoted most of his time after his return to public life. As a writer, he was more productive than ever before. His essays appeared in all the leading black journals of the period, as well as in such white-edited publications as the *Atlantic* and *Arena.* For a time, he produced a regular column for the New York *Age,* and he also maintained an active schedule as a public speaker. No less important was his role as a member of the American Negro Academy, founded by Alexander Crummell and others shortly before his return to the United States. He entered into its activities almost at once, giving some of his major

    1. Angelina W. Grimké, "A Biographical Sketch of Archibald H. Grimké," *Opportunity,* III (February, 1925), 47. The relationship between McKinlay and Grimké is noted in Whitefield McKinlay to Theodore Roosevelt, April 23, 1913, copy in Archibald H. Grimké Papers, Box 5, Folder 99, Moorland-Spingarn Research Center, Howard University, Washington, D.C.

addresses to that body. At the end of 1903, he became its third president—following Crummell and Du Bois—and used the opportunity
of delivering the annual presidential address to present some of his
most important work. He remained president of the group until the
end of 1919.

Necessarily an important place in his life was occupied by the developing debate over Booker T. Washington's ideas and leadership.
This debate involved ideological questions, matters of class and identity, and personal friendships. It was a complex and ambiguous situation. Eventually it insinuated itself into much that he did in making
his place in the communities in which he lived.

When Archibald Grimké returned to the United States during the
summer of 1898, he was able to resume directly his role of father to
Angelina, who, having herself an academic home at Wellesley, where
she studied physical culture, was giving him increasing pleasure. She
had never stopped writing poetry, and these efforts, too, made him
happy.

Angelina ultimately did well at Wellesley, both academically and
socially. There were a few black students in the school, but certainly
important for Angelina was her friend Tessa Lee, the daughter of an
old friend of her father's from Charleston, Joseph Lee, a Boston res-
taurateur, hotelier, and caterer. From the time of Grimké's return to
the United States until Lee's death in 1908, Grimké lived part of the
year in the Lee home on Columbus Avenue, several blocks from the
Boston Common, as, apparently, did Angelina, at least during her
time at school.[2]

From his base at the Lees', Grimké seems to have moved easily back
into the Boston community he had left four years earlier. He renewed
his contacts with such influential white Bostonians as Thomas Wentworth Higginson and Albert E. Pillsbury and collaborated with many
of them in the years to come. He also resumed his friendship with
Nelly Stebbins. And he renewed his ties to some of the more influential black Bostonians, including the emerging young leader William
Monroe Trotter.[3]

But Grimké did not completely pick up where he had left off upon

2. "Joseph Lee and His Bread Machines," *Colored American Magazine*, V (1902),
9–14; Archibald Grimké to Angelina Weld Grimké, June 6, 1899, in Angelina Weld
Grimké Papers, Box 4, Folder 69, Moorland-Spingarn Research Center, Howard University, Washington, D.C.; *Boston City Directories*, 1900–1909, *passim*.

3. Stephen R. Fox, *The Guardian of Boston: William Monroe Trotter* (New York,
1970), 12–14.

becoming a diplomat. Before he had lived a public life in a decidedly interracial circle in Boston, but on his return he began something of a split existence. In Boston, he maintained his interracial circle, whereas in Washington, his contacts were almost entirely within the black community. Washington was, of course, very much a southern city, segregated and lacking the traditions of interracial friendship and cooperation that characterized Boston. Moreover, because his entrée to the city came largely through his brother, Archie could not easily have entered any other world.

Even in Boston, Grimké increasingly inhabited a black world. Although he maintained his long-standing friendships with such whites as Pillsbury, Higginson, and Nelly Stebbins, more and more of his daily social contacts were with black Bostonians, the Lees, the Trotters, the Butler Wilsons, and others. Not returning to predominantly white Hyde Park but moving into the city and into the home of the Lees seems to have been a major step toward a life in the black community, even if he did not make a drastic break from the way he had lived before.

Grimké did not explain at the time why he made the change in his life, especially in Boston, and one can only speculate on the reasons. America was becoming even more of a Jim Crow society at the close of the 1890s, and this was as true in Boston as anywhere. Grimké would later show his own awareness of this change as he spoke in ways that conveyed a greater distrust of whites than he had before, although he said nothing along these lines in the beginning.

In Boston, the change in society was especially noticeable in politics, in which blacks were being given a much smaller place than they had held during Grimké's most active days, gerrymandered out of a significant role as voters. Politics had earlier been a key area for Grimké's interracial activities, and no interracial organizations had yet developed to replace the political ones. There were still mass meetings in which blacks and whites spoke and took part together, and Grimké continued to appear prominently at these, but they lacked the practical character of the old political affairs.

In any case, he seems to have found primarily, if not exclusively, black paths the best avenues for reentering public life and to have derived satisfaction from his participation in a largely black world. This was notably true of his involvement with Washington's black elite, which began through his brother Francis, with whom he lived during his increasingly long stays in the city. The Washington that Grimké inhabited had become the center of black cultural and intellectual life in the United States, attracting men and women of talent and achievement who formed the core of a Washington "society." The Grimké home was the scene for regular evenings of cultured, intellectual entertainments; the leading black men and women of the period were among the guests. Moreover, both Francis and Charlotte Grimké were active participants in the civic and cultural life of the community—school board members, active at Howard University and in the leading civic organizations.[4]

Two organizations were to be of crucial importance in Archibald Grimké's return to a full life in the United States. One of these was Washington's noted Bethel Literary and Historical Association. Founded in 1881 by Bishop Daniel Payne, a close friend of Francis Grimké, the Bethel was one of the oldest black literary societies and the most prestigious. Leading black Americans from throughout the country appeared at its meetings, which attracted the cream of Washington's elite. Its members discussed a range of topics, debating them hotly, from racial questions to history, from science to literature. Not surprisingly, it soon took on an importance that went beyond the cultural and intellectual, becoming a significant force in Washington and even in national black political life.[5]

By the time of Archibald Grimké's return from Santo Domingo, Francis had been an active participant in the Bethel for several years. Within a few months of his return, in December, 1898, Archibald Grimké began to appear regularly on the program of the Bethel, and he continued to do so for many years.[6]

A second organization that was to become increasingly important to Grimké's career was the American Negro Academy. Founded at the end of 1896 and holding its first real meeting in March, 1897, this organization, under the leadership of its first president, Alexander Crummell, was intended to bring together the intellectual elite of black America. With stringent membership requirements—and membership by invitation only—its earliest members included such outstanding figures as Crummell, W. H. Crogman, Kelly Miller, W. E. B. Du Bois (elected the academy's second president in 1898),

4. The most vivid account is in Anna J. Cooper, *Personal Recollections of the Grimké Family* (2 vols.; N.p., 1951), I, 9–11; see Willard B. Gatewood, *Aristocrats of Color: The Black Elite, 1880–1920* (Bloomington, 1991), chap. 2.

5. Constance McLaughlin Green, *The Secret City: A History of Race Relations in the Nation's Capital* (Princeton, 1967), 123–24, 150–51; Mary Church Terrell, "Society Among the Colored People of Washington," *Voice of the Negro,* I (1904), 156.

6. Washington *Colored American,* December 24, 1898, October 7, 1899.

and Francis Grimké. Francis Grimké had been one of the leading figures in the founding of the academy, helping to work toward its creation as early as 1894 and taking a leading role in its initial organization. Archibald Grimké was made a member at the academy's third
annual meeting in December, 1899, and invited to deliver the principal
address.[7]

Grimké quickly found a home in black Washington's intellectual
and cultural elite, and it gave him not only a ready welcome but a
good deal of recognition. He was always "the Hon. Archibald
Grimké" in acknowledgment of his former consular post. He received
a steady stream of invitations to present his thoughts and ideas in the
most distinguished organizations. And he could hold his own with
the cream of the Washington black elite. In 1899, for example, he was
elected over Register of the Treasury Judson W. Lyons in a vote of
students from his alma mater, Lincoln University, to represent the
Philosophian Society at the university's commencement.[8]

Grimké also joined avidly in protests against the increasingly re-
pressive and violent racial order that had been taking shape in the
United States, and especially in the South, in the years before the turn
of the century. In November, 1898, while in Washington, for example, he joined vigorously in the protests inspired by the terrible
Wilmington, North Carolina, race riots, an orgy of violence directed
against blacks immediately following the elections of that year. In one
of his first responses, a letter to the editor of the Washington *Times,*
written only a few days after the riots, he showed that he had lost none
of his old fire as he warned white southerners that they were "busy
sowing today the storm of race hatred for yourselves and posterity"
and urged them to "remember Nat Turner; remember that in your
midst live and brood over their wrongs not one but a thousand Nat
Turners!"[9]

Much the same militance is evident in one of the more noted

7. Alfred A. Moss, Jr., *The American Negro Academy: Voice of the Talented Tenth*
(Baton Rouge, 1981), 26–27; Henry Justin Ferry, "Francis James Grimké: Portrait of a
Black Puritan" (Ph.D. dissertation, Yale University, 1970), 213; William H. Crogman
to Francis Grimké, September 24, 1894, in Francis J. Grimké Papers, Box 2, Folder 71,
Moorland-Spingarn Research Center, Howard University, Washington, D.C.; John W.
Cromwell to John E. Bruce, February 26, 1899, in John E. Bruce Papers, Box 2, Folder
12, Schomburg Center for Research in Black Culture, New York Public Library;
American Negro Academy, Third Annual Meeting, program, December 27–28, 1899,
in W. E. B. Du Bois Papers (microfilm), University of Massachusetts, Amherst.
    8. Washington *Colored American,* March 11, 1899.
    9. Washington *Times,* November 14, 1898.

speeches Grimké made following his return, a widely publicized attack on lynching delivered on the evening of May 9, 1899, before a
large, enthusiastic crowd gathered in Boston's People's Temple, where
he joined a distinguished interracial group of speakers including William H. Lewis, an early black Harvard Law School graduate and a city
councilman, Thomas Wentworth Higginson, Massachusetts' former
governor J. Q. A. Brackett, A. A. Berle, and Grimké's old friend
Albert E. Pillsbury.[10]

Grimké's remarks took central place in the meeting, and they were
strong. Asserting that the black victim of lynching was no less "the
victim of an iniquitous understanding and arrangement between the
mobocrats of the South and the good Christian people of the country
in order to blacken his character, and to render him odious to the
world as a brute who did nothing but assault white women and children," he concluded his speech prophetically declaring that "all the
piled-up agony and wrongs of this simple and patient people, will be
exacted of thee in the coming years when thou shalt be judged at the
bar of some life and death crisis and emergency in thy history," and
warning, "If thou dost not soon kill the mob, the mob will ultimately
make an end in the North as it has already done in the South of all that
good men value highest in American character, institutions and
civilization."

The speech attracted much attention. It received more coverage in
the Boston *Transcript* than did the remarks of any other speaker and
was the only speech printed in full. But it also shows that Grimké
remained wedded to a language of protest that asked and gave "no
quarter," continuing the abolitionist tradition he had celebrated in the
lives of such heroes as Phillips, Garrison, and Sumner. He undoubtedly felt that the world of racial crisis, of lynching, disfranchisement,
and Jim Crow, which was taking shape in late nineteenth-century
America, made that tradition more appropriate than ever.

It was in this context that he confronted that other key fact of turn-
of-the-century race relations, the emergence of Booker T. Washington
as a visible leader among black Americans. August Meier's conclusion
that black leaders at this time were forced to confront the prestige and
influence of Washington as a key factor in their own work applied to
Grimké, his work being taken up increasingly with the division in the
black leadership over Washington's policies and ideas—a dispute often

10. This discussion and the account of the speech that follows are taken from the
Boston *Evening Transcript,* May 10, 1899.

characterized by historians as a conflict between Washington and his followers on one side and W. E. B. Du Bois and his on the other. In the late 1890s, of course, that dispute had not taken shape because neither Du Bois nor anyone else had emerged as a leader in opposition to Washington. But Washington was an important figure whom no black leader could afford to ignore.[11]

For Grimké, the emergence of Washington inserted two new variables into the American racial equation that had not been there before he left for Santo Domingo. One was the simple fact of Washington's stature. There had been important black leaders before, but none had achieved the widespread popular attention of Booker Washington in white and black America alike. To many, Washington "represented" black America nationally and internationally in a way not even Frederick Douglass had done before. Every other black leader, including Grimké, stood in his shadow.

The second variable consisted of Washington's own well-publicized views on race relations in America. Not only was Washington's leadership something new, also new was the prominence he gave to a message of conciliation in the relations between white and black Americans. Although there were certain ambiguities in Washington's conciliatory stance, there is no doubt that conciliation was a hallmark of his public reputation and a reason for his lionization by a large part of white America. His 1895 Atlanta Exposition address, delivered while Grimké was gone, summarized what was widely taken to be the Washingtonian message, as he strongly disavowed "agitation of questions of social equality" and urged a compromise with the white South on segregation and disfranchisement. Speaking calmly and soothingly, there and elsewhere, treating basic rights as privileges to be earned, and counseling patience in the struggle for their achievement—he was pointedly opposed to what he called the "incendiary utterances" that were so much a part of Grimké's repertory— Washington could have adopted a no more different approach from Grimké's fiery language and sense of crisis in responding to the events of the 1890s.[12]

Thus, upon his return Grimké not only faced what he saw as a crisis in American race relations but one that had to be defined in a new and

11. August Meier, *Negro Thought in America, 1880–1915: Racial Ideologies in the Age of Booker T. Washington* (Ann Arbor, 1963), 165.

12. Booker T. Washington, *Up From Slavery* (1901), in *Three Negro Classics,* ed. John Hope Franklin (New York, 1965), 149; Louis R. Harlan and Raymond Smock, eds., *The Booker T. Washington Papers* (14 vols.; Urbana, 1972–89), VIII, 378.

unsettling way by the presence of Washington. What did he think of Washington, and what did Washington think of him? There is no doubt that Grimké was aware of Washington and of his role and ideas, an awareness Washington himself cultivated. A relationship between the two men began to take shape soon after Grimké's return, when Washington contacted him in response to Grimké's powerful and militant speech on lynching. Francis Jackson Garrison, an old friend of both men, was so impressed with Grimké's speech that he sent a copy to Booker T. Washington, then in Europe, describing it as "very good." Washington, who was working on a paper of his own on lynching, agreed and wrote to Grimké his view that the remarks "will do good and I thank you for them."[13]

Grimké must have appreciated the compliment, but his own view of Washington at the time was neither entirely friendly nor clear. Even before Washington's response to the lynching speech began what was to be a long-term relationship between the two men, Grimké showed his discomfort with Washington's views. As early as his 1898 reaction to the Wilmington riots, though he did not mention Booker Washington by name, his language had to refer to the ideas Washington had been espousing for some time, including the Atlanta address. Declaring his own lack of hope for action by the national government on behalf of southern blacks, Grimké added: "Let me not be understood by what I am about to say as in any way countenancing even by implication the new folly which has been launched as the cure-all of our woes, namely our voluntary political self-effacement in the South. . . . Palsied be the parricidal hand of one of us, that lifts a pen at this moment of our deepest agony to utter one treacherous word against his race. May the blood in its veins turn to the color of ink, and the ink to the tint of blood before it commits so unnatural, so foul a deed!" Such were hardly the words of a man ready to accept Washingtonian views.[14]

Such words would not, incidentally, have played badly in Boston, which had already emerged as a center for opposition to Washington as the nineteenth century drew to a close, even though the sides in the later dispute had not fully taken shape. Only a few months after Grimké's Wilmington remarks—and less than a month before he spoke at the People's Temple—a group of black Bostonians met at

13. Harlan and Smock, eds., *Washington Papers,* V, 114, 125, 126.
14. Archibald Grimké, "Lessons of the Hour," in Archibald Grimké Papers, Box 20, Folder 381.

Young's Hotel to commemorate the anniversary of Charles Sumner's election to the Senate and used the occasion not only to criticize the failure of the national government to prevent southern lynchings but also to level intense criticisms at Booker T. Washington. Among the most vocal were William H. Lewis and another Harvard alumnus and former class orator, Clement G. Morgan. Whether Grimké's earlier remarks had helped to coalesce such sentiments is hard to say. Certainly, in making them, he found himself in distinguished company.[15]

On the subject of lynching, Grimké also maintained a distance from Washington, despite Washington's compliments on the Boston address. Responding to southern outrages, Washington, under pressure from other black leaders, had sent a letter to leading newspapers in the South advising white southerners to do what they could to prevent the crime and even urging blacks to try to prevent the "crimes" that led to lynching. He had his secretary send Grimké a copy. Grimké sympathized with Washington's appeal to the whites but made clear that he saw little hopeful in Washington's approach because "the whole body of the white people of that section, excepting possibly a righteous remnant of 5 per cent., seems to have gone mad on the subject of the Negro and his rights."[16]

The exchange that took place between Washington and Grimké was important, particularly in light of coming events in the lives of both. That there was an exchange at all is significant. That Washington felt a need to send Grimké a copy of his speech shows that he wanted to create some level of collegiality between them. That Grimké chose to reply in a friendly if not wholly agreeing way shows that he, too, was willing to maintain contact, despite the obvious and strong disagreement between them.

There were, most likely, several reasons why the relationship between the two men was fairly cordial if also, on Grimké's side, somewhat frank. For Washington, there was an obvious benefit to be gained from cultivating a man of Grimké's prestige, especially since one of Grimké's home bases, Boston, was already giving him trouble. Washington was always on the lookout for allies, even those whose views differed from his own, and Grimké represented one more part in what was already becoming a well-functioning Tuskegee machine. Not to be discounted, too, was Grimké's control of the Cushing estate, which the two had earlier discussed. The estate was not large,

15. Boston *Evening Transcript,* April 25, 1899; Fox, *Guardian of Boston,* 26–27.
16. Harlan and Smock, eds., *Washington Papers,* V, 152, 226.

but Washington was an inveterate fund-raiser, and he tried to persuade Grimké to turn the entire amount over to him for use at Tuskegee.[17]

Part of the reason for Grimké's positive response may have been personal. Grimké seems to have genuinely liked Washington and, despite their disagreements, to have felt positively about him. Washington contributed to such feelings by saying nothing to give the sensitive Grimké offense; quite the contrary, he was actively demonstrating his respect for Grimké as both a thinker and an individual, to make him feel at home in the world to which he had returned.

Moreover, Grimké was influenced by his brother Frank's friendship with Washington and the acquaintance of both with Washington over a period of several years. He also saw value in the work Washington was doing. Although he was later to express strong differences with Washington over educational philosophy, as well as over accommodationist strategies, he was never to deny the worth of Tuskegee. It may be a measure of this appreciation that his initial inclination was to turn the entire Cushing fund over to Tuskegee. It is a measure of the ambivalence he soon developed, however, that by early 1899 he had changed his mind, although Tuskegee did receive a gift of about fifty dollars a year into the 1920s. Unfortunately, his explanation for changing his mind has not survived.

Part of the reason for his adopting a connection with Washington may have been political. Not only was Washington the leading black American figure at the time of Grimké's return to the United States, but, despite such occasions as the Young's Hotel meeting, his power was on the rise. Although there had been some criticism of him immediately following his Atlanta address, from that time until about 1900, support for both Washington and his views was increasing, and even many future critics, like Du Bois, were among his supporters. Anyone who wanted to be in the thick of black reform activity had to recognize that Washington's was the major, if not the only, organization so that it is not surprising that Grimké maintained an open attitude toward Washington. Never adopting a Washingtonian line, he probably knew that he could not afford to cut Washington off either.[18]

But as Grimké's comments in the exchange on lynching indicate, he may also have hoped that Washington could be made to see the problems of a conciliatory line and that he could move Washington to

17. William Bowditch to Archibald Grimké, January 17, 1895, in Archibald Grimké Papers, Box 15, Folder 283.
18. Meier, *Negro Thought*, 171, 196.

use his already enormous influence directly for more militant efforts for change. Grimké had every reason to see in Washington a man whose strategies went beyond his words, who was more as a man than first met the eye. It is well-known now, and was then, that Washington, under cover of conciliation, used his influence and money to work against the worst forms of discrimination; even as he urged a withdrawal from political agitation, he covertly sought to slow the march of disfranchisement and segregation in the South. August Meier has argued that even Washington's strongest opponents knew this side of Washington and were aware of his strategy of placating whites while trying to improve conditions for blacks.[19]

Grimké, who had grown up in Charleston's slave society, knew firsthand of the strategies of dissimulation which blacks had used in dealing with whites and of the lore that underlay those strategies. As an insider in the black elite, he would have known as well as anyone what Washington had been up to over the years. He had further confirmation in the supportive letters Washington wrote him, approving Grimké's words that were so different from and so much more militant than Washington's own.

Dissimulating strategies were on Grimké's mind at the end of his first year and a half of dealing with Washington. His thinking about them was at the core of a major paper he presented a few months after the exchange on lynching, "Right on the Scaffold, or the Martyrs of 1822," an account of the Denmark Vesey revolt, which had taken place in Charleston, and his initial lecture before the American Negro Academy. He attached great importance to this paper, sending copies to all his friends, including Nelly Stebbins, and trying to get it published in the *Atlantic*.[20]

There are no notes in the published version of Grimké's paper, no references to give one a clue as to his sources. The Vesey story had been largely ignored by white historians before Grimké's paper appeared, and, although black writers had referred to Vesey in their works, their accounts were more evocative than detailed. Grimké felt that he was rescuing Vesey's history from oblivion, "from the bottom of that pool where I found it, to give it once more to the light." He must have studied the major surviving documents; he may also have

19. *Ibid.,* 118.
20. Archibald Grimké to Ellen B. Stebbins, December 31, 1899, in Archibald Grimké Papers, Box 6, Folder 105; Editors of the *Atlantic* to Archibald Grimké, April 18, 1900, *ibid.,* Box 8, Folder 146.

learned the story as a child. As narratives collected from former slaves by the Federal Writers' Project in the 1930s show, some slaves in South Carolina had kept the Vesey story alive throughout the antebellum period and drawn inspiration from it. This was especially true of slaves whose families and friends, like Grimké's, talked much about the politics of the war and of freedom.[21]

He may also have heard the story from his aunts. As Angelina Weld's biographer, Katherine Lumpkin, shows, Angelina was strongly affected by the Vesey uprising, which occurred when she was about seventeen. Although there is no record of her reaction at the time, she later sent to Charleston for the official records, and, as Lumpkin says, the possibility of rebellions such as Vesey's entered into her thinking about the institution of slavery and its character. It is a measure of the importance of the Vesey revolt to her thinking and of her talking about it later in life that her daughter Sarah Weld got the impression, not at all accurate, that Denmark Vesey had been a slave of her grandfather, John Faucheraud Grimké.[22]

Whatever the sources, much of Grimké's paper focused on Vesey the dissimulator. Vesey knew, Grimké said, "that his oppressors were strong and that he was weak" and that any successful revolt would require "discretion and self-control." He began with "the sowing of seeds of discontent, the fomenting of hatred among the blacks, bond and free alike, toward the whites," preaching with great patience "his new and terrible gospel of liberty and hate." He encouraged "that *ars artium* of slaves in their attempts to break their chains—a habit of smiling and fawning on unjust and cruel power, while bleeds in secret their fiery wound, rages and plots there also their passionate hate, and glows there too their no less passionate hope for freedom." In what he called "the dark subterranean world" of black Charleston, the "underworld" which Grimké himself had known so well, Vesey kindled a revolutionary fire that could be contained only for so long and that ultimately, if briefly, flared up.[23]

21. Archibald Grimké to Ellen B. Stebbins, December 31, 1899; George P. Rawick, ed., *The American Slave: A Composite Autobiography,* supplement 1, series 1 (12 vols.; Westport, Conn., 1977), XI, 149–50, 261–63.

22. Katharine Du Pre Lumpkin, *The Emancipation of Angelina Grimké* (Chapel Hill, 1974), 16–17; Sarah Weld Hamilton, "Memories of Theodore Dwight Weld, the St. John of the Abolitionists," notebooks, in Weld-Grimké Papers, Box 18, William L. Clements Library, University of Michigan, Ann Arbor.

23. Archibald H. Grimké, *Right on the Scaffold, or The Martyrs of 1822,* Occasional Papers of the American Negro Academy, no. 7, 1901, in *The American Negro Academy Occasional Papers 1–22* (New York, 1969), 8–9.

Whether Grimké saw in Booker Washington another Vesey, or potential Vesey, is difficult to say, but in the context of turn-of-the-century America, and in light of what he knew about Washington, it is not difficult to believe that the Vesey paper helped him to wonder whether there was another Washington behind the veil of public utterance. Grimké himself, of course, having faced racism directly all his adult life and having adopted strategies of confrontation and violent language, could no more be a Vesey, or a Washington, than he could give up a life of activism and independence. But he could see from his own experiences the possibility that, whatever Washington said in public, there might still be an angry man open, with enough encouragement, to a more forthright stand on racial questions.

Perhaps it was in hopes of encouraging the "hidden" Washington that Grimké continually tried to keep his own ideas and militance before Washington. The exchange on lynching was one example of this, but there were others. In early October, 1899, at a mass meeting at the Charles Street Church in Boston, under the auspices of an organization called the Colored National League—whose officers included such longtime associates of Grimké's as Edward E. Brown, Edwin S. Walker, and James Wolff, as well as Grimké himself—Grimké presented a draft which he had written, in typically strong language, of an open letter to William McKinley, condemning the president both for his imperialist policies in the aftermath of the war with Spain and for his indifference to the problems facing black Americans at home. He read the draft to great applause, and it was adopted "with significant unanimity" and forwarded to the president.[24]

Basking in his triumph, Grimké took the trouble to send a copy of the Boston *Transcript*'s flattering account of the meeting and his letter to Booker Washington, noting that the *Transcript* had compared Grimké's letter and Washington's Atlanta address. Although he did not directly say so, it seems as though Grimké, seeing a dissimulating character in Washington, was trying to keep the language and message of militant protest before his eyes to ensure that what Grimké hoped was only a stance would remain only a stance.[25]

He seems to have done something similar in another major paper

24. Willard B. Gatewood, Jr., *Black Americans and the White Man's Burden, 1898–1903* (Urbana, 1975), 209–10; Boston *Globe,* October 2, 4, 1899; Archibald H. Grimké, "Resolution to Hon. William McKinley, from Colored People of Massachusetts," in Archibald Grimké papers, Box 21, Folder 407.

25. Archibald Grimké to Booker Washington, October 19, 1899, in Washington Papers.

that he produced at this time, "Modern Industrialism and the Negro in the United States," delivered initially at a center of Washingtonian thinking, Booker Washington's alma mater, Hampton Institute in Virginia, at the annual Hampton Negro Conference held in July, 1899, and subsequently at the Bethel. In 1907, Grimké presented the same paper as an address before the American Negro Academy, which published it as an Occasional Paper the following year. Later, the paper occupied a central place in a dispute that developed between Grimké and W. E. B. Du Bois, editor of the *Crisis,* which was also to involve such important figures as Oswald Garrison Villard and A. E. Pillsbury. He made few changes in the paper's various versions—certainly the main ideas remained constant.[26]

In the paper Grimké elaborated further on the "irrepressible conflict" idea in terms of the economic questions he had begun to think about in the late 1880s. He looked at the two sections not as competing social or political entities but as irreconcilable industrial systems and traced the history of the sectional conflict as the story of the steady march of northern industrial capitalism into the southern states and of the South's futile but persistent attempt to resist that advance, which led to much of the racial oppressiveness characterizing the region. He ascribed virtually everything in postemancipation northern racial policy to that industrial conflict in a way that had some affinities with the progressive history of such earlier scholars as E. Benjamin Andrews (which Grimké knew) but also looked back to his political thinking in the 1880s and forward to the work of some of the progressive historians in the 1920s and 1930s. He found cause for optimism in the story. The South's system of racial serfdom could not work in an advanced capitalist democracy, he said, nor could the North, in the modern economic world, allow an anachronistic southern outpost to continue to exist. It was an unusual argument for its time, and it showed Grimké's continuing effort to think originally about the bases of the racial problem, to formulate approaches that went beyond the usual strategies then being offered.[27]

The paper had political significance as well. At various points, Grimké took a line that was superficially Washingtonian, as when he located the solution to racial oppression in industrial development.

26. Boston *Evening Transcript,* July 24, 1899.

27. E. Benjamin Andrews, *Brief Institutes of Our Constitutional History: English and American* (Providence, 1886); see, *e.g.,* William B. Hesseltine, "Economic Factors in the Abandonment of Reconstruction," *Mississippi Valley Historical Review,* XXII (1935), 191–210.

Like Booker Washington, he urged, in Social Darwinist terms, the need for black people to prepare themselves through education and hard work for a place in the emerging industrial order in the South. But as he continued, his opinion of the limitations of Washington's most noted views could not have been clearer.

Although he urged blacks to be prepared to participate in the triumphant system of industrial democracy, he placed the chief responsibility on the white South to recognize its own ultimate acceptance of that system and to emancipate black labor so it could participate fully in the worldwide industrial competition that was taking shape. Black Americans were ready, he declared; the South needed only to give them their rightful place in the industrial order. He further departed from Washington by ignoring the notion that by proving themselves to whites, blacks would earn the "privileges" or rights which whites seemed so eager to deny them. This was particularly true, he said, of the right to vote, which Washington, in public at least, was willing to set aside. The ballot, Grimké argued, was essential to black survival in a competitive world. He showed how Booker Washington's premises inevitably led to a more militant political stance than Washington presently was taking—and, clearly, he wanted Washington to know it.[28]

Thus, early after his return from Santo Domingo, Archibald Grimké had created an uneasy but continuing tie to Booker Washington. That tie was not to get any easier as Grimké worked over the next few years to make a place for himself and his people in the new American century.

28. Archibald Grimké, "Modern Industrialism and the Negroes of the United States," 1902, in Archibald Grimké Papers, Box 20, Folder 388.

7

Anti-Washington

Over the next three years, and up to the end of 1903, Archibald Grimké's relationship with Booker Washington provided a central focus at least for his public life. He remained on cordial terms with Washington until about the middle of 1903, while preserving his own ideological independence, and his ideological development took him increasingly far from Washington's ideas, which he had not thought too much of to begin with. Nevertheless, until well into 1903, neither man seems to have been eager to let the other go entirely, Grimké, in particular, continuing to press on Washington the need for a more militant stance. But even though cordiality remained, others had begun to notice the differences between the two men, placing Grimké at the forefront of a potential anti-Washington coalition. This story is complex and difficult to trace.

Much of what Grimké did in the earliest years of the twentieth century consolidated and built on his earlier activities. He became better acquainted with Booker Washington, with whom his brother Francis remained on good terms, and even worked with Washington. Grimké took a leading and not unfriendly role at a meeting of the Bethel Literary and Historical Association in May, 1900, at which Washington delivered a major address setting forth in detail his own approach to American racial oppression. Not surprisingly, he championed industrial education and the need for conciliation with whites. Nothing was to be gained, he said, "in mere badinage of words of blame or censure" directed toward whites; he again asserted the value of accommodation and cooperation. On the difficult issue of disfranchisement, he asserted a belief that educational requirements for suffrage were valuable and urged linking them with property requirements, though he said that these should be administered even-handedly. And he reiterated his view that the focus of racial activity ought to be on uplift rather than politics. He acknowledged, correctly, that there were many present who would disagree with him, but his reception was cordial, and Grimké entered into its spirit, a token of the personal relationship that continued to exist between the two men.[1]

They acted together in other ways as well. Throughout this period, they met socially, and when the "secret" Washington was contemplating working behind the scenes against revisions to the Louisiana state constitution designed to disfranchise blacks, Grimké was one of those with whom he discussed the matter, confirming yet again Grimké's sense that there was hope for the man. Grimké appears to have introduced him to Albert E. Pillsbury—who had a few months earlier written Washington to express his own reservations about Washington's accomodationist views—for advice on whether a court test had any chance of success.[2]

Still, philosophical differences remained as important as friendly cooperation and were evident in several ways. Showing his political independence from the Republican Washington, Grimké reasserted his allegiance to the Democratic party and joined a few other black leaders in supporting William Jennings Bryan for the presidency. Although he was not an active participant in the 1900 campaign, he did sign a lengthy open letter, also signed by several other black Massachusetts leaders, setting forth reasons for the endorsement. Its arguments indicate that Grimké wrote the letter condemning the Republicans and urging support for Bryan as the only alternative, however unpleasant it might be.[3]

As a writer and lecturer Grimké revealed still more about his disagreements with Washington and Washingtonian ideas, speaking and writing with a militance that was decidedly un-Washingtonian. On

1. New York *Age,* May 31, 1900; Washington *Star,* May 23, 1900, in Hampton University Peabody Newspaper Clippings File (Microfiche ed.; Alexandria, Va., 1987).

2. Louis R. Harlan and Raymond W. Smock, eds., *The Booker T. Washington Papers* (14 vols.; Urbana, 1972–89), V, 449–50, 649–50; Archibald Grimké to Booker T. Washington, April 27, 1900, December 20, 1900, in Booker T. Washington Papers, Library of Congress.

3. August Meier, "The Negro and the Democratic Party, 1875–1915," *Phylon,* XVII (1956), 182–83; Boston *Herald,* October 15, 1900; *Colored American Magazine,* I (1900), 185.

many occasions after about mid-1900, he seems to have tried to answer, point by point, the very detailed speech Washington had made at the Bethel in May of that year. Grimké continued to press for equal social and political rights and with the violent language Washington had decried as "mere badinage of words." He engaged in such "badinage" often.

Not only did he speak militantly, but he began to sharpen his definition of the grounds for his disagreements with Booker Washington. Most notably, and in response to Washington's oft-expressed hope that blacks and whites could learn to work together in a spirit of goodwill, Grimké began to stress the inveterate hostiliity of white America to black aspirations. This view had been implicit in his withdrawal from interracial activity as well as in the Vesey paper and in "Modern Industrialism and the Negroes," but it now became clearer and more important in his works.

Toward the close of a 1900 address, tellingly entitled "The Negro's Case Against the Republic," he described a consensus among both northern and southern whites that blacks were to be "forever an alien race, an inferior race, a servile race, allowed to live here in strict subordination and subjection to the white race." Noting as exceptions from his general indictment "the small band of noble white men and women who are in very truth our dear and devoted friends, the best ever race had," he nevertheless added, in words eschewing Washington's Bethel advice not to waste time condemning white America, "Blood proves thicker than water," and "in any contest between the white race and the black race in this country, you will find all white men like birds of a feather, flocking together regardless of all standards of right and ethics or religion." The exceptions, he concluded, only proved the rule.[4]

He made a similar point in a widely noted address delivered on January 1, 1901, in commemoration of the anniversary of Lincoln's Emancipation Proclamation. He was in distinguished company. The mayor of Boston sat on the platform and made brief remarks, as did Bishop Alexander Walters of New Jersey and a longtime Grimké associate, Edward Brown. For much of the speech, Grimké focused on what he was increasingly coming to see as competition between the races. Looking back into history to define the problem, he decried the

---

4. Archibald H. Grimké, "The Negro's Case Against the Republic," 7–8, in Archibald Grimké Papers, Box 21, Folder 397, Moorland-Spingarn Research Center, Howard University, Washington, D.C.

betrayal of the Negro by the North after Reconstruction, especially the abandonment of the cause of equal rights for blacks by the Republican party which had upset him as a young politician. In the 1880s, he had ascribed that abandonment to white indifference based on a willingness to subordinate black rights to other concerns, but now he saw in that abandonment an act of hostility, declaring: "On the race question, a white man is a white man. Scratch the skin of a Republican or a Democrat, and you will find close to the surface race prejudice." Although such words described a foundation for his own most recent political activity, they left little room for the conciliatory approach Washington continued to espouse.[5]

Grimké's focus on racism was not a rejection of the economics-based arguments he had been developing, summarized in the "Modern Industrialism" paper. Such arguments ascribed much of white behavior, northern and southern, to a cynical use of blacks for political and economic ends. Now he made the foundations for such a cynicism more explicit, stressing in yet another way that white America was not to be counted on, despite the presence of a few moral heroes in its midst. Washington's conciliatory approach counted on white cooperation, and Grimké's words rejected that approach out of hand.

Thus despite his cordiality to Washington, Grimké was staking out his own position on specific issues. This is not to say that he could not wax as optimistically as anyone on the future for black Americans, despite his strong and negative sense of the nature of racial conflict in the United States. In August, 1901, the Boston *Globe* asked him, along with several other "representative colored men of Boston"— including William H. Lewis and George W. Forbes—to participate in its weekly "symposium" feature, in this case on the topic "Will the Negro Ever Attain to Perfect Equality with the White Man?" Grimké, in his contribution, wrote, "If I were to forecast the future by the present it would seem that the riddle propounded by the *Globe* must be answered in the negative." But, he said, there were better indicators for responding to the question, and one should try to "forecast the future by the past." Doing so would show a historical trend toward equality that made the present difficulties appear only "transitional and temporary," ultimately to be overcome. Going back to his earlier thought, he cited those "everlasting principles of justice and truth" that had produced emancipation in the past and would guarantee equality in the future. But he also made clear that the victory would

5. Boston *Evening Transcript,* January 2, 1901.

come only after a battle in which agitation, not temporary surrender, had to be the dominant strategy.[6]

Such views were important, but even as he put them forth, he was creating at least as much impact by his participation in a range of activities that also put him on a path leading directly away from Washington and Washingtonianism. Boston and Washington, D.C., the two cities in which Grimké was most prominent, were the centers for opposition to Booker T. Washington. Although hardened pro- and anti-Washington factions had not yet emerged, the bases for those factions were beginning to take shape. In the city of Washington, both organizations in which Grimké was most active, the American Negro Academy and the Bethel Literary and Historical Association, were developing strong anti-Washington components, despite the cordial reception Washington had received for his May, 1990, address at the Bethel. In Boston, where Grimké spent most of his time, his closest relationships were with such figures as William Monroe Trotter, George W. Forbes, Clement Morgan, William H. Scott, and others who were also emerging as visible critics of Washington. Several of these men worked to create, by the end of 1901, the leading organ of anti-Washington opinion in the United States, the *Guardian,* a newspaper under the editorship of the outspoken Trotter.[7]

Grimké and Trotter were especially close, not only socializing frequently, their friendship augmented by a friendship between Angelina Grimké and Trotter's sister Maude, but associated in public affairs as well. Grimké and Trotter worked together to create what was to become the center of the city's anti-Washington faction, the Boston Literary and Historical Association, an organization modeled on the venerable Bethel organization in the District of Columbia. The Boston Literary got its start in March, 1901, when Grimké, along with Joseph Lee and W. H. Dupree, sent an invitation to a number of leading Bostonians, including Trotter and such other critics of Washington as Morgan, Forbes, Granville Martin, and Pauline Hopkins, suggesting the formation of such a society. That Grimké could command respect in such company is shown by his unanimous election at the first meeting as the association's first president. Grimké's leadership in the founding and development of the Boston Literary did much to co-

6. Boston *Globe,* August 18, 1901.

7. Louis R. Harlan, *Booker T. Washington: The Wizard of Tuskegee, 1901–1915* (New York, 1983), 34; Henry Justin Ferry, "Francis James Grimké: Portrait of a Black Puritan" (Ph.D. dissertation, Yale University, 1970), 216.

alesce that group of Bostonians who had already begun to speak out in opposition to Washington.[8]

Of all those Bostonians who ultimately came to be seen as opponents to Washington, Grimké was the first to garner a reputation as a Washington critic. In a review of Washington's 1901 autobiography, *Up from Slavery,* W. E. B. Du Bois expressed for the first time his own misgivings about Washington's leadership and program. In the review, Du Bois differentiated three strains of black leadership: the Washingtonians, the spokesmen for emigration from the South (in whom he had little faith) and "the large and important group represented by Dunbar, Tanner, Chesnutt, Miller, and the Grimkés, who, without any single definite programme, and with complex aims, seek nevertheless that self development and self-realization in all lines of human endeavor which they believe will eventually place the Negro beside the other races." These men, he said, respected what Washington was doing but "believe it falls far short of a complete programme." Specifically, he noted, they favored higher education and the right to vote and also "believe in self-assertion and ambition," a belief which Washington, he implied, did not hold. The characterization was prophetic because, although Grimké remained on good terms with Washington personally, he was increasingly seen as an opponent, ultimately by Washington himself.[9]

The characterization inaugurated, symbolically at least, a period during which Grimké, in his early fifties and one of the elder statesmen of African-American political and cultural life, found himself in a situation of general turmoil, even extending to his personal life. He had the most serious conflict he ever had with his daughter in which his deep devotion became possessiveness. Over 1901 and 1902, before her graduation from Wellesley, which gave him great pleasure, he used his ties with the District of Columbia elite—chiefly with Bruce Evans, a school administrator and brother-in-law of Butler Wilson—to get her a job as a teacher in Washington. She joined her father in living and boarding with his brother. But she was now a young woman and more independent than ever.[10]

8. Constitution and By-Laws of the Boston Library and Historical Association, and Minutes of the Boston Literary and Historical Association, March 18, 1901, both in William Monroe Trotter Papers, Box 11, Mugar Memorial Library, Boston University; Stephen R. Fox, *The Guardian of Boston: William Monroe Trotter* (New York, 1970), 43; *Colored American Magazine,* II (1901), 471.
9. Harlan and Smock, eds., *Washington Papers,* VI, 178.
10. Boston *Guardian,* September 27, October 4, 1902; W. Bruce Evans to Roscoe

Their relationship suffered a severe strain when, in the summer of 1903, Angelina fell in love. Her feelings were recounted in a diary, deeply colored by her poetic leanings (when her biographer, Gloria Hull, refers to the first thirty years of Angelina Grimké's life as "a long period of adolescence" she is not referring to this diary specifically but could have been) in which, unfortunately, the identity of the object of her affection remains hidden.[11]

Archibald Grimké knew about the romance and did not approve. Father and daughter fought several times about it; at one point Archibald referred to the man as a "consummate ass" and sarcastically called him her "platonic friend" until, as she said, "I loathed and hated it." This was not the first time her father had questioned her taste in men, nor would it be the last, although on other occasions he tried to show his concern in a joking manner. This time, however, he gave his daughter an ultimatum, asking that she choose either him or her friend. She chose her father, but not before they had gone through some battles, both of them showing that gift for invective Archie himself had so long prized.[12]

In Grimké's public life, confirming Du Bois' remarks, his relations with Booker Washington became increasingly hostile. Some still saw him as a leader among Booker Washington's Boston critics, although Trotter had emerged as Washington's most visible and vociferous opponent. Grimké cemented his reputation over the next couple of years through his activities in the Boston Literary, as well as in a more recently founded group, the St. Mark's Literary and Musical Union, of which he also served as president. In both, he made a point of inviting anti-Washington figures—even the recently revealed Washington critic W. E. B. Du Bois—as speakers and gave each group a distinctly anti-Washington cast.[13]

That he retained the respect of the Boston Literary circle is shown not only by his continuing leadership of the organization but by its effort to use the influence of its notable membership to get Grimké a political appointment in Boston in early 1902. The group's executive

Conkling Bruce, January 29, 1908, in Angelina Weld Grimké Papers, Box 3, Folder 30, Moorland-Spingarn Research Center, Howard University, Washington, D.C.

11. Gloria T. Hull, *Color, Sex and Poetry: Three Women Writers of the Harlem Renaissance* (Bloomington, 1987), 116; Angelina Weld Grimké, Diary, 1903, undated entry, in Angelina Grimké Papers, Box 15, Folder 248.

12. Angelina Weld Grimké, Diary, 1903, undated entry.

13. Boston Literary and Historical Association programs, in Trotter Papers, Box 11.

committee, which included Trotter, contacted Democratic mayor Patrick Collins urging Grimké's appointment "for any suitable office in your power to bestow" and noting Grimké's past record of public and party service. The effort did not succeed, but it showed, as the letter to Collins said, "the esteem in which he is held by the colored citizens of Boston."[14]

Moreover, that such esteem was not damaged by the growing anti-Washington character of his leadership was shown by Grimké's role as a featured speaker at a major rally in May, 1902, called to protest southern disfranchisement. With Trotter in the chair, the Boston Literary membership was well represented. The meeting strongly condemned disfranchisement, Grimké calling it "wrong to blacks and peril to the republic." He especially excoriated the literacy and property qualifications which Washington continued to support, describing them as subterfuge. Trotter praised Grimké for his "clear and incisive logic," saying that "his speech of itself would have been worth going miles to hear."[15]

To be sure, some among Booker Washington's lieutenants continued to feel that Archibald Grimké was not entirely unapproachable. When the South Carolina Republican officeholder Edmund H. Deas spoke in Boston in the spring of 1902, he had dinner with "Mr. Archie Grimkie," to whom he defended Washington, and from whom, he felt, he received a sympathetic hearing. In early 1903, Washington himself invited Grimké to take his brother Francis' place at a Tuskegee function, although Grimké apparently did not attend.[16]

Nevertheless, his anti-Washington reputation was growing. At a mass meeting in Faneuil Hall, where he appeared on a Lincoln's birthday, 1903, program with, among others, his old friend Albert Pillsbury, he spoke with typical militance. Although he never mentioned Booker Washington by name, one correspondent, perhaps reading between the lines, felt that Grimké had "assailed" Washington and his work "in some way."[17]

14. John Daniels, *In Freedom's Birthplace: A Study of the Boston Negroes* (1914; rpr. New York, 1968), 269; Charles Steward to Hon. Patrick A. Collins, January 16, 1902, in Trotter Papers, Box 6.

15. Boston *Guardian,* May 17, 1902.

16. Harlan and Smock, eds., *Washington Papers,* VI, 473; Booker T. Washington to W. E. B. Du Bois, January 2, 1903, in W. E. B. Du Bois Papers (microfilm), University of Massachusetts, Amherst.

17. Boston *Guardian,* February 14, 1903; Harlan and Smock, eds., *Washington Papers,* VII, 77; Harlan, *Booker T. Washington: Wizard of Tuskegee,* 41.

By the spring of 1903, Grimké's anti-Washington credentials were strong. W. E. B. Du Bois' powerful text *The Souls of Black Folk* made its appearance and again singled out the Grimkés as being among those who had held back from Washington and his policies. In the book, Du Bois' attack was stronger than that in the earlier review, and so was his characterization of the Grimkés' opposition to Washington, which he said had been moderated only to preserve harmony among black leaders, not because of any sympathy with Washington's policies.[18]

Grimké had not stopped trying to make clear that he disliked Washington's views, not the man himself. In early June, 1903, he wrote Washington a brief letter acknowledging "the difficulty and danger" of Washington's "relations with the South" but urging him to clarify and to stop supporting the literacy and property qualifications which Grimké had attacked in the Boston meeting. He particularly criticized a recent statement by Washington that the revised southern state constitutions put "a premium on property, intelligence, character, and thrift." (Grimké's first law partner, whom he continued to see, William I. Bowditch, had written a similar letter to Washington only a few weeks before.)[19]

Grimké's ideological and political course was set. He regularly spoke publicly and angrily on the injustice of disfranchisement, on what he called, in a contribution to another Boston *Globe* symposium near the end of July, 1903, the "brutal assumption" that black Americans have no rights "which white men are bound to respect," echoing, again, the terrible words of the *Dred Scott* decision from a half-century before. And he unceasingly argued that disfranchisement, basely motivated, endangered all of American society and that "one cannot so cheapen the lives and rights of some men without in time cheapening the lives and rights of all men," echoing beliefs he had expressed as far back as his Garrison biography.[20]

Thus the stage was set for Grimké's sharpest turn against Washington, which came at the end of July, 1903, as a result of the episode known as the Boston Riot. The riot occurred at a meeting of the Boston branch of the National Business League, a Booker Washington organization, which Washington had been invited to address.

18. W. E. B. Du Bois, *The Souls of Black Folk* (1903), in *Three Negro Classics,* ed. John Hope Franklin (New York, 1965), 241–42, 248.

19. Harlan and Smock, eds., *Washington Papers,* VII, 142–43, 170–71.

20. Boston *Guardian,* July 25, 1903; Boston *Globe,* July 19, 1903.

Trotter was the catalyst for the riot. Angered over mistreatment by the Washington machine at a meeting in Louisville a few weeks before, he confronted Washington and his allies with a powerful challenge as the Boston meeting got under way. Pandemonium erupted, and in the confusion, fighting broke out. Trotter, among others, was arrested, charged with disrupting a public meeting. Along with others he was tried, found guilty, and, with Granville Martin, spent some time in jail.[21]

Trotter's jailing had profound effects. Francis Grimké, who had begun to incorporate some anti-Washington ideas in his public addresses and sermons, wrote Trotter a letter of support. Moreover, as both Washington's biographer, Louis Harlan, and Du Bois', Elliott Rudwick, have suggested, the events surrounding the riot helped to undermine any sympathy Du Bois might have had for Washington, pushing him into the opposition camp.[22]

And all of this was to have tremendous implications for Grimké. Because Du Bois had, especially after the publication of *The Souls of Black Folk,* achieved substantial notoriety as the leading intellectual in the black community, his coming over to the anti-Washington side at a time when factions were hardening virtually assured that he would be its leader, eclipsing Trotter, Grimké, and anyone else, their prestige within their own communities notwithstanding. For Grimké, this meant that henceforth his public activities would be framed by what was coming to appear to be a Washington–Du Bois debate.

More immediately, Archibald Grimké's involvement in the events surrounding the riot had implications for his activities over the next few weeks and months. He did not participate in the riot. He and Angelina had gone together to the meeting, but when the situation became nasty, he had taken her out. Archibald Grimké later returned to the hall, where he learned that Trotter and others had been arrested.[23]

Grimké stood by Trotter during his subsequent trials and imprisonment. He served as Trotter's chief witness before the courts—first at Trotter's appearance before the municipal court, then, after Trotter

21. Harlan and Smock, eds., *Washington Papers,* VII, 232–33; Fox, *Guardian of Boston,* 54–56.
22. Louis R. Harlan, *Booker T. Washington in Perspective: Essays of Louis R. Harlan,* ed. Raymond W. Smock (Jackson, Miss., 1988), 169; Elliott M. Rudwick, *W. E. B. Du Bois: Propagandist of the Negro Protest* (New York, 1969), 72; Ferry, "Francis J. Grimké," 241; Emma Lou Thornbrough, *T. Thomas Fortune: Militant Journalist* (Chicago, 1972), 249.
23. Angelina Weld Grimké, Diary, 1903, entry for July 31, 1903.

appealed a guilty verdict reached by the municipal court judge, at his jury trial before the superior court beginning in early October. Grimké defended Trotter's good character and urged the extremity of the provocation that had led him to present his questions to Washington in the manner he did. After Trotter had served his time in jail, Grimké addressed a small crowd of Bostonians gathered to celebrate his liberation.[24]

All of this had a powerful effect on Washington, who turned violently against Archibald Grimké. Publicly, of course, Washington responded in his usual statesmanlike manner. Privately, and perhaps encouraged by reports of questionable validity that Trotter and the other radicals were planning something worse for him, he was vindictive. He indicted Du Bois as a co-consipirator and, in the wake of the riot, drew up an enemies list on which even his old friend Francis Grimké had a place. And he excoriated Archibald Grimké, encouraging a press release, probably written by his secretary Emmett Scott, which said that "the men who were sentenced were not the most guilty. Behind them, and urging them on, it is currently reported, are George Forbes, A. H. Grimké, and C. G. Morgan, who were not so brave as those who were arrested, but in the most cowardly manner stood in the dark, urging them on, without showing their own hands." From Washington's point of view, Archibald Grimké had ceased to occupy middle ground but had wholly gone over into the camp of his opponents.[25]

Over the next few months, this view of Washington's played a role in Grimké's work as a racial activist. Washington attempted a master stroke to strengthen his position as a black leader and within the black community by calling a conference to include the most prominent black leaders, both his friends and those he saw as the most reasonable among his opponents, to find a common ground and to call a truce to what was becoming extremely bitter intraracial warfare. Neither Grimké nor Trotter was to be invited, but Washington did work closely with that most respected of his opponents, Du Bois, in planning the conference.[26]

24. Fox, *Guardian of Boston*, 55, 58; Boston *Guardian*, August 8, 1903; Angelina Weld Grimké, Diary, 1903, entry for August 10, 1903; William Toll, *The Resurgence of Race: Black Social Theory from Reconstruction to the Pan-African Conferences* (Philadelphia, 1979), 101.

25. Harlan, *Booker T. Washington: Wizard of Tuskegee*, 49, 50; Harlan and Smock, eds., *Washington Papers*, VII, 258.

26. August Meier, *Negro Thought in America, 1880–1915: Racial Ideologies in the Age of Booker T. Washington* (Ann Arbor, 1963), 245.

Actually, Washington had begun to plan for the conference early in 1903, before the Boston Riot. In February, Du Bois had been at Tuskegee negotiating for a position in the institution, and Washington had proposed the conference to him, planning to hold it in New York in March or April, although it proved impossible to complete the planning so quickly. Even at that time, Du Bois was suspicious, writing to Kelly Miller—that most moderate of men but no strong Washingtonian—that he did not want to go to the conference unprepared, leaving it open to Washington's control. He fought to ensure invitations for Miller and for the Boston Trotterite Clement G. Morgan and to develop an agenda of his own, raising such thorny issues as higher education and "a stoppage to the campaign of self-depreciation." He hoped that with the cooperation of Miller, Morgan, and a few others, he could turn the conference into a chance for "a heart to heart talk with Mr. Washington."[27]

As planning for the conference went ahead, led by Washington and Du Bois, any effort for "unity" was made within the context of hardening lines of division of which the planners were acutely aware. The Grimkés were put in the middle of this situation, whether they knew it or not, when Du Bois fought to ensure that the conference not "degenerate into a B.T.W. ratification meeting," as he put it, and each man tried to ensure that his side would be well represented among the delegates. At first, of the two brothers, they argued mainly over Francis Grimké, whom Du Bois suggested be issued an invitation, in early November. Washington asked rhetorically, "Do you really think that Dr. Grimké would represent some idea or element that would not be represented by somebody else already invited?" He ultimately acquiesced, however, and, later that month, tendered the invitation.[28]

Francis Grimké apparently was not sure he could attend, but he sent Washington a list of other people he thought should be there and suggested that his brother Archibald be invited. Washington immediately wrote back—in a letter that he copied to Du Bois—urging Francis Grimké not to decline and expressing reservations about an invitation to Francis' brother. First, he noted, Archibald was from Boston, which was already well represented; second, Archibald was a Democrat, and that party was well enough represented. Francis Grimké

27. W. E. B. Du Bois to Kelly Miller, February 17, 25, 1903, in Du Bois Papers.

28. Harlan, *Booker T. Washington: Wizard of Tuskegee*, 67–68; W. E. B. Du Bois to Kelly Miller, November 2, 1903, W. E. B. Du Bois to Booker T. Washington, n.d., in Du Bois Papers; Harlan and Smock, eds., *Washington Papers*, VII, 339.

sought to defend his brother, writing that "my brother is not a demo-crat and never has been. He is what is known as a Mugwump or In-dependent in politics" and urging that he be invited. Washington took no action, and for the next several weeks both sides jockeyed for po-sition, with Francis, whose invitation was firm, clearly in the anti-Washington camp.[29]

In the meantime, Archibald Grimké was keeping busy in ways that would hardly endear him to Booker Washington. Toward the middle of December, representing the newly formed Boston Suffrage League, which he and Trotter had started, he met with leaders of other local bodies—his brother Francis was a vice-president of the Washington, D.C., branch—to consider the creation of a national organization to counterbalance the Tuskegee machine. The effort collapsed, however, when some representatives urged an endorsement of the candidacy of Theodore Roosevelt for the presidency in the 1904 elections, while Grimké, Trotter, and a few others sought to make the organization nonpartisan.[30]

More significant was his assumption that month of the presidency of the American Negro Academy. During the years of Du Bois' pres-idency, the academy had been on ground that was far from firm. The commitment of many of its members was not strong, and its annual meetings were sparsely attended and poorly publicized. Even Du Bois had not been particularly active, and some of the more com-mitted members, and even Du Bois, recognized that this was a prob-lem. As early as 1901, John W. Cromwell, who had long been a mov-ing spirit in the organization, began to cast about for someone to replace Du Bois.[31]

Cromwell contacted several potential candidates, including Archi-bald Grimké, who was willing to serve. He was unanimously elected to the post at the academy's meeting on December 29, 1903. There was apparently little controversy or even much discussion surround-ing his election. His willingness to serve, compounded with his liter-ary and intellectual credentials and his sometime residence in Washing-ton, were enough to recommend him to the academy's membership.

29. Booker T. Washington to W. E. B. Du Bois, December 4, 1903, Booker T. Washington to Francis J. Grimké, December 5, 1903 (copy), W. E. B. Du Bois to Fran-cis J. Grimké, December 28, 1903, in Du Bois Papers; Harlan and Smock, eds., *Wash-ington Papers,* VII, 363.

30. Toll, *Resurgence of Race,* 102; New York *Age,* September 24, December 24, 1903.

31. Alfred A. Moss, Jr., *The American Negro Academy: Voice of the Talented Tenth* (Baton Rouge, 1981), 66.

Grimké celebrated his election with an address titled "Industrial Competition and the Right to Vote." Its anti-Washington message was conveyed in its title.[32]

His election and address did not help him with Booker Washington, who continued to oppose inviting him to the New York conference, scheduled to begin on January 6, 1904. Only when the pressure became too great did he relent. When Francis finally refused to attend, and Washington had been "urged strongly" by others to invite Archibald Grimké, he sent the invitation, "strongly against my own will."[33]

Washington was far from gracious in defeat. He wrote to one associate that he did not believe Archibald Grimké had done anything to entitle him to membership in the conference. Beyond that, he said, "he represents a noisy, turbulent and unscrupulous set of men to such an extent that I cannot feel that he would enter into the serious and far-sighted deliberations of such a conference in the way that we plan to enter into it." And in what may have been a reference to the abortive Boston Suffrage League meeting but could have referred to the more recent American Negro Academy meeting, Washington warned "that if he attempts to have the same kind of 'nigger meeting' that was had in Washington a few days ago, it will be much wiser for him not to go to New York."[34]

But Archibald Grimké did attend the conference in New York, and with a result that even Washington would have found impossible to predict.

32. *Ibid.*, 66–67, 113–15.
33. Harlan, *Booker T. Washington: Wizard of Tuskegee,* 68; Booker T. Washington to T. Thomas Fortune, January 2, 1904, in Washington Papers; Francis J. Grimké to W. E. B. Du Bois, January 4, 1904, in Du Bois Papers.
34. Harlan and Smock, eds., *Washington Papers,* VII, 383.

8

Carnegie Hall

The New York meeting took place on January 6, 7, and 8, 1904, at Carnegie Hall, with Archibald Grimké in attendance. Among the others present were Washington and Du Bois, of course, T. Thomas Fortune, E. H. Morris, Clement Morgan, P. B. S. Pinchback, Kelly Miller, Judson Lyons, Hugh M. Browne, Whitefield McKinlay, and Emmett Scott. To Du Bois' dismay, several prominent whites also addressed the Carnegie Conference, as the meeting came to be known, and they were mainly friends of Washington. They included Andrew Carnegie himself, William H. Baldwin, and Oswald Garrison Villard, grandson of the abolitionist. The proceedings of the conference were supposed to be secret, but such secrets are hard to keep, and historians have been able to discover much about what took place and its significance.[1]

The partisans had gone to the conference prepared to do battle. Du Bois, as historians have noted, had created a classification system for the delegates, including those "unscrupulously for Washington," those who were for or against Washington in more moderate degrees, and those who, like himself and Francis Grimké before his withdrawal, were "uncomprisingly anti-Washington." That Du Bois had emerged nationally as the leader of an anti-Washington faction, apart from the conspicuously absent Trotter, was confirmed by the sched-

---

1. Louis R. Harlan and Raymond W. Smock, eds., *The Booker T. Washington Papers* (14 vols.; Urbana, 1972–89), VII, 186; Louis R. Harlan, *Booker T. Washington: The Wizard of Tuskegee, 1901–1915* (New York, 1983), 71; W. E. B. Du Bois to Kelly Miller, February 25, 1903, in W. E. B. Du Bois Papers (microfilm), University of Massachusetts, Amherst.

uling of Washington and Du Bois each to give a brief, ten-minute opening address.[2]

Despite Washington's desire to use the meeting to create harmony among the black leadership, the sessions were often tense, hardening rather than lessening the divisions Washington wanted to heal. Nevertheless, the conference was able to reach unanimity on a series of resolutions, bearing all the marks of compromise, that grew out of the discussions. These included a stand on behalf of the right of suffrage, at least where it had not yet been abridged; an agreement to continue filing suits challenging Jim Crow in public accommodations and travel; a recognition of the validity of both industrial and higher education; a denunciation of lynching; and a declaration that "the Northern white man, the Southern white man and the Negro" would have to work together for a solution to the American race problem. The conference also called for the formation of a twelve-member Committee of Safety. Washington, Du Bois, and Hugh M. Browne were appointed to it at the conference and delegated to select the other nine members.[3]

Archibald Grimké, though undoubtedly in the anti-Washington camp, occupied an ambiguous position at the close of the conference. Washington had given a closing address at the very end of the meeting, and Grimké was reported to have been greatly impressed by it, saying to one Washington lieutenant that its arguments were "unanswerable" and to another that he had been "completely overcome" by it. The address has not survived in any form other than a hostile account, but apparently it was highly emotional, Washington even breaking into tears on occasion, assuring the delegates of his good faith, of his genuine belief in higher education and universal suffrage, and, as one observer put it, "any old thing," despite impressions to the contrary. All he wanted was unity in the ranks. These were the stands that Grimké had long urged Washington to take.[4]

Washington's words were not only encouraging to Grimké but reached out to him personally as well. Despite his ugly remarks about Grimké before the meeting, Washington showed trust in Grimké as an emissary to the enemy by asking him for help with one important

2. Harlan, *Booker T. Washington: Wizard of Tuskegee,* 70–71; Elliot M. Rudwick, *W. E. B. Du Bois: Propagandist of the Negro Protest* (New York, 1969), 80–81; W. E. B. Du Bois, Memoranda on the Washington Meeting, n.d., in Du Bois Papers.

3. Harlan and Smock, eds., *Washington Papers,* VII, 384–87.

4. Harlan, *Booker T. Washington: Wizard of Tuskegee,* 72; Boston *Guardian,* January 30, 1904.

problem that arose in the aftermath of the conference. When it appeared that Trotter planned to publish an account of the "entire proceedings" of the conference, Grimké was entrusted with the job of restraining Trotter from doing so. Grimké promised to try, vainly as it turned out, and despite a surreptitious effort by Washington, belying his show of trust, to mobilize some of his more faithful lieutenants to work behind the scenes both to keep pressure on Grimké and to prevent Trotter from acting.[5]

But a more important product of the conference, especially for Archibald Grimké, was the formation of the Committee of Safety, soon to be known as the Committee of Twelve for the Advancement of the Negro Race, and the selection after the conference of its remaining nine members, one of whom was to be Grimké himself. The formation of the committee had been no easy matter. Du Bois and Washington argued over its structure and size, until they and Hugh Browne actually did the appointing. The presence of Washington and Browne, in opposition to Du Bois, ensured that the committee was stacked with pro-Washington men. Only Grimké, Du Bois, and Dr. Charles Bentley of Chicago (who, as Louis Harlan has noted, also had ties to Washington) represented anything like a radical presence.[6]

If anything, the formation of the committee exacerbated rather than decreased the tension between Washington and Du Bois. Grimké, despite his apparent place in the opposition, found himself at first caught in the middle and then driven back toward the Washington camp. This situation grew initially out of a dispute over whether Du Bois had been properly invited to the first full meeting of the body held in July. Du Bois felt he had not and, after a lengthy exchange of letters among the principals, in which Grimké described Du Bois as "acting queerly," left his allies to go it alone against Washington's forces. Grimké later said he felt "let down flat" by Du Bois' apparent refusal to attend. Grimké was still among Washington's most vocal opponents.[7]

5. Harlan and Smock, eds., *Washington Papers,* VII, 389; Harlan, *Booker T. Washington: Wizard of Tuskegee,* 73–74.

6. Harlan, *Booker T. Washington: Wizard of Tuskegee,* 79–80; Hugh M. Browne to Archibald Grimké, March 25, 1904, in Archibald H. Grimké Papers, Box 8, Folder 155, Moorland-Spingarn Research Center, Howard University, Washington, D.C.

7. Kelly Miller to W. E. B. Du Bois, July 8, 1904, in Du Bois Papers; Archibald Grimké to Angelina Weld Grimké, June 11, July 3, 1904, in Angelina Weld Grimké Papers, Box 4, Folder 72, Moorland-Spingarn Research Center, Howard University, Washington, D.C.

The situation then became astonishingly muddled. Despite his sense of being let down, Grimké felt fairly comfortable at the July meeting. He even agreed to serve as treasurer for the group; Washington was the chairman, Browne, the secretary. A few weeks later, when Du Bois, still angry, decided to resign and to try to start a counter-organization, a "body of fearless people" who could back those willing to fight both discrimination and Booker T. Washington, Grimké agreed to go along. Then, contradicting that move almost immediately, he withdrew his resignation, urging Du Bois to do the same.[8]

The reasons for Grimké's actions are not at all clear. But over the next few months it became apparent that he had settled on a strategy much like the one he had earlier adopted for dealing with Washington's leadership, working with the Washington group and hoping to use it for more militant ends. He tried to explain this to Du Bois, arguing that he had come to feel, as a result of conversations with other committee members, that Washington's domination of the committee was not so complete as to make working with it impossible and that he thought that, by participating, "we cannot lose anything." Indeed, he wrote, their cause "may gain much." Du Bois was not much persuaded.[9]

Grimké had cause to believe that such a strategy made sense. He did not feel compromised by his participation on the committee. In a later letter to Charles Bentley, who was also thinking about creating a competing group, he wrote that, despite his participation, he had remained his own man. "I am not in consonance with its two principal officers," Washington and Browne, and "I am a member of the Committee & do not thereby surrender one jot of my well known convictions on the equal civil & political rights of the colored race. And in the councils of the Com. I have never hesitated to advance these opinions."[10]

Washington and his allies encouraged Grimké to believe that his ideas were not simply tolerated but listened to by both Washington and the committee. He was regularly praised for his work and even his views. Moreover, he received confirmation of the hearing his ideas could get in the reaction of Washington and the rest of the body to one of his most noticed published pieces from this time, "Why Dis-

8. Archibald Grimké to W. E. B. Du Bois, August 13, 1904, in Du Bois Papers.
9. *Ibid.*
10. C. E. Bentley to Archibald Grimké, March 20, 1905 (Grimké draft reply on back), in Archibald Grimké Papers, Box 4, Folder 85; Stephen R. Fox, *The Guardian of Boston: William Monroe Trotter* (New York, 1970), 89.

franchisement Is Bad," which appeared in the July, 1904, issue of the *Atlantic*. The article elaborated on ideas that Grimké had long expressed. Evoking yet again a black "underworld" filled with potential Veseys and Nat Turners and noting the role of disfranchisement and other forms of oppression in the South's effort to maintain an anachronistic industrial system, he argued that the right of suffrage was a fundamental issue for anyone interested in racial equality and economic progress.[11]

One would be hard-pressed to see Grimké's "Why Disfranchisement Is Bad" as a Washingtonian piece. But soon after it appeared, Washington wrote to Grimké that he found the piece "one of the strongest and most statesmanlike articles that I have ever read on this subject," adding, "I am sure that it will accomplish good." Two days later, Grimké heard from one of Washington's closest white associates and philanthropic sources, William H. Baldwin, who told him that he also had liked the article, calling it, "the best exposition of the subject that I have ever seen," no doubt encouraging Washington's own positive reaction.[12]

More important for Grimké's place in the tense setting of black political alliances, Washington was not content merely to compliment Grimké on the article. Shortly after its appearance, he contacted Grimké about the possibility of reprinting it and distributing it under the imprimatur of the Committee of Twelve. By November, he had had the article reprinted and had drawn up a list of people to whom it should be sent. The following year, Grimké's article played an important practical role in one of Washington's efforts to work behind the scenes, in this case to defeat constitutional "amendments pertaining to voting" that would have disfranchised blacks in Maryland. On Washington's motion, the Committee of Twelve authorized a printing of five thousand copies of Grimké's article to be distributed in the state. The amendments were defeated, and one of Washington's friends gave particular credit to the "literature" the committee had sent out, although partisan politics—the familiar Republican desire to maintain a bloc Negro vote and a split in the Democratic party—probably had as much to do with the outcome. Even so, it was a victory, one more victory than Du Bois' would-be opposition could claim, which

11. Archibald H. Grimké, "Why Disfranchisement Is Bad," *Atlantic*, XCIV (1904), 72–73.

12. Booker T. Washington to Archibald Grimké, July 13, 1904, in Archibald Grimké Papers, Box 6, Folder 121; William H. Baldwin to Archibald Grimké, July 15, 1904, *ibid.*, Box 4, Folder 85.

would have confirmed Grimké's decision to stay, in factional terms, where he was.[13]

Grimké thus had much reinforcement for his decision to work with the Committee of Twelve. He was further reinforced because, except for Du Bois, he lost no friends on either side of the dispute as he continued to work with the committee. For instance, his circle of friends and associates in Boston remained the same. He had left the presidency of the Boston Literary in March, 1903, after two years, but this had little effect on his relationship with the Boston community. He had been succeeded in the office by two friends, Maria Baldwin and Butler Wilson, and he had remained active in the association's affairs, speaking before it on several occasions. Anti-Washington activity remained as strong as ever within this community, as Washington himself was well aware. But for all the conflict between the two camps and Grimké's willingness to cooperate with the Committee of Twelve, he remained a member in good standing of Boston society, even being given a testimonial dinner for his services toward the end of 1904.[14]

His life in Boston seems to have been generally satisfying to him at this time, both in public matters and in his private life, which was organized around his long-standing friendships, black and white, within the city. He engaged in a wide range of social and cultural activities. He was joined in Boston by his daughter, who spent her summer break in the city. Both stayed, as always, with the Lees, Angelina using her time in Boston to take a summer course at Harvard, as she was to do every summer for the next six years.[15]

He escaped from the problems of black factionalism sufficiently to reenter party politics in 1904, breaking with the Democratic party for the first time since 1886 to support Theodore Roosevelt's campaign for reelection to the presidency. Grimké tried to make clear that he was not changing parties but acting, as always, as an Independent. He claimed to be motivated chiefly by the South's reaction to

13. Booker T. Washington to Archibald Grimké, [date illegible], in Booker T. Washington Papers, Library of Congress; Harlan and Smock, eds., *Washington Papers,* VIII, 146, 373, 484; New York *Tribune,* October 9, 1905, in Hampton University Peabody Newspaper Clippings File (Microfiche ed.; Alexandria, Va., 1987).

14. Boston Literary and Historical Association programs, in William Monroe Trotter Papers, Box 11, Mugar Memorial Library, Boston University; Harlan and Smock, eds., *Washington Papers,* VIII, 75, 110–12; Card for dinner, November 10, 1904, in Archibald Grimké Papers, Box 39, Folder 764.

15. Archibald Grimké to Angelina Grimké, October 29, 1904, in Angelina Grimké Papers, Box 4, Folder 72; Angelina Grimké to Archibald Grimké, June 11, 1904, in Archibald Grimké Papers, Box 3, Folder 60.

Roosevelt's famous 1901 White House dinner with Booker Washington; its opposition to Roosevelt's appointment in 1902 of a black man, William D. Crum, as collector of the port of Charleston; and its violent response to Roosevelt's persistence in supporting Minnie Cox as postmaster of Indianola, Mississippi. Grimké appreciated Roosevelt's stand on all three issues, ignoring the president's increasingly mixed record on racial questions in general and arguing that the white South's hatred for Roosevelt ought to be enough to convince any black voter that his interests lay with the president.[16]

Whether his political position was related to his revitalized relationship with Booker Washington is hard to say. Washington's own role in the Republican party was large and significant; his support for Roosevelt was strong and well-known. That Grimké was making a gesture toward Washington by supporting Roosevelt is possible but not certain. There were other good reasons for moving away from the Democratic party in the early 1900s, which Grimké stressed in his public comments.

His independence in other areas made it unlikely that he would feel obliged to support Roosevelt simply because of any ties to Washington. Grimké's public statements continued to develop along the same lines they had taken two decades before, sounding much more like an opponent of Washington than a friend. During the early fall, he issued an attack on southern suffrage restrictions that put him in definite opposition to Washington's views. This attack came in an article in the *Voice of the Negro* in which he condemned as sheer subterfuge the education and property requirements for voting that were being enacted in various parts of the region. The *Voice* was a relatively new magazine and initially had included writings on both sides of the Washington–Du Bois debate. But it had quickly taken an anti-Washington turn, and Grimké's article fit right in, in both tone and substance.[17]

In about October, 1904, Grimké produced one of his most original and demanding essays on the meaning of race and racism. In it he took new and surprising directions, indicating how little his Committee of Twelve membership had moved him toward Washington's ideas. He apparently had been working on the essay for some time, and with the help of E. H. Clement, editor of the Boston *Transcript,* got it pub-

16. Clipping, n.d., in Archibald Grimké Papers, Box 36, Folder 729; New York *Age,* October 13, November 3, 1904. On Roosevelt's record see Seth Scheiner, "President Theodore Roosevelt and the Negro," *Journal of Negro History,* XLVII (1962), 179–80.

17. Archibald H. Grimké, "An Education and Property Basis," *Voice of the Negro,* I (1904), 384–85.

lished in 1906 in a general interest magazine, the *Arena* (edited by B. O. Fowler, who had spoken earlier at the Boston Literary). He entitled it "The Heart of the Race Problem." The heart of the race problem, as he described it in this paper, had less to do with economics and politics than with biology and, above all, sex.[18]

Looking back to history, Grimké wrote that "the ship which landed at Jamestown in 1619 with a cargo of African slaves for Virginia plantations, imported at the same time into America with its slave-cargo certain seed-principles of wrong." What he meant was that "the enslavement of one race by another produces necessarily certain moral effects upon both races, moral deterioration of the masters, moral degradation of the slaves." The result was the "evolution of the double moral standard," in which "the master or superior race will have one standard to regulate the conduct of individuals belonging to it in respect to one another, and another standard to regulate the conduct of those selfsame individuals in respect to individuals of the slave or inferior race." This had happened in the South, he wrote.[19]

The effects of this double moral standard were enormous. White men profited from it. They were able to "live in licit intercourse with a woman of his own race, and at the same time in illicit intercourse with a woman of the other race" without facing the sanctions of law. The result, he said, using a metaphor that went well back in his thinking, was that the chief effect was to create an "under world of the under race." And, he wrote, "Down there, there is no law, no public opinion, to curb the gratification of the sexual instinct of the men of the upper world." He said, "In the upper world, they are members of a civilized society, amenable to its codes of law and morals; in the lower one, they are merely male animals struggling with other male animals for possession of the females."[20]

Black men, by contrast, suffered by being forced to confront a triple barrier of monogamous standards, a restriction to women of their own race, and a continuing invasion of their "under world" by men of the dominant race.[21]

For white women, he wrote, the main effect was to increase race hatred. "The white women of the South," he said, "are not fools."

18. Archibald Grimké to Angelina Weld Grimké, November 10, 1905, in Angelina Grimké Papers, Box 4, Folder 74; Fox, *Guardian of Boston,* 28; Archibald Grimké, "The Heart of the Race Problem," October 16, 1904, in Archibald Grimké Papers, Box 19, Folder 374, published in *Arena,* XXXV (1906), 29–32, 274–787, 606–10.
19. "The Heart of the Race Problem," *Arena,* XXXV (1906), 30–31.
20. *Ibid.,* 275.
21. *Ibid.,* 276–77.

When "they see black mothers with light-colored children, they need not ask the meaning of it, the cause of such apparent wonder." It angered them, and their hatred found its fulfillment in segregation and in the laws, by then current in every southern state, forbidding inter-marriage, laws that were counterproductive insofar as they permitted concubinage while denying the black woman the one possible sanction she might have should she become pregnant from such a relationship. Far from preventing "amalgamation," Grimké asserted, such laws made it "appallingly easy."[22]

For black women, the problems were critical. The position of the black woman outside the restraints and laws protecting the white woman made her terribly vulnerable to being pursued by the white man without fear, on his part, of any consequences. If she resisted, she simply became a more attractive prey. When she succumbed, she became a "moral plague-spot in the midst of both races" and part of a vicious circle of moral ruin for both races in the South.[23]

So long as there was segregation and inequality, and so long as the law gave no protection to black women, Grimké wrote, the problems would continue to exist for everyone. Should the South persist in in-equality, it must be prepared to "continue to gather the bitter fruits of it in the darkened moral life, in the low moral standards of both races." As he rather biblically predicted, "what the South sows, whether it be cotton or character, that it shall surely reap."[24]

There is no small temptation to read Grimké's own life and expe-riences into this essay, especially those of his mother and his brother and the racial concerns that had led his wife to break up their marriage. But no less significantly, one can also identify public concerns that would have encouraged Grimké's interest in the sexual dimension of racial oppression. In this period of epidemic lynchings, Grimké was not the only black writer to address the topic. At the time he wrote, several essays appeared under black authorship intended both to con-tradict radical racist charges of black sexuality and to document the sexual brutality of southern white men and the phoniness of white southern pretensions to sexual purity.[25]

Grimké could have drawn on other sources than his own experi-ences. In addition to other contemporary writers, long black tradition, both popular and literary, exhibited the same awareness of the irony

22. *Ibid.*, 606–608,
23. *Ibid.*, 609–10.
24. *Ibid.*, 610.
25. See, *e.g.*, essays in Gerda Lerner, *Black Women in White America: A Documentary History* (New York, 1973), 149–71.

of white sexual behavior and of its brutality, including its brutalizing effects on white women. The madly jealous slave mistress, for example, was a hoary figure in both folklore and literature, as was the desire of white men to take advantage of black women without fear of sanction. And, of course, abolitionists, both black and white, had stressed the significance of sexuality as a symbol of the slave system's brutality.

The paper reflected the continuing influence of his aunts, particularly Angelina Weld, whose own view of sex, as manifested in the "orgy of restraint" that marked her courtship with Theodore Weld and was manifested in her persistent condemnation of the opportunities for licentiousness provided by slavery, was revitalized in her nephew's essay linking slavery, segregation, and a continuing state of moral corruption in the white South.

But none of this should detract from the striking originality of Grimké's paper for its time. Although many writers had stressed the importance of sex to white racism, none had done so before in quite the way Grimké did, particularly in his focus on a system of sexual gain for white men that gave them a powerful stake in maintaining a well-defined caste system in the South. The argument Grimké advanced here was new, and it strongly anticipated a later statement of the same position by the psychologist John Dollard in his influential study from the 1930s, *Caste and Class in a Southern Town*. Whether Dollard knew of Grimké's paper is uncertain. Neither the paper nor its ideas met a sudden death. As late as 1925, Arthur Spingarn asked for a copy to give to Carl Van Vechten; as late as 1933, in a passage Dollard cited, James Weldon Johnson echoed Grimké when he wrote, "In the core of the heart of the American race problem the sex factor is rooted." But whether the paper influenced Johnson or Dollard, in it Grimké took a familiar tradition in very new directions, anticipating what, after Dollard, would be a central idea in theories of American racism.[26]

Its sources and its prescience should not detract from the paper's significance as an indicator of the direction toward which Grimké's thought had been tending for some time. Above all, its shows a Grimké who was deeply convinced of the irrationality of what he had always called "colorphobia" and who knew that any solution to the

26. John Dollard, *Caste and Class in a Southern Town* (1937; 3rd ed., Garden City, N.Y., 1957), 135; Arthur Spingarn to Archibald Grimké, November 28, 1925, in Archibald Grimké Papers, Box 5, Folder 104; James Weldon Johnson, *Along This Way* (New York, 1933), 170.

problem, if any solution were possible, had to take that irrationality into account. And this made it a commentary, as well, on the specific political situation in which Grimké found himself. Its stress on irrationality in racism made all appeals to goodwill impossible and gave lie to any notions such as those of Booker T. Washington that black people could earn themselves a place in American life. White people alone caused the problems; only when white people could be persuaded that it was in their own interests to overcome their instincts and dismantle the racist system they had created would anything like a solution begin to appear. Grimké's view of racism here represented an indictment of white America more deeply rooted and more militant than even Washington's opponents, Du Bois included, were engaging in at the time. It might not be too much to claim that his paper shows, more than any other, the strange position Grimké occupied at the close of 1904, at the leading edge of the creation of an ideology in opposition to Booker Washington's, while working mainly from within the Washington camp. It was a position he was not to give up quickly.

The year following the Carnegie Conference was a full one for Grimké, largely because of the continuation of conflicts that the conference had been called to resolve. Grimké continued to write, spurred, perhaps, by the ongoing debates but not always dominated by them. He also acted with enthusiasm in his new role as president of the American Negro Academy. He brought his longtime friend and the sometime Trotterite Butler Wilson into the organization, augmenting the organization's anti-Washington tendencies. And in the spring, he handled his first real controversy in that role, approving the publication, as an Occasional Paper, of a highly critical piece titled *Defects of the Negro Church* by academy member Orishatukeh Faduma. It had been referred to him by the academy's executive committee, which had no questions about the paper's quality but worried about what might be seen as its hostility to black ministers, including those among the academy's membership.[27]

Despite all the other activity, the now well-defined Washington–Du Bois conflict remained ubiquitous and inescapable, and it was to continue to occupy a major portion of Archibald Grimké's life.

27. Alfred A. Moss, Jr., *American Negro Academy: Voice of the Talented Tenth* (Baton Rouge, 1981), 117, 151; Harlan and Smock, eds., *Washington Papers,* VIII, 92–93; Wilson Jeremiah Moses, *The Golden Age of Black Nationalism, 1850–1925* (1978; rpr. New York, 1988), 203–204, 231.

Francis and Archibald Grimké, probably in their late teens
Archibald Grimké Papers, Box 40, Folder 819. Courtesy Moorland-Spingarn
Research Center, Howard University

Francis, Archibald, and John Grimké
Archibald Grimké Papers, Box 40, Folder 821. Courtesy Moorland-Spingarn
Research Center, Howard University

Archibald Grimké, around the time of his political activity in Boston, *ca.* 1880s

Archibald Grimké Papers, Box 40, Folder 794. Courtesy Moorland-Spingarn Research Center, Howard University

Grimké, on the right, as consul to Santo Domingo

Archibald Grimké Papers,.Box 40, Folder 802. Courtesy Moorland-Spingarn Research Center, Howard University

Grimké, *ca*. World War I
Archibald Grimké Papers, Box 40, Folder 799. Courtesy Moorland-Spingarn
Research Center, Howard University. © Scurlock Studio, Washington, D.C.

Grimké, late in life
Archibald Grimké Papers, Box 40, Folder 804. Courtesy Moorland-Spingarn
Research Center, Howard University. © Scurlock Studio, Washington, D.C.

Angelina Grimké and Sarah Stanley Grimké, *ca.* 1881
Photograph by J. J. Hawes. Archibald Grimké Papers, Box 40, Folder 807. Courtesy Moorland-Spingarn Research Center, Howard University

Angelina Grimké (front row, third from right) in school in Hyde Park,
Massachusetts
    Archibald Grimké Papers, Box 40, Folder 813. Courtesy Moorland-Spingarn
    Research Center, Howard University

Angelina Grimké
    Archibald Grimké Papers, Box 40, Folder 812. Courtesy Moorland-Spingarn
    Research Center, Howard University

Archibald and Angelina Grimké, early twentieth century
Archibald Grimké Papers, Box 40, Folder 817. Courtesy Moorland-Spingarn
Research Center, Howard University

Nancy Weston, Archibald Grimké's mother
Archibald Grimké Papers, Box 40, Folder 838. Courtesy Moorland-Spingarn
Research Center, Howard University

Francis Grimké, as a young man
   Archibald Grimké Papers, Box 40, Folder 825. Courtesy Moorland-Spingarn
   Research Center, Howard University

Charlotte Forten Grimké, wife of Francis Grimké
   Archibald Grimké Papers, Box 40, Folder 836. Courtesy Moorland-Spingarn
   Research Center, Howard University

Francis Grimké, in middle age
Archibald Grimké Papers, Box 40, Folder 829. Courtesy Moorland-Spingarn
Research Center, Howard University

Francis Grimké, as an older man
Archibald Grimké Papers, Box 40, Folder 834. Courtesy Moorland-Spingarn
Research Center, Howard University

Sarah Moore Grimké and Angelina Emily Grimké Weld,
Archibald Grimké's aunts
  Sarah, from the Library of Congress. Angelina, from *Dictionary of American Portraits*.

Theodore Dwight Weld, Angelina Grimké's husband
Archibald Grimké Papers, Box 40, Folder 892. Courtesy Moorland-Spingarn
Research Center, Howard University

T. Thomas Fortune, editor of the New York *Age*
Archibald Grimké Papers, Box 40, Folder 857. Courtesy Moorland-Spingarn
Research Center, Howard University

Booker T. Washington
From *Dictionary of American Portraits*

W. E. B. Du Bois
Library of Congress

Joel Spingarn
Library of Congress

William Monroe Trotter
Courtesy Photographs and Prints Division, Schomburg Center for Research in
Black Culture, The New York Public Library, Astor, Lenox and Tilden
Foundations

Roscoe Conkling Bruce
Courtesy Moorland-Spingarn Research Center, Howard University

Mary White Ovington
Library of Congress

Ulises Heureaux
Library of Congress

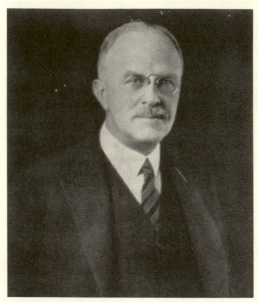

O. G. Villard
Library of Congress

Wendell Phillips
Library of Congress

9

The *Age*

Over the next year and a half, factions between African-American leaders continued to harden. Archibald Grimké pursued the independent course he had set for himself, working mainly within the structure Washington had built, believing that he could gain little by aiding Washington's most visible opponents, but also giving voice to views that provided a framework for that opposition which Du Bois, in particular, was working hard to build.

As 1905 opened, Grimké was publicly associated with the Washington organization. Washington's opponents did much to ensure that he stayed there, providing a negative reinforcement that complemented Washington's more positive efforts. Setting a pattern that would continue over at least the next year and a half, Du Bois, for instance, who had already been difficult and disappointing from Grimké's point of view, became positively offensive, discouraging any thought that he might offer a more congenial alternative to the Washington machine. Calling Grimké to task for remaining with the Committee of Twelve, Du Bois wrote, in a letter addressed to both Grimké and Kelly Miller, "I count it a great misfortune to the Negro race when two clear headed and honest men like you can see their way to put themselves under the dictation of a man with the record of Mr. Washington." In a way that could hardly have appealed to a man of Grimké's temperament, he cited, by contrast, his own refusal "to wear Mr. Washington's livery, or to put on his collar." [1]

1. W. E. B. Du Bois to Archibald Grimké and Kelly Miller, March 21, 1905, in Archibald H. Grimké Papers, Box 4, Folder 91, Moorland-Spingarn Research Center, Howard University, Washington, D.C.; Stephen R. Fox, *The Guardian of Boston: William Monroe Trotter* (New York, 1970), 92.

Grimké continued to act as he had, not moderating his ideological differences with Washington and avoiding the enemy camp identified with Du Bois. The differences between him and Washington remained strong and clear. The two men disagreed strongly, for instance, over a revival of an idea dating from the post–Civil War era to reduce southern representation in Congress as a result of disfranchisement by basing it on the voting population rather than on the population as a whole, which, of course, included disfranchised blacks.

Washington, typically, opposed the idea of reducing representation, but Grimké, joining Trotter and others among Washington's vocal opponents—and reversing his own stance on the coercive features of the Force Bill twenty years before—was clearly on the other side. He campaigned vigorously on the issue in the press and on the stump, and he made the reduction a central focus for a meeting of the American Negro Academy timed to coincide with President-elect Roosevelt's inauguration. The theme chosen for the meeting was "The Negro and the Elective Franchise," and speakers included Archibald and Francis Grimké, John Hope from Atlanta (along with Du Bois, Booker Washington's most vocal southern critic), and Kelly Miller. Each of the papers attacked Washington's apparent willingness to compromise on questions of suffrage; each placed the right to vote at the foundation of American citizenship. Archibald Grimké's position was summarized in the title of his paper, "The Meaning and Need of the Movement to Reduce Southern Representation." In it he reiterated arguments initially stated in "Modern Industrialism," applying them specifically to the issue of reduction. All of this gave cause for more than one of Washington's men, including Whitefield McKinlay, to worry about the strength of his commitment to the Washington organization.[2]

Grimké's ability to offend both sides equally makes the next stage of his career both particularly fascinating and particularly important. In mid-March, 1905, he decided to resume his journalistic career, signing on with the New York *Age,* perhaps the leading black newspaper of the day. He did so in response to an invitation from its editor, the staunch Booker Washington ally Thomas Fortune, and assumed the role of the paper's Washington, D.C., correspondent.[3]

2. New York *Age,* January 26, 1905; Archibald H. Grimké, *The Meaning and Need of the Movement to Reduce Southern Representation,* Occasional Papers of the American Negro Academy, no. 11, 1905, in *The American Negro Academy Occasional Papers 1–22* (New York, 1969).

3. Thomas Fortune to Archibald Grimké, March 6, 1905, in Archibald Grimké Papers, Box 4, Folder 92.

It is not clear whose idea it was that Grimké should write for the *Age*. It may have been an attempt by Fortune, encouraged by Washington and complementing the flattery of Washington's people on the Committee of Twelve, to keep Grimké within the organization and out of a connection with the Du Bois–Trotter group. Nor is it clear why Grimké responded positively. Fortune did offer him a small compensation, though probably not enough to be the deciding factor. But his joining the *Age* was of great significance because, by 1905, not only was Fortune well-known as a Booker T. Washington ally, despite some disagreements between them, but the *Age* was known as a Booker Washington paper. Since January, 1904, Fortune and Washington had worked to strengthen the paper's Tuskegee connection and had even discussed Washington's buying the *Age* to make it "a large national weekly paper that will control in a very large degree the whole Negro situation," obviously from a Washingtonian point of view. The sale did not go through, but after that time, and especially during 1905 and 1906, Washington made regular financial contributions to subsidize the newspaper.[4]

Grimké's connection to the *Age* increased the frustration of Washington's most dedicated opponents. Du Bois confronted him on the matter, and Grimké replied only that Washington's "attitude on the race question is changing for the better." Trotter, who now classified Grimké with the enemy, received a copy of Grimké's letter to Du Bois and found it "disgusting." He took Grimké's actions personally, noting that his own relations with Grimké had been going downhill for some time—which may have encouraged Grimké to feel more comfortable in the Washington orbit—and noting that his wife had lost faith in Grimké as well. (The Trotters and Grimké were to have a complete falling-out by the end of the year, and, although the immediate cause is unclear, it was likely a culmination of these already worsening relations.) He accused Grimké, who had no regular employment, of compromising himself for the salary Fortune was paying and seemed to suggest that, apart from money considerations, Grimké's signing with the *Age* was directly aimed at Trotter himself. Trotter hoped he would return to the fold but believed he would do so "a broken and empty vessel."[5]

4. Hugh Browne to Archibald Grimké, June 15, 1905, *ibid.*, Box 8, Folder 155; Emma Lou Thornbrough, *T. Thomas Fortune: Militant Journalist* (Chicago, 1972), 264–65; Emma Lou Thornbrough, "American Negro Newspapers, 1880–1914," *Business History Review*, XL (1966), 484; Booker T. Washington to Thomas Fortune, January 27, 1904, in Booker T. Washington Papers, Library of Congress.
5. Louis R. Harlan and Raymond W. Smock, eds., *The Booker T. Washington Pa-*

Despite the apprehensions of Trotter and Du Bois, Grimké as a columnist for the *Age* did not become a Washington mouthpiece. Instead, he continued to attack positions that might be identified with Washington, often with a militance rarely matched even by Du Bois, while working within the framework of the Washington organization. His first column was an indictment of "colorphobia" in Washington, D.C. Despite an almost Washingtonian headline proclaiming "Each Race Responsible," what Grimké wrote was hardly a call for further uplift on the part of blacks, as one might expect. Rather, condemning white aggression in discriminating against blacks, he used the column to inveigh against any acquiescence by blacks in the face of discrimination against them.[6]

Subsequent columns described incidents of discrimination in the nation's capital, urged resistance, and praised those who showed fight in the face of segregation, subtly but clearly questioning Washington's more conciliatory approach. But occasionally Grimké was more pointed in expressing his differences from Washington. In one column, for example, he picked up on ideas that had figured prominently in his Vesey paper, applying them squarely to his own time and even taking them a step further than he had a few years before. Here, he focused on a black southern educator, Richard Carroll, who, like Washington, seemed to have made a career of pleasing white people to gain support for his activities. Noting as he had in the Vesey piece the mask of servility Carroll had adopted, behind which were "dark unseen passions and forces" that were "crouching like so many tigers," he asserted that every black man in the South is a Richard Carroll, "Janus-faced," hiding a seething anger behind a mask of lies and duplicity.[7]

Grimké discussed the strategy of dissimulation Carroll represented. Describing "this crop of fraud, of deceit, of baffling dissimulation on the part of blacks" as the result of seeds sown by white prejudice and oppression, he said that it was a crop "choking and starving all that is best and brightest in both races." However useful the technique, Grimké concluded, it was ultimately not good for either race, perverting the principles of blacks even as it allowed whites to wallow in

---

pers (14 vols.; Urbana, 1972–89), VIII, 227; William Monroe Trotter to W. E. B. Du Bois, March 26, 1905, in W. E. B. Du Bois Papers (microfilm), University of Massachusetts, Amherst.

6. New York *Age,* March 23, 1905.
7. *Ibid.,* May 4, 1905.

their self-delusion. A man like Carroll was not to be praised, however well he might be understood. Whether Grimké intended his remarks to apply to Washington, he never said. But it is not difficult to read the column as both a defense of his own belief that Washington could change—that there was a layer of anger below that of accommodation—and as a warning to Washington that he must.[8]

He raised other issues in his columns, including those prompting a crusade to try to force the replacement of John B. Gordon, president of Howard University, with a black man (Francis Grimké was mentioned, though not by Archibald). The chief ground for Grimké's effort was prejudice, and for several weeks he documented instances of Gordon's bigotry. The columns were not without effect. Based on a consensus Grimké did much to create, Gordon was forced to step down at the end of 1905, though he was not replaced by a black. But this was merely an interlude in a longer-running series of pieces demanding, in language as militant as ever, equal rights and privileges for black Americans, with not a conciliatory passage to be seen. Indeed, one wonders how Washington maintained his patience with Grimké, a patience that can only be explained by his desire to keep the articulate writer from adding his voice to an already increasingly noisy opposition.

The demands of a weekly column occupied much of Grimké's time after his appointment to the *Age,* but he could not keep entirely removed from the factional battles. As ever, and as he was doing in the *Age,* he persisted in his effort to make Booker Washington's Committee of Twelve work for him. And he felt encouraged about his progress, as when, for example, the committee accepted his recommendation to appoint the Ohio writer Charles Chesnutt, a man who, like Grimké, could get along personally with Booker Washington but who strongly opposed Washington's ideas—thus potentially increasing the radical sentiment—to fill any vacancy that might occur.[9]

The factional battles were becoming stronger, exacerbated by the founding by Du Bois during the summer of 1905 of the Niagara Movement to serve as a counterforce to Washington, the Tuskegee machine, and the Committee of Twelve. This movement grew out of a meeting held at Buffalo, New York, during the week beginning July 9, 1905, to which Du Bois had invited such noted anti-Washingtonians as Trotter, Clement Morgan, Washington *Bee* editor

8. *Ibid.*
9. Hugh Browne to Archibald Grimké, June 15, 1905.

Calvin Chase (an on-again, off-again Washington ally, currently off, who had recently called Grimké a "hireling of Tuskegee" because of his work for the *Age*), and Granville Martin. Neither Grimké brother was invited, mainly at Trotter's insistence.[10]

Trotter probably did not have to insist very hard. By that summer, relations between Du Bois and Grimké had gone from bad to worse, especially from Grimké's point of view. Du Bois, perhaps recognizing the Grimké's prestige, seems to have made an effort to improve them. In mid-June, Du Bois wrote to Charlotte Grimké, Francis' wife, asking if his wife and daughter might stop off in the Grimké home on their way to Boston. Archibald wondered cynically, "Are Mrs. Du Bois & Yolande a sort of peace embassy," though he had every intention of receiving them cordially. Given what had gone before, the Grimkés were all somewhat surprised by the request. Angelina wrote, "One would think that he would have asked any one else in Washington to do him a favor before he asked the Grimkés."[11]

Du Bois even apologized for failing to send a Niagara invitation. In mid-August, he reversed course and, aware of the stature they could lend to his young organization, invited both the Grimkés to join the movement. He justified his delay, somewhat lamely, by saying that he did not want to ask them "to go through the rocks of organization with us but now that we are launched I feel we have something worthy of confidence & we need your help." He also added that he had been reluctant because Archibald Grimké remained with Washington's Committee of Twelve.[12]

Not surprisingly, Grimké was not placated. He felt, as he even told Washington, that he had been insulted by Du Bois—whether by

10. Louis R. Harlan, *Booker T. Washington: The Wizard of Tuskegee, 1901–1915* (New York, 1983), 84–85; Kelly Miller, *Race Adjustment: Essays on the Negro in America* (1908; rpr. New York, 1968), 15; Thomas Fortune to Archibald Grimké, May 29, 1905, in Archibald Grimké Papers, Box 4, Folder 92; Call for the meeting of the Niagara Movement, in Du Bois Papers; Fox, *Guardian of Boston*, 92–93; August Meier, *Negro Thought in America, 1880–1915: Racial Ideologies in the Age of Booker T. Washington* (Ann Arbor, 1963), 200.

11. Archibald Grimké to Angelina Weld Grimké, June 24, 1905, in Angelina Weld Grimké Papers, Box 4, Folder 73, Moorland-Spingarn Research Center, Howard University, Washington, D.C.; Angelina Weld Grimké to Archibald Grimké, June 27, 1905, in Archibald Grimké Papers, Box 3, Folder 61.

12. Fox, *Guardian of Boston*, 93; Harlan and Smock, eds., *Washington Papers*, VIII, 337; W. E. B. Du Bois to Francis J. Grimké, [August, 1905], in Francis J. Grimké Papers, Box 3, Folder 86, Moorland-Spingarn Research Center, Howard University, Washington, D.C.; W. E. B. Du Bois to Archibald Grimké and Kelly Miller, August 13, 1905, in Archibald Grimké Papers, Box 4, Folder 91.

Du Bois' angry letter from earlier in the year or by his failure to send a Niagara invitation Grimké did not say—and it was an insult he never got over. Subsequently, Grimké kept his distance from Du Bois, even on occasions when Du Bois seemed to propose a rapprochement. In this instance, Grimké left Washington with the belief that he had "broken completley from Du Bois and his crowd."[13]

For the next few months, Grimké confirmed that impression, working closely with Washington and the Committee of Twelve, even as he continued to express his own ideas in the *Age*. In June, he helped Washington quietly schedule a meeting for Boston, calling on the assistance of his old friend Joseph Lee to help find places for members to stay, without causing difficulties involving the predominantly white clientele of Lee's own establishment. Toward the end of August, he attended a banquet in Boston for William D. Crum, the controversial Roosevelt appointee to the post of collector at the port of Charleston, joining such notable Washingtonians as William H. Lewis, Dr. Samuel Courtney, and his old friend Butler Wilson, who had also broken with Trotter. By September, Washington, Du Bois, and even Whitefield McKinlay, despite his earlier fears, felt quite certain that Grimké had, indeed, abandoned Washington's critics and gone over to Washington's side.[14]

This perception led to one of the strongest attacks on Grimké in his career, in a black newspaper championing Du Bois as "the head of a great movement for freedom and manhood rights" and tying together Grimké, Kelly Miller, and Fortune for their fidelity to Washington as men who "put on airs and advertize themselves as fighting to the death the Negro-hating white man" while they "lay on their bellies and lick the dust in admiration of the big white folks' Negro who is spending his life to encourage these white men to keep the Negro down." According to the writer, "Grimké loves the public praise of Tom Fortune and Booker too well to forsake them for the race, and Kelly Miller has always hunted a soft place by straddling." He urged Du Bois to spend no more time trying to woo Grimké and Miller to the cause. The column was far from accurate, but it was an important indicator of where, in the perception of Washington's opponents, Grimké now appeared to stand.[15]

Hostility was high, and Grimké had few chances to escape it. His

13. Harlan and Smock, eds., *Washington Papers,* VIII, 337.

14. Booker T. Washington to Archibald Grimké, June 10, 1905, in Archibald Grimké Papers, Box 6, Folder 121; New York *Age,* August 31, 1905; Harlan and Smock, eds., *Washington Papers,* VIII, 363.

15. Clipping, n.d., in Archibald Grimké Papers, Box 36, Folder 728.

time in Boston provided some relief, especially during the summer, when he was there with Angelina boarding with the Lees. Angelina had been having some difficulties back home in the District of Columbia. She was not very happy as a teacher, mainly because she did not get along with the principal, W. Bruce Evans, despite his help in getting her the job. For the moment, Archie offered little more than moral support—once calling Evans a "contemptible fellow"—but the situation was to drag on for several years, and Grimké was to become more personally involved.[16]

When they were in Boston, however, most of this was forgotten. Angelina attended her summer course at Harvard while Archie socialized with his Boston friends and engaged in his usual round of public activities, including, despite his tense relationship and ultimate falling-out with Trotter, those of the Boston Literary and the St. Mark's Union. Samuel Courtney, a Washington lieutenant, wrote to his boss toward the end of the year that Grimké had been "ostracized" by the Boston radicals, but, Trotter excepted, this seems hardly to have been the case. His circle of friends changed little. It was to be augmented when Archie and Angelina were joined at the Lees' by a young New Orleans woman, Bertha Bauman, about five years Angelina's junior, just beginning her course in piano at the New England Conservatory of Music. Both Archie and Angelina liked Bertha and got to know her well; both, but Archie in particular, thought her a talented musician.[17]

But the demands of faction could be escaped only momentarily, even during the time in Boston. Grimké continued to write for the *Age,* and the factional problems remained on his mind, leading to one of his more important columns for the paper "Right Afro-American Leadership." The column, reflecting his own unhappiness with an almost inescapable necessity to be visibly for one side or another, was, above all, a call for unity and a tacit indictment of both sides in the battle, arguing for a new leader who would be known primarily "by

16. Gloria T. Hull, *Color, Sex and Poetry: Three Women Writers of the Harlem Renaissance* (Bloomington, 1987), 116; Archibald Grimké to Angelina Weld Grimké, September 30, 1904, in Angelina Grimké Paper, Box 4, Folder 72; Archibald Grimké to Angelina Weld Grimké, June 24, September 26, 1905, both in Angelina Grimké Papers, Box 4, Folder 73; Archibald Grimké to Angelina Weld Grimké, October 6, 1905, in Angelina Grimké Papers, Box 4, Folder 74.

17. Fox, *Guardian of Boston,* 93; Bertha Bauman to Angelina Grimké, October 6, 1905, in Angelina Grimké Papers, Box 1, Folder 2; Archibald Grimké to Angelina Grimké, November 21, 1905, in Angelina Grimké Papers, Box 4, Folder 74.

what he stands for to promote Union, to introduce or extend the principle of organization among his race." He condemned "the false leader" who worked only "for Division, for strife, for race narrowness and intolerance."[18]

Without mentioning names, Grimké make clear that none of the existing leaders could escape condemnation. He identified three distinct groups among the black community—"the industrial education group, the higher education group, and the political rights group"— each going its separate way, or "apparently separate" way, rather than trying to find a common ground. Existing leadership, all the way around, could only be considered false.[19]

The column attracted a great deal of comment, most of which proved Grimké's point by its defensiveness. Fortune, in an accompanying editorial, sought to remind Grimké that the real culprits were the anti-Washingtonians, men who sought to "exalt frenzied mediocrity into an oracle and criminals [probably Trotter] into spokesmen of a race." Whitefield McKinlay praised the column but also felt that Grimké had let his former associates—"would be leaders," he called them—off too easy.[20]

As these responses make clear, the Washington people were no more interested in unity than they accused the Du Bois people of being. Ever since the Niagara meeting, Washington had been trying to infiltrate that organization and to stir up problems. In the same month that Grimké's piece was published, he was busily preparing a vicious attack on Trotter and the Niagara Movement that he wanted to put into the *Age*. Grimké, of course, knew this, and there is no doubt that his rebuke was aimed as much at Washington as at his former associates—as McKinlay and Fortune quickly recognized.[21]

Grimké continued along his way, expressing his views, working with the man who at least did not respond with insults, and using that same man's media, especially the *Age,* to make his case. Sometimes he did so pointedly, as he had in the "leadership" column; sometimes more subtly, as in the piece on Richard Carroll. And sometimes, ingeniously, he tacitly subverted Washington's rhetoric, as he did in a sequence of columns on his friend Maria Baldwin, in the first showing how "merit and character" had allowed her, "in spite of her color and

18. New York *Age,* September 14, 1905.
19. *Ibid.*
20. *Ibid.;* Harlan and Smock, eds., *Washington Papers,* VIII, 363–64.
21. Harlan and Smock, eds., *Washington Papers,* VIII, 382–83.

race," to achieve recognition in the broader community; in the second, showing how even her character had not protected her from the insults and indignities to which every black American was vulnerable.[22] But always he worked in the same vein, indicting racism, rejecting accommodation, urging militance in the fight against oppression, never mentioning Washington by name, but always and unmistakably keeping free of Washington's ideas.

He also pressed his case outside the *Age*. He did a piece for *Alexander's Magazine,* edited and published by Charles Alexander, a Tuskegee graduate, and Washington lieutenant living in Boston, on Talladega College. The magazine was supported by Washington, and the publication of the piece seems to have been subsidized by Washington. Grimké praised Talladega in his essay, but though he noted the existence of an industrial department, he singled out for attention its strong academic program. He cited, especially, the accomplishments of two Talladega graduates who had gone on to honors at Yale. Taking a Washingtonian view that places such as Talladega were helping to improve racial harmony in the South, he gave most of his attention to those areas in which Talladega was improving the intellectual as well as the material character of its graduates, hardly a Washingtonian point of view.[23]

Grimké seems to have been working hard throughout 1905 to influence both sides—especially Washington's—in the violent debate within the black leadership and to create a new, better-focused approach to combating racial oppression. It is hard to say that he made any headway because the lines were drawn so tightly, neither side talking to the other, neither listening to the other.

It was also hard for him, or anyone, to make any headway because virtually everything of any significance became embroiled in the factional dispute within the leadership. Grimké was to have this reality forcefully brought home to him before the end of the year in the controversy surrounding the commemoration in December, 1905, of the centenary of the birth of William Lloyd Garrison. Grimké was not one to let the centenary pass unobserved. He wrote two columns on Garrison for the *Age* and also produced, with Francis Garrison, a leaflet containing a biographial sketch and a selection from Garrison's writ-

22. New York *Age,* December 14, 21, 1905.
23. Charles Alexander to Booker T. Washington, December 18, 1905, in Washington Papers; Harlan, *Booker T. Washington: Wizard of Tuskegee,* 59–61; Meier, *Negro Thought,* 226; Archibald H. Grimké, "Talladega College," *Alexander's Magazine,* I (September, 1905), 3–8.

ings for the use of schools. For *Alexander's Magazine,* he did a brief piece on the mobbing of Garrison in Boston in 1835, praising the abolitionist's bravery for standing up to popular threats and violence.[24]

The controversy arose over the planning of events for more public commemorations of the Garrison centenary. Since at least early October, Booker Washington had been involved in preparing celebrations around the country. Around the end of October, Washington tried to get the Committee of Twelve to plan for such a commemoration and sought to get Grimké involved in the planning. He was responding, in part, to plans of William Monroe Trotter's, also beginning around the end of the month, to organize a celebration under the auspices of the anti-Washington New England Suffrage League. The rivalry soon became open. Although Angelina had urged her father to stay in Washington, D.C., and to deliver an address there, Archibald Grimké became a public figure in the Boston conflict. There was strong sentiment in the league, in which Grimké still had many friends—Courtney's views to the contrary notwithstanding— to have Grimké deliver the address at its celebration, but Trotter was viciously opposed and beat back every attempt to extend Grimké the invitation. Grimké's old friend the Washingtonian W. W. Bryant, writing for the *Age* as its Boston correspondent, made the appropriateness of Grimké's giving the commemorative address a point on which to attack Trotter's plans for any commemoration held under the auspices of the league.[25]

The result was two Boston celebrations, one held early on the afternoon of December 10, 1905, under Trotter's auspices; the other, later, involving a more diverse crowd, but including the Washingtonians. A few people attended and spoke at both—and there was general harmony between the two, once things were under way—but the Garrison family and Grimké took part in the second gathering. James Wolff presided, and speeches were given by Grimké, Frank B. Sanborn, Moorfield Storey (who had addressed the earlier gathering), and Robert Taylor of Tuskegee. Grimké was the first speaker, offering a

24. New York *Age,* November 2, 9, 1905; Archibald H. Grimké and Francis J. Garrison, comps., *Garrison Centenary, 1805 December Tenth 1905* (Cheyney, Pa., n.d.); Archibald Grimké, "The Broadcloth Mob," *Alexander's Magazine,* I (December, 1905), 24–29.

25. Fox, *Guardian of Boston,* 100; Booker T. Washington to Archibald Grimké, October 26, 1905, in Washington Papers; Archibald Grimké to Angelina Weld Grimké, November 3, 10, 1905, in Angelina Grimké Papers, Box 4, Folder 74; New York *Age,* November 2, 9, 1905.

biographical sketch praising Garrison's bravery and freedom from prejudice.[26]

Grimké was no easier to place at the end of the 1905 than he had been at the year's beginning. If his views were notable for anything, it was for their independence, despite his relations with the leaders of the debate swirling around him, and particularly his close associations with some elements of the Washington machine. This association was to become increasingly problematic for him and for Washington, too, and the next several months were to find Grimké looking for still other ways to make his presence felt and to change the course of black politics.

26. Fox, *Guardian of Boston*, 100, 119; Charles Alexander, "The Garrison Centenary Celebration," *Alexander's Magazine*, I (January, 1906), 11–15; Archibald H. Grimké, "Biographical Oration," *Alexander's Magazine*, I (January, 1906), 17–22; Charles Alexander to Booker Washington, December 11, 1905, in Washington Papers.

10

Brownsville

For at least a year, Archibald Grimké had been cooperating well with Booker T. Washington, in his actions if not in his thoughts. He continued to work closely with Washington on a variety of issues. But the relationship was far from natural, despite its appearances, and it was not destined to endure beyond the next several months. By the end of 1906, largely as a result of the Brownsville incident, Grimké had become increasingly unhappy in Booker Washington's world.

The first part of 1906 saw Grimké as busy as he had ever been. He became involved with an organization that was to become extremely important to him, the Constitution League led by John Milholland. Milholland was a white civil rights activist and a Republican who had tried to work both with Du Bois and Trotter and with Washington, but who was strongly supportive of black suffrage rights, which had more than once brought him to loggerheads with Washington and Washington's supporters.[1]

Milholland intended for the Constitution League to lend support to the cause of equal rights. Grimké and a number of other leaders were involved from the beginning. An organizational meeting held on February 1 in New York attracted a distinguished cast, including Grimké, Du Bois, Kelly Miller, George H. White, and Mary Church Terrell. Grimké was there at Milholland's request, an invitation to speak having been tendered through Booker Washington. Washington's version

1. Stephen R. Fox, *The Guardian of Boston: William Monroe Trotter* (New York, 1970), 123–24; Louis R. Harlan, *Booker T. Washington: The Wizard of Tuskegee, 1901–1915* (New York, 1983), 82; New York *Age,* September 14, December 21, 1905; Louis R. Harlan and Raymond W. Smock, eds., *The Booker T. Washington Papers* (14 vols.; Urbana, 1972–89), VIII, 374–81, 392–94.

of the invitation indicated his rather tepid feelings about the meeting. He said to Grimké simply, "I think it well for you to take up the subject directly with him," meaning Milholland, and noting that "the meeting is in the interest of general suffrage." Grimké accepted nonetheless.[2]

The meeting drew three thousand people, about four-fifths of them black. Grimké's remarks were not reported, but the tenor of the meeting was strong and in keeping with his own views. Mary Church Terrell attacked northern neutrality and southern "treason"; Kelly Miller focused on the character of Reconstruction governments and described the revised southern constitutions as a regression to barbarism. Du Bois, in remarks Grimké must have appreciated, focused on the ways in which southern laws served to keep the worker down. The meeting went on all night and concluded with the approval of a set of resolutions for the reduction of southern representation in Congress.[3]

Grimké's participation in the Constitution League meeting had little effect on his relationship with Washington, despite Washington's lukewarm feelings about the meeting and the cause it espoused. As he had with the *Age,* Washington was giving Grimké room to operate and counting on the opposition to do at least some of the work of keeping him in the fold. The opposition continued to oblige. At about the same time as the Constitution League meeting, for example, Du Bois had published an essay in the *Voice of the Negro* titled "The Growth of the Niagara Movement." Although he set forth principles of free suffrage and equality which Grimké could only have agreed to, Du Bois also celebrated his own leadership and rehearsed some old grudges against the Committee of Twelve, describing it as Washington's tool.[4]

Grimké was livid about the article and especially about the characterization of the committee, on which he had felt himself an independent voice. He considered making a reply, but, in a way that indicated his continuing alienation from Washington's opponents, however

2. New York *Age,* December 21, 1905; Booker T. Washington to Archibald Grimké, January 9, 1906, Archibald Grimké to Booker T. Washington, January 27, 1906, in Booker T. Washington Papers, Library of Congress; Announcement for meeting of the Constitution League, January 22, 1906, in W. E. B. Du Bois Papers (microfilm), University of Massachusetts, Amherst.

3. New York *Times,* February 2, 1906.

4. W. E. B. Du Bois, "The Growth of the Niagara Movement," *Voice of the Negro,* III (1906), 45.

much he shared their views, decided that it would not be a good idea because it would involve the committee in precisely the kind of controversy that "Du Bois & The Guardian people" seemed to be trying to encourage.[5]

If anything, Grimké's participation in the Constitution League probably strengthened his sense that he could work with Washington by providing, in one key event, a possibility for him to take still more militant, independent action based within the Washington organization, but action with which Washington was not entirely comfortable.

This opportunity was created unwittingly by Washington himself when, early in 1906, before the Constitution League meeting, he asked Grimké and Kelly Miller to form a subcommittee of the Committee of Twelve to keep an eye on pending legislation, the Hepburn Act to regulate railroad rates. Washington had taken notice of the act from the time of its introduction, concerned that, because Jim Crow had been widely imposed in southern rail travel over the preceding years, the act might be used by southern congressmen as a pretext for introducing still further provisions harmful to black Americans. Miller and Grimké had consulted with Washington on the matter in New York at the time of the Constitution League meeting, when they decided to engage former New Hampshire senator Henry W. Blair as "Counsel," paying him a small retainer to watch the progress of the bill and to "look after the interests of the colored race."[6]

This modest effort was soon to be expanded independent of Washington. About the first of March, the Constitution League again met, this time in Philadelphia—Grimké was a vice-president for the meeting—and appointed a committee, consisting of former congressman George White, A. B. Humphrey (like Milholland a white radical and the league's secretary), William Sinclair, and Grimké himself, to pursue the possibility of amending the pending legislation to challenge Jim Crow on the railroads. Kelly Miller was added to this group, and it became a joint operation of the Committee of Twelve and the Constitution League. Grimké was made chairman, and he, Miller, and White represented the "local working force" on the issue, with Blair also deeply involved.[7]

5. Harlan and Smock, eds., *Washington Papers,* VIII, 453–54, 495.

6. Archibald Grimké to Booker T. Washington, January 27, 1906, in Washington Papers; Harlan and Smock, eds., *Washington Papers,* VIII, 504, 517–18.

7. New York *Age,* July 5, August 2, 1906; Constitution League badge in Archibald H. Grimké Papers, Box 39, Folder 764, Moorland-Spingarn Research Center, Howard University, Washington, D.C.

The committee met with several congressmen, most notably Senator Joseph Foraker of Ohio, a powerful member of the Interstate Commerce Committee, who had a strong and not entirely friendly interest in the Hepburn Act and who agreed to offer an amendment requiring that all passengers paying the same fare be given "the same or equally good accommodations and a like and equally good service." The amendment was far from what the Grimké committee had desired. Moreover, as the historian of the controversy, Daniel Crofts, has noted, it created a dilemma for blacks by promising an improvement of service and a guarantee of decent accommodations while also giving implicit sanction to the practice of segregation. Those, including Grimké, who realized this, were unable to get it changed, however, and, after much discussion, it made its way to the Senate floor with the wording but not the substance slightly altered. Sponsored by Senator William Warner of Missouri and supported by Foraker, it passed, incorporated into the rate bill package forwarded to a House-Senate conference committee formed to work out a final version of the legislation.[8]

The Grimké committee now began working to defeat the well-intentioned Warner-Foraker amendment. They met first with House-Senate conferees to ask for assistance; they organized a letter-writing campaign; they brought to bear pressure from key black leaders, including Clement Morgan, William Monroe Trotter, H. T. Keating, and, later, William Sinclair and Judson W. Lyons. Ultimately, they succeeded when Republican conferees rescinded the amendment from the final legislation.[9]

Despite such apparent unity, however, the effort to defeat the amendment had become an issue in black factional politics. Trotter, though cooperating in the campaign, had used the pages of the *Guardian* to suggest that Miller and Grimké, along with Blair, had been responsible for the amendment. Blair wrote a long letter, later published in the *Age,* acknowledging his own faith in the amendment, which he felt would do more good than harm, but documenting Miller and Grimké's consistent opposition. Others made similar charges. Calvin Chase, in his Washington *Bee,* wrote that Miller, "Grimkie,"

8. New York *Age,* July 5, August 2, 1906; Daniel W. Crofts, "The Warner-Foraker Amendment to the Hepburn Bill: Friend or Foe of Jim Crow?" *Journal of Southern History,* XXXIX (1973), 341, 346–47; Harlan and Smock, eds., *Washington Papers,* IX, 3–4.

9. New York *Age,* July 5, August 2, 1906; Harlan and Smock, eds., *Washington Papers,* IX, 12–13.

and White had gone to Foraker and had gotten him to introduce an amendment providing for "equal accommodations" without perceiving its implications. According to Chase, a delegation of more distinguished "colored citizens" had undone the damage Grimké, Miller, and White had almost done. Chase never named his sources. But a week later, he printed a long letter from White, providing documentation for a more accurate account of the events. Still, such charges could hardly have made Grimké feel better about the character of the opposition.[10]

Booker Washington also seems to have been less than happy about the affair, although for different reasons from Trotter and Chase. As Crofts notes, in trying to do more than ensure against "negative legislation," Grimké and Miller went beyond their initial agreement with Washington, and there is good evidence that he did not approve of what they were doing. He later told Miller that he thought "the Warner Amendment would have been a good measure, and very helpful." As Crofts says, in this instance, the man actually was the mask, forced to conceal the extent of his own accommodationism from black allies. In any case, he preferred to work behind the scenes. When Humphrey asked him to work publicly against an amendment that "nationalizes Jim Crow Cars," he replied that Miller and Grimké were in charge, representing the Committee of Twelve, and could be trusted to handle the matter.[11]

But, significantly, and unlike Trotter or Chase, he did not reveal his irritation to Grimké. To the contrary, once the victory was won, recognizing its popularity, he tried to capitalize on it. He tried to get Grimké to write an account of the amendment's defeat for the *Bee,* although the only piece to appear there was White's letter. He also contacted other black journalists urging them to give credit to Miller and Grimké as agents of the Committee of Twelve. At the end of July, Miller and Grimké together did write an article for the *Age* on their efforts to defeat the amendment. The article was not exactly what Washington had wanted, although he said he was pleased with it. It was more in line with the "right leadership" piece, praising the Constitution League, along with the Committee of Twelve, and generally using the victory as evidence that black Americans could organize for their own protection if they made the effort to do so.[12]

10. Washington *Bee,* June 2, 9, 1906; New York *Age,* July 5, 1906.
11. Crofts, "Warner-Foraker," 353, 355; Harlan and Smock, eds., *Washington Papers,* VIII, 24–25.
12. Archibald Grimké to Angelina Weld Grimké, July 25, 1906, in Angelina Weld

But the article indicated nothing of a move away from Washington on Grimké's part because whatever discomfort Washington felt in the event he kept to himself. By maintaining his apparent position against the amendment—or at least by doing nothing to stop Miller and Grimké either from their efforts or from their continuing cooperation with people Washington did not like—Washington, from Grimké's point of view, continued to act like a man behind a mask, making a change that Grimké had been encouraging, implicitly and explicitly, for a long time. He continued to give Grimké reason to cooperate with him and to believe that he might ultimately confront the questions of colorphobia and civil rights that Grimké found important and against which Grimké continued to hope he would bring about a united front.

Thus, particularly through the first half of 1906, Grimké continued to believe that he could work with and have a cordial relationship with Washington. He continued to write for the *Age,* and he corresponded with Washington about his columns, although Washington never hinted that Grimké should tone them down. In March, Washington invited him to Tuskegee, which was celebrating its twenty-fifth anniversary. Although Grimké was unable to attend, he used the occasion to celebrate the quality of the institution and its work. He later strongly praised a special issue of *Alexander's Magazine* devoted to the Tuskegee anniversary.[13]

Of more significance, perhaps, was his cooperation with Washington, at the same time as the Warner-Foraker effort, on a project that was personally important to him, the preservation of the Frederick Douglass home at Cedar Hill. The project had been taking shape for some time, despite controversy between the children of Douglass' first wife, Anna, and his widow, Helen, who had been urging such an effort almost from the time of his death. Archibald Grimké knew Helen through his brother, to whom she had been close, and in one of his rare forays into the legal profession had served as her attorney on the Douglass home matter, handling her estate, including her desire for the home's preservation, after her death in 1903. He had helped set

---

Grimké Papers, Box 4, Folder 75, Moorland-Spingarn Research Center, Howard University, Washington, D.C.; New York *Age,* August 2, 1906; Harlan and Smock, eds., *Washington Papers,* IX, 26–27, 49.

13. Archibald Grimké to Booker T. Washington, March 8, 1906, Archibald Grimké to Emmett J. Scott, June 6, 1906, in Washington Papers; *Alexander's Magazine,* II (1906), 6.

up the Frederick Douglass Memorial and Historical Association, acting as its president, to raise additional funds needed primarily to pay
off a mortgage on the property.

Washington initially had not been involved in the project, although, as early as 1902, Douglass' widow had written to ask him to
help raise money. In early 1906, however, Judge Robert Terrell—an
ardent Washingtonian—had written to Washington asking him to take
part in the campaign, and Washington had said he would, provided he
received full authority to do so in his own way from the Frederick
Douglass Memorial and Historical Association. Grimké and the board
were happy to do this and invited Washington to join the board.[14]

Washington worked to raise money, and initially he was optimistic
that the mortgage on the Douglass home could be paid off in a very
short time. Over the next two years, though funds failed to come in
as quickly as Washington had expected, Grimké and Washington corresponded regularly about the Douglass home. They talked about
fund-raising strategies and arranged for advertising and supporting
editorials to appear in newspapers and magazines. Grimké continued
as president of the Frederick Douglass Memorial and Historical Association, with Whitefield McKinlay serving as secretary and Francis
Grimké as treasurer, while Washington appears to have been the chief
fund-raiser. (Trotter sardonically headlined a neutral account picked
up from another paper of Washington's participation in the effort "Eager—Estate Thought to Have Had Money.") They had trouble getting subscribers and also getting subscribers to submit the money
pledged. As late as 1908, they had collected only about $600 toward
the total of $5,400 needed to pay off the mortgage.[15] The effort to
preserve the Douglass home was a relatively nonpartisan activity
within the black community.

Toward the end of June, 1906, Archibald, Francis, and Angelina
Grimké joined Kelly Miller, Richard Greener, and Whitefield Mc-
Kinlay for a visit to Charleston, South Carolina, where Archibald addressed the graduating class of the Hospital and Training School for
Nurses, an institution founded for black women by A. C. McClennan
in response to the exclusion of blacks from South Carolina's state institutions. He recounted his childhood in the city and urged the im-

14. Harlan and Smock, eds., *Washington Papers*, VI, 400, VIII, 525–26, 531–32.

15. New York *Age*, August 16, 1906; Archibald Grimké to Booker T. Washington,
June 1, 1906, Francis J. Grimké to Booker T. Washington, February 21, 1907, June 6,
1908, in Washington Papers; Harlan and Smock, eds., *Washington Papers*, VI, 408, IX,
623–24; Boston *Guardian*, August 25, 1906.

portance of health in mind and body in the struggle for life. He and
his companions also toured the city and even visited the grave of
John C. Calhoun, the subject of one of Grimké's earliest public
addresses.[16]

But such respites were few and, in mid-1906, deceptive as well.
Over the preceding couple of years, Grimké had balanced his independence as a thinker and actor with his sense that the Washington
group offered a positive framework for effective action. Both Washington and his opponents had done much to create this situation.
But the balance was not easy to maintain in the difficult climate of
black factionalism in the first decade of the 1900s, and it was made
even harder by the still more difficult situation of American racial
oppression.

Even in the spring, while he was working—as he thought—with
Washington on the Warner-Foraker amendment, some of the difficulties were beginning to take concrete shape. He was still writing for
the *Age*, and although he covered a range of topics—one may note
particularly an account of the characteristics of the District of Columbia elite—he was devoting increasing effort to attacking the racial
policies of President Theodore Roosevelt, whose hostility to African-
American rights was becoming more and more pronounced and who
had not lived up to the promise Grimké saw 1904. Referring sarcastically to Roosevelt's famous slogan of speaking softly and carrying a
big stick, Grimké accused Roosevelt of carrying that big stick abroad
but of refusing to wield it to protect the rights of the nation's black
citizens. "Where there is a will there is a way," he quoted in a column
a month later, and again decried the national government's unwillingness to protect the lives and rights of black Americans. "When the
South growls the President heeds instantly," he wrote, accusing Roosevelt of putting his own ends above the welfare of even his black
supporters.[17]

Grimké's views of Roosevelt and his own past separated him politically from Washington. Washington was not only friendly with Roosevelt but was deeply involved in Republican party politics and patronage. Grimké, by contrast, remained a champion of independence
in voting. Only when blacks became politically independent, he ar-

16. New York *Age,* June 21, July 5, 1906; Charleston, South Carolina, *Reporter,*
June 30, 1906, clipping in Archibald Grimké Papers, Box 36, Folder 729.
17. New York *Age,* April 26, May 24, 1906; see Willard B. Gatewood, *Aristocrats of
Color: The Black Elite, 1880–1920* (Bloomington, 1991), 63–64.

gued, could they make either party responsive to their demands and needs.[18]

His urging of independence set him clearly apart from the Washington camp on other issues than Roosevelt. Spending time in Boston as usual during part of 1906, he became interested in the Massachusetts election for governor. The Republican party had renominated the incumbent, Curtis Guild, and Guild had the strong support of the Washington organization, expressed in its Boston-based *Alexander's Magazine*. Grimké, writing in the other Washington publication, the *Age,* made clear his own support for Guild's opponent, the Democrat John Moran, whom Trotter also supported because of Moran's superior record on racial issues.[19]

For all this, Washington continued to praise and encourage his work in their correspondence. Washingtonian organs such as *Alexander's Magazine* praised him as a writer, as did Washington's lieutenants. Certainly, for most of 1906, he had no reason to doubt his sense, expressed a year or so earlier to Du Bois, that he was getting a hearing in Washingtonian circles and that Washington's racial views were improving.

His optimism and sense of the value of working with Washington remained until well into the fall. It was not to last much longer, however, because events soon took control of politics and factionalism in ways that shook the entire black leadership, including Grimké, and redefined his sense of what he could and should be doing. The key event was the Brownsville incident, which had its origins in the summer, when a group of black soldiers stationed in that Texas city were accused of rioting and, when tried, recommended for discharge without honor, despite their excellent military records and protestations of innocence. The incident came to a head in late October and early November, when Roosevelt instructed his secretary of war, William Howard Taft, to carry out the recommendation. Booker Washington, it was widely known, had pleaded in vain with the president to take a different course, but Taft did as he was told.[20]

Grimké reacted violently to the president's order. Within a week, he had become involved in a protest against the president's action,

18. New York *Age,* November 15, 22, 1906.

19. *Alexander's Magazine,* III (1906), 14; New York *Age,* November 15, 22, 1906; Fox, *Guardian of Boston,* 104.

20. Harlan, *Booker T. Washington, Wizard of Tuskegee,* 309–10; Emma Lou Thornbrough, "The Brownsville Episode and the Negro Vote," *Mississippi Valley Historical Review,* XLIV (1957), 470.

taking part in a mass meeting held in Boston to mobilize opposition, joining both his old friend Joseph Lee and his former old friend William Monroe Trotter.[21]

Grimké also used the *Age,* in which Fortune had called Roosevelt's action an exercise in "presidential lynch law," to make his case. In late November, he forwarded for its columns a letter from his longtime friend Albert Pillsbury, decrying the president's decision. In that letter, Pillsbury urged both public protest and a "full and immediate investigation into the legality of the order." Such an investigation was, in fact, being carried out under the auspices of John Milholland's Constitution League, of which Grimké was a member.[22]

For several weeks his column protested the presidential action, condemning Roosevelt's exercise of "despotic" power and his "colorphobia" as well. He also used his column to attack Secretary of War Taft for knuckling under to Roosevelt's order, pointing out that Taft was Roosevelt's heir apparent for the office of the presidency.

But no less significant were his somewhat veiled comments on Washington. As many historians have noted, Roosevelt's action in the Brownsville case put Washington in a horrible position. Knowing in advance what the president had decided to do and believing it to be wrong, he nonetheless thought he should remain silent until the decision was made public to preserve any future influence he might have. The decision, however, revealed strikingly the limits of Washington's influence on the president. Not surprisingly, many of Washington's critics took his silence on the issue as tacit compliance, or worse. Du Bois, for example, took this tack in his own response to the situation.[23]

Grimké was among those who disapproved of Washington's silence, despite his unwillingness to go over to the opposition faction, and echoed the opposition's words in the strongest tones. In a column, not mentioning Washington by name or focusing directly on Brownsville, he made his own views clear. Ironically putting his argument in

21. Thornbrough, "Brownsville," 470–71; New York *Age,* November 22, 1906; "Protest by Citizens of Boston in Mass Meeting Assembled in Faneuil Hall, Friday, November 16, 1906, Against the Discharge, Without Honor, by President Roosevelt, of the Battalion of Colored Troops of the 25th U.S. Infantry," in Archibald Grimké Papers, Box 39, Folder 758.

22. New York *Age,* November 29, 1906; James A. Tinsley, "Roosevelt, Foraker, and the Brownsville Affray," *Journal of Negro History,* XLI (1956), 49–50.

23. Thornbrough, "Brownsville," 475; W. E. B. Du Bois, *Writings by W. E. B. Du Bois in Periodicals Edited by Others,* ed. Herbert Aptheker (Millwood, N.Y., 1982), 345.

the language of uplift, he wrote: "There are some qualities, mental and moral, which the colored people of America need to acquire or develop in order to get what belongs to them as American citizens. And one of the chief of these qualities is courage—the courage to take a manly position on the race question and to stand by such position in the face of the frowns of power and the teeth of hostile public sentiment, and under the falling axe of persecution, loss and even death itself." There were not enough such men among black America's leaders, he said, who seemed more commonly to be "ever ready to have other people throw their whole bodies to the lions of American colorphobia and power, but who are strangely reluctant to risk a little finger in the mouth of those same lions." He then directed his wrath at black officeholders—Roosevelt appointees—who refused to protest their boss's action. But the more obvious target was clear, if implicitly, when he closed the column in Du Boisian—and prophetic—tones, declaring of such leaders that "they cannot serve God and Mammon, party and their race, at one and the same time."[24]

Grimké's frustration and the price of Washington's silence, as well as Washington's dilemma, soon increased. In his December, 1906, message to Congress, Roosevelt chose to address such issues as racial violence and the rise of lynching in the South. As Washington's biographer Louis Harlan says, that speech made clear the racial bias underlying the Brownsville decision. The cause of lynching in the South, Roosevelt declared, was nothing less than the "perpetration, especially by black men, of the hideous crime of rape." He placed additional onus on the black community when he asserted that one way to prevent lynching was for blacks to quit harboring their own criminals. The message was clear and as classic a statement of the "blaming the victim" approach to crime as one can find, built on the most brutal white racial stereotypes and assumptions. Washington had known about this speech in advance, too, and, as everyone knew, had been unable to do anything to alter it.[25]

Grimké reacted bitterly to the speech and to the situation. As usual, he did not use the occasion as a pretext to attack Washington, at least not by name. Connecting the speech, as many did, to the Brownsville decision, he wrote that "too much power, too much world-adoration, too much vaulting ambition we are afraid are unseating the President's reason." He took particular offense at Roosevelt's lumping all black

24. New York *Age,* November 29, 1906.
25. Harlan, *Booker T. Washington: Wizard of Tuskegee,* 319–20.

Americans together—recognizing the white criminal as an individual wrongdoer but the black one as a representative of the entire race. Even though he still refrained from directly attacking Washington, he made clear that the existing situation could not continue. The two incidents taken together, he urged, called for a real challenge to Roosevelt and the administration, something he knew Washington was unwilling to do.[26]

Grimké did see one such challenge taking shape. This was an effort by Senator Joseph Foraker to reopen an investigation of the Brownsville incident. He was encouraged to do so, he said, by a growing conviction that the case was "flimsy, unreliable and insufficient, and untruthful," drawing on findings gathered by the Constitution League in the aftermath of the affair.[27]

Foraker's effort was widely praised in the black press, and no one praised it more highly than Grimké. Even as he characterized Roosevelt as a would-be autocrat, he praised Foraker for attempting to reopen the inquiry and commended the effort as a needed check on presidential tendencies. As the battle over Foraker's effort continued, so, too, did Grimké's championing of the senator. Over the next several weeks, Grimké's language grew more prophetic in tone, harking back to his earlier biographies, and the senator himself grew more heroic, almost Sumnerian in his virtues.[28]

But the praise of Foraker led Grimké to do something he had never done before. He felt the need to contrast the senator's actions directly with those of Booker Washington, actually mentioning Washington by name and expressing concern about Washington's failure to stand forthrightly against injustice. Roosevelt, according to Grimké, was using Washington as a pawn in a political battle for survival in the face of Foraker's challenge. This, Grimké said, neither the country nor the race could afford. By allowing it to happen, Washington was a part of the president's selfish efforts. It was his strongest direct expression of reservations about Washington to date and all the more important for its appearance in the Washington-backed *Age*.[29]

Despite this strong contrast between the verbal Foraker and the silent Washington, Grimké did not break with Washington, at least not decisively, over the Brownsville incident. Nor, despite the tone of

26. New York *Age,* December 13, 1906.
27. Tinsley, "Roosevelt," 49–50; Thornbrough, "Brownsville," 476–77; Joseph B. Foraker, *Notes of a Busy Life* (2 vols.; Cincinnati, 1916), II, 234, 251.
28. New York *Age,* January 3, 17, 1907.
29. *Ibid.,* February 14, 1907.

Grimké's Brownsville columns, did Washington break with him. This is something of a surprise because Washington, by the beginning of 1907, seemed to set about making a certain companionable "silence" over Brownsville and Roosevelt a litmus test for friendship. Washington, in fact, seems to have tried to remain on Grimké's good side. He did not deny Grimké's remarks about him, nor did he use them as a pretext for breaking with Grimké. Rather, he took the occasion to send a "personal and confidential" letter, saying that Grimké's description of the situation was entirely correct, as was his assesment of the risks involved in that situation.[30]

Grimké and Washington continued to work together, collaborating, for example, on the Douglass project—a cause that blurred factional lines, particularly in the District of Columbia. As late as the summer of 1907, Grimké was carrying on a positive correspondence with Washington. At the end of March of that year, Washington had spoken at the Vanderbilt University School of Theology on the topic "How can the young Southern man help in the lifting up of the Negro race?" Washington expressed his optimism that the two races in the South would eventually live in harmony and friendship. The speech was widely circulated the following July, at which time Grimké wrote to tell Washington that it had the potential to do "a world of good, i.e., if the Southern white people are amenable to common sense & logic on this race question" and praised Washington for his words.[31]

Thus even in the aftermath of Brownsville, cordial relations existed between Grimké and Washington. But the seeds of change were planted, and by the end of the year, Grimké had become troubled about the leadership Washington was providing. He expressed his concerns not only in the *Age* but privately, as when he wrote to Charles Chesnutt that he was losing some of his earlier optimism and that the only hopeful sign he saw was "the manly & independent speech & conduct of such educated leaders like yourself." Although he did not soon break completely with Washington, he was no longer as comfortable as he had been as a member of the Washington camp.[32]

30. Tinsley, "Roosevelt," 53; Booker T. Washington to Archibald Grimké, February, 1907, in Washington Papers.

31. Harlan, *Booker T. Washington: Wizard of Tuskegee,* 296; Washington *Bee,* July 27, 1907; Archibald Grimké to Booker T. Washington, July 24, 1907, in Washington Papers.

32. Archibald Grimké to Charles Chesnutt, December 3, 1906, in Charles Chesnutt Papers, Special Collections, Fisk University Library, Nashville, Tenn.

11

Niagara

The fallout from Brownsville was to have profound effects on Archibald Grimké's place in black politics for the next several years. It did not take long for those effects to become visible, chiefly in his steady movement away from the Washington organization and into the opposition camp. His relationship with the Washington organization through the New York *Age* was the first to be affected.

In the immediate aftermath of Brownsville, Grimké continued to use the *Age* as his main public forum, and most of his columns focused on the Brownsville issue. He loudly defended the soldiers' innocence, especially after Senator Joseph Foraker's investigation got under way. He questioned Roosevelt's integrity, his loyalty to black Americans, and his apparent choice for a successor, William Howard Taft. He began to campaign enthusiastically for a possible Foraker candidacy for the Republican nomination. In only one column, opposing a proposed bill outlawing intermarriage in the District of Columbia, did he write about anything else. As a result, he finally gave Booker Washington more than Washington could tolerate. Toward the middle of April, Fortune, who was finding himself in a touchy situation for his criticism of the Brownsville action, wrote to Grimké asking him, for the first time, to back off. "Some of the brethren in interest complain that you do not treat President Roosevelt and Secretary Taft in a dignified way in your letters," Fortune said. He added, "Complaint is also made by the same brethren in interest that you do not diversify your subjects of discussion sufficiently." Fortune returned Grimké's most recent column for the latter reason.[1]

1. New York *Age,* February 28, March 7, 21, 1907; T. Thomas Fortune to Archi-

The episode was important for Grimké. He had continued to work pretty much within the Washington camp, expressing very un-Washingtonian views yet being made to feel that those views could have a respectful hearing and even an influence within the organization. Now, an effort was being made to muzzle him. Although Grimké made no immediate reply to this effort, at least none that has survived, his actions made his feelings clear. Grimké ended his association with the *Age* immediately and permanently.

Leaving the *Age* was a major step for Grimké. He did not follow it up, surprisingly, with recriminations against Washington himself, perhaps because Washington had not made any attacks on Grimké's ideas or character—unlike others with whom Grimké had dealt. The two men maintained a personal relationship, encouraged by Washington, which Grimké found valuable. But it did lead to a severing of political relations as Grimké demonstrated that he was being pushed out of the Washington camp and drawn to the ranks of the opposition.

The process was not immediate, but over the next several months it took shape. In July, 1907, Grimké took part in an extraordinarily stormy meeting of the Afro-American Council in Baltimore. He spoke, served on the Committee on Address, and was named head of the council's Literary Bureau. At first glance, his participation in the meeting might appear to confirm his continuation of older associations. The council, which dated back to the 1890s, had long had Washingtonian ties, and it had recently been widely viewed as an effort to counteract any influence that the Niagara Movement might be gaining among blacks.[2]

The impression was misleading. As historian Emma Lou Thornbrough has noted, the council was becoming increasingly independent by 1905 and 1906. The council's head, Bishop Alexander Walters of the African Methodist Episcopal (AME) Zion church, had tried to develop a closer relationship with the Niagara group, and, though he would later deny it, the Baltimore meeting seems to have been strongly influenced by Niagara people and to have included strong condemnations of Booker Washington's Republican party—in language much like that Grimké had been using for several months—and

bald Grimké, April 15, 1907, in Archibald H. Grimké Papers, Box 4, Folder 92, Moorland-Spingarn Research Center, Howard University, Washington, D.C.

2. Emma Lou Thornbrough, "The National Afro-American League, 1887–1908," *Journal of Southern History,* XXVII (1961), 509; Washington *Bee,* July 6, 1907.

of Washington himself, who was called a "Judas to his race," more interested in "the almighty dollar" than in education for black Americans. Grimké's participation was thus at least as much a measure of his growing independence as of any past ties to Booker Washington.[3]

More significantly, Grimké was moving toward the Niagara Movement during the summer of 1907. The story is complicated and difficult to sort out, in part because of the records that have survived. When Du Bois invited Grimké to join the movement near its inception, Grimké had not acted on the invitation, seeing little positive benefit in doing so. But much had happened since, and with the approach of the movement's third annual conference in the summer of 1907 in Boston, Du Bois and the head of the Boston branch, Clement Morgan, again encouraged Grimké to join. This time he responded positively.[4]

Not everyone in Boston was pleased that Grimké had been invited, and no one was unhappier than Grimké's onetime friend and ally William Monroe Trotter. When he found out what Du Bois and Morgan had done, Trotter was livid. As the national meeting approached, Trotter continued to oppose Grimké's admission to the movement, and he carried his opposition into the meeting itself. In a private session, however, the Executive Committee of the movement affirmed Du Bois' and Morgan's leadership and Grimké's membership.[5]

The controversy created a great deal of ill will; at the close of the meeting, Grimké told his daughter, "Both Du Bois & the Morgans have come to something very like an open breach with Trotter." Trotter did not allow the matter to rest. During the following month, he continued to protest. The issue dragged on into October, with Du Bois growing increasingly angry, saying at one point, "I am reluctantly compelled to believe that Mr. Trotter is a burden to the Niagara Movement at present." He concluded the matter by polling charter members of the branch, who gave resounding support to Grimké, in effect reading Trotter out of the movement.[6]

3. Thornbrough, "Afro-American League," 510; Washington *Bee,* July 6, 1907; August Meier, *Negro Thought in America, 1880–1915: Racial Ideologies in the Age of Booker T. Washington* (Ann Arbor, 1963), 180–81.

4. Ballot, Boston branch, Niagara Movement, 1907, in W. E. B. Du Bois Papers (microfilm), University of Massachusetts, Amherst; Washington, *Bee,* September 14, 1907.

5. Stephen R. Fox, *The Guardian of Boston: William Monroe Trotter* (New York, 1970), 105; W. E. B. Du Bois, "A Brief Resume of the Massachusetts Trouble in the Niagara Movement," 1907, in Du Bois Papers.

6. Du Bois, "Brief Resume"; Fox, *Guardian of Boston,* 108; Archibald Grimké to

Trotter's biographer, Stephen Fox, has suggested that in the Boston contest, Du Bois and Trotter had clashed, and Du Bois had won. But among the others winners was Grimké, who had, wittingly or not, forced Du Bois to make a choice between him and Trotter, to demonstrate that Grimké had sufficient standing with the radicals to allow him to receive the respect and to have the influence he had earlier felt he could achieve within the Washington group. Since Brownsville, he had been given reasons to look for a new place, and, whatever he felt about Du Bois personally, he had been offered one, and made to feel wanted, in the Niagara Movement.[7]

The victory of Du Bois and Grimké was probably owing to more than Du Bois' efforts. It probably was also related to Grimké's still prominent place in the Boston community. Even as the battle raged, Grimké had remained a visible figure within the Boston elite. He led a very active social and public life in the city during that time, visiting often and happily such people as the Butler Wilsons, the Edward Everett Browns, and the Morgans. In addition, he remained active in the St. Mark's Union, attending regularly and speaking. In early October, for example, he delivered a well-received address on the recently deceased poet Paul Laurence Dunbar. Such ongoing ties with the Boston elite, many of whose members had had problems with Trotter, undoubtedly strengthened his position in the contest over his membership in the movement.[8]

His social life seems to have been especially rewarding during that summer of 1907, distracting him from the conflicts, even as it enhanced his position in them. Among the more pleasant distractions was his development of a close relationship with the young New England Conservatory student Bertha Bauman, who had been boarding with him and Angelina at the Lees since 1905. While he was battling with Trotter, he and Bertha were becoming a topic of conversation in Boston circles because she was often his social companion. Angelina teased him unmercifully about Bertha. At one point, in response to Archie's effort to encourage a friendship between the two women, she wrote that she would certainly try to be friendly: "I may as well learn to like my new mamma now, don't you think?" She continued to twit

Angelina Grimké, August 31, 1907, in Angelina Weld Grimké Papers, Box 4, Folder 76, Moorland-Spingarn Research Center, Howard University, Washington, D.C.; Meier, *Negro Thought,* 241.

7. Fox, *Guardian of Boston,* 106.
8. New York *Age,* October 17, 1907.

Archie about Bertha through the summer, but the relationship between Archie and his young companion remained close for some time.
They continued to see each other, with varying degrees of intimacy,
for many years, even after the death of Joseph Lee in the summer of
1908 broke up the Lee household at the end of that year and after
Bertha's graduation in 1909.[9]

Angelina was the cause of concern for Archie during this time, especially because of problems related to her job, which ultimately made
their way into the factionalism that had developed over Grimké's joining the Niagara Movement. Angelina again felt threatened by her
principal in Washington, Bruce Evans, and she asked her father for
help. Evans seemed to have a grudge against her and had used his
authority to give her a bad rating as a teacher, even recommending
her dismissal. Grimké decided to go to members of the school board
on her behalf. The effort was long and drawn out, but the board gave
her a sympathetic hearing and finally decided, as the new school year
began, to transfer her to the M Street High School.[10]

Angelina seems to have been fairly happy with the outcome, and
her father was happy that she was away from "that scapegrace" Evans.
But the affair left both Grimkés open for an attack from Trotter, who,
smoldering over his earlier defeat, used Angelina's transfer as the basis
for an attack on Grimké. Offering an account of the transfer that reflected badly on Angelina, Trotter, according to Grimké, was trying
to "hurt me more easily & deeply by hurting you." The motive of the
attack, he said, grew out of Trotter's belief "that I had something to
do with Monroe's overthrow in the Niagara Movement, which seems
to be complete." Grimké could not deny his own enmity for Trotter.
Referring to Trotter and his associates, Grimké wrote, "I think that
before long we shall extract the fang of the reptile in them when they
will be able to hiss only."[11]

These feelings carried over into his public life. "Extracting the

9. Angelina Grimké to Archibald Grimké, July 14, 25, 1907, in Archibald Grimké
Papers, Box 3, Folder 61; Archibald Grimké to Angelina Grimké, July 27, October 9,
1907, in Angelina Grimké Papers, Box 4, Folder 76.

10. Memoranda for Captain J. F. Oyster, January 29, 1908, in Angelina Grimké
Papers, Box 3, Folder 30; Archibald Grimké to Angelina Grimké, June 23, July 18,
August 31, 1907, *ibid.*, Box 4, Folder 76; Wm. E. Chancellor to the Board of Education,
District of Columbia, August 24, 1907, in Minutes of the Board of Education, D.C.
Public Schools, Washington, D.C., Public Library,

11. Archibald Grimké to Angelina Grimké, August 31, September 25, October 2,
1907, in Angelina Grimké Papers, Box 4, Folder 76.

fang" apparently meant consolidating his place within the Niagara Movement. Not that he was above attacking Trotter. In October, for example, he publicly denounced Trotter at a meeting of a Boston literary society. Trotter continued to denounce him in the pages of the *Guardian*. But usually his approach was more positive, simply speaking out strongly on behalf of the movement, identifying himself closely with it, and helping to build support for it.[12]

Much of this positive effort found an outlet in what earlier would have seemed the most unlikely of places, *Alexander's Magazine*. Beginning in September, 1907, Archibald Grimké took over, for three issues, the editorship of *Alexander's,* and he clearly intended to take the magazine in the directions he had been carving out for himself over the preceding several months. He took responsibility for its editorial pages and also produced articles of his own. In his first issue, the lead editorial, headed "Foraker vs. Taft," returned to the Brownsville decision, tarring the secretary with Roosevelt's decision. Virtually all of the editorial matter in Grimké's initial issue attacked Roosevelt and Taft, as Grimké adverted again and again to Brownsville and to Taft's apparent friendliness with southern whites.[13]

But Grimké also in that issue made his own new loyalties known in an article he entitled "A Brief History of the Niagara Movement." It was not a history so much as a representation of the movement within the framework of the historical principles that had been basic to Grimké's thought since early in his career. Grimké described the Niagara Movement as "an organization composed of radicals who believe heart and soul in the supreme efficacy of agitation and the divine mission of agitators" and stressed both the rightness of their methods and his own rejection of anything else, including compromise and conciliation. The Niagara radicals were the new abolitionists, he said, and deserved support. Du Bois at this time reached out to Grimké, remarking in his own magazine, the *Horizon,* the organ of the movement, that the "vigorous matter" of Grimké's first number of *Alexander's* "at once puts the magazine in a different class."[14]

Grimké stuck to his uncompromising stance in subsequent issues of *Alexander's* during his term as editor. In the next issue, he attacked racism in Boston, condemned racism in American churches, and at-

12. Archibald Grimké to Angelina Grimké, October 13, 1907, *ibid.,* Box 4, Folder 76.

13. *Alexander's Magazine,* IV (1907), 235–43.

14. Archibald H. Grimké, "A Brief History of the Niagara Movement," *Alexander's Magazine,* IV (1907), 249–52; *Horizon,* II (October, 1907), 22.

tacked both the Republican and Democratic parties of Massachusetts, reserving special scorn for his former classmate Senator Henry Cabot Lodge and Lodge's indifference to the problems of black Americans. He also did a telling essay on the Berean Manual Training and Industrial School, headed by his friend and his brother Francis' Princeton classmate Matthew Anderson. The article was singled out by Du Bois, who recommended it to readers of his *Horizon*. Anderson was a graduate of Oberlin, but his work bore a surface similarity to that of Booker Washington. His school was a trade school for young black men and women. But Anderson did not champion industrial education in the same way Washington did because, as a member of the American Negro Academy, he was also a dedicated proponent of liberal education and had publicly criticized Washington for taking a negative stance toward it.[15]

Grimké focused on this aspect of Anderson's thinking and quoted him approvingly as saying, "I do not believe in manual training for the Negro because I think him so different from other men that this is the only kind of training to which he is adapted; but it is because I believe him to be like other men, especially white men, in physical and mental composition, that in order to become a civil force he must be trained industrially as well as mentally and morally." Grimké documented Anderson's friendliness to higher education and his unwillingness to compromise with white racism and social inequality. It was a highly laudatory article in which Booker Washington was never mentioned by name but was ubiquitous by implication. Anderson appreciated and remembered the essay; later he asked Grimké to become a trustee of the school to counter those whites and "truckling Negroes" who might pressure him into adopting a more Tuskegee-like approach.[16]

Following the November, 1907, issue, Grimké left *Alexander's* without fanfare—indeed, without notice—but apparently the parting was amicable. Although he ceased to be a regular contributor, he did write one other article for the magazine, a brief, admiring piece on the African Methodist Episcopal church published in the May, 1908, issue. But if the parting was amicable, it was undoubtedly necessary from Charles Alexander's point of view. Alexander's newfound inde-

15. *Horizon,* II (December, 1907), 17; New York *Age,* January 9, 1902.
16. Archibald H. Grimké, "Berean Manual Training and Industrial School," *Alexander's Magazine,* IV (1907), 314; Matthew Anderson to Archibald Grimké, May 29, 1914, in Archibald Grimké Papers, Box 25, Folder 498.

pendence after Brownsville was far from complete or permanent; Grimké's presence did not mean an end to articles praising Washington and presenting his ideas or to Washington's financial assistance. Such articles often appeared incongruously juxtaposed with Grimké's own work, as when his first editorials, attacking the Republican party, faced a magazine frontispiece portrait of Washington and when his Niagara piece followed one on Washington's National Negro Business League. With Grimké's departure, any appearance of independence in the magazine disappeared. It returned to a tone that was positively sycophantic and became a devoted champion of the campaign for the presidency of William Howard Taft.[17]

After leaving *Alexander's*, Grimké redoubled his efforts against Taft and for his opponents. At the end of November, 1907, Foraker had formally announced his candidacy for the presidency, and Grimké, who had been supporting him for some time, went to work in earnest for his nomination and against Taft's. Immediately following Foraker's announcement of his candidacy, Grimké had joined a group in Boston supporting the campaign of Democratic mayor John Fitzgerald for re-election and used that campaign not only to help the mayor but also to establish among black voters a sentiment for Foraker and against the "Roosevelt-Lodge Republican Administration" on a "Remember Brownsville" platform. He had a more direct opportunity to help Foraker a few months later, in February, 1908, in conjunction with a meeting of the bishops of the AME Zion church in Washington, D.C. The gathering was seen as much more than simply a meeting of churchmen. Booker Washington had discussed the meeting with Roosevelt, and both his side and Foraker's lobbied the bishops to try to gain support. Grimké was a mainstay of what proved to be a successful effort for Foraker.[18]

At a public meeting in New York a short time later, he spoke out virulently against Roosevelt, Taft, and Booker Washington and, taking a position also held by Du Bois, urged that black voters desert the Republican party should Foraker fail. He joined in a more formal expression of the same view in early April, 1908, at a National Negro

17. Charles Alexander to Emmett Scott, October 19, 1907, in Booker T. Washington Papers, Library of Congress; Louis R. Harlan, *Booker T. Washington: The Wizard of Tuskegee, 1901–1915* (New York, 1983), 61.

18. Boston *Guardian*, November 30, December 7, 1907; Louis R. Harlan and Raymond W. Smock, eds., *The Booker T. Washington Papers* (14 vols.; Urbana, 1972–89), IX, 455; N. F. Mossell to Archibald Grimké, February 12, 1908, in Archibald Grimké Papers, Box 8, Folder 138; New York *Age*, February 20, 23, 1908.

Conference in Philadelphia called by Trotter and Walters. This meeting was as stormy as the earlier Boston Niagara meeting and, like it, was marked by yet another attempt by Trotter to exclude Grimké, along with other "race traitors, spies, and stool-pigeons"—a substantial group from Trotter's point of view. Again Trotter lost, and Grimké played an active role, joining others who declared their support for the Democrat William Jennings Bryan in the event that Taft were nominated.[19]

When Taft received the nomination, Grimké was as good as his word, joining such others as Du Bois and Walters in favoring Bryan. He had few illusions about the Democratic nominee, who had long been on record in support of white southern racial policies, but he felt strongly that Roosevelt and Taft had to be punished for what they had done about Brownsville.

After the Taft victory, Grimké continued to show his dissatisfaction with the Roosevelt administration and Taft's role in it. At about the time of Taft's inauguration, in March, 1909, Grimké appeared as the featured speaker at a huge mass meeting held in Washington to present a "loving cup" to Senator Foraker, who, having announced for the presidency, had not stood for reelection and was retiring from office. Grimké used the opportunity to declare yet again his opposition to the Republican administration and its black allies, especially those close to Booker Washington.[20]

The election of 1908 signaled the end to any residual ties Grimké might have had with Booker Washington's organization, even if he retained some connection to the man. Washington did what he could to maintain the relationship. Throughout 1907, he worked to enhance the discord surrounding Grimké's admission to the Niagara Movement by fomenting the enmity between Grimké—along with other Niagarites—and Trotter. In the aftermath of the Boston Niagara meeting, he had surreptitiously encouraged his ally William H. Lewis to give a banquet in honor of W. E. B. Du Bois. Among the guests were Grimké, Forbes, and Morgan, but, pointedly, not Trotter. In November of that same year, he sponsored the publication of a long

19. Harlan and Smock, eds., *Washington Papers,* IX, 510–11; New York *Times,* March 27, 1908; Fox, *Guardian of Boston,* 111–12; *Horizon,* III (February, 1908), 24; Washington *Bee,* April 11, May 23, 1908; New York *Age,* April 16, 1908.

20. Archibald H. Grimké, "Address on the Occasion of the Presentation of a Loving Cup to Hon. Joseph Benson Foraker, United States Senator," in *Masterpieces of Negro Eloquence: The Best Speeches Delivered by the Negro from the Days of Slavery to the Present Time,* ed. Alice Moore Dunbar (1914; rpr. New York, 1970), 337–46.

attack on Trotter by the former Trotterite William H. Ferris. In the piece, Ferris often singled out both the Grimké brothers for praise in ways designed to cement Trotter's hostility. Ferris argued that the brothers' support for Trotter after the Boston Riot had given Trotter a prestige he could not otherwise have earned; he described Trotter as hating the Grimkés out of envy for their "power and influence." It was a piece of sheer flattery, designed to preserve the discord in the Niagara Movement while reaching out to men like Grimké.[21]

Washington also seems to have reached out to Grimké in one of the more pathetic episodes of 1907, the publication in the *Age* of an editorial entitled "Brownsville Ghouls." Fortune was removed from the editorship of the *Age* in September, 1907, to be replaced by the more loyal Fred R. Moore. At this time, Washington and his secretary, Emmett Scott, also sought to reverse the paper's strong stand against the president on Brownsville. They had persuaded Moore to take on another loyal lieutenant, Ralph Tyler, as an editorial writer, and for the October 17 issue Tyler produced a blockbuster. Describing those who criticized the president's order, and particularly those who "raised the black flag of Race discrimination," as "human ghouls," he went on to say that "no sane and honest man" could believe that the president's action was based on color and to condemn the critics for raising the color question at all. They had done it, he averred, only to enrich themselves.[22]

As Washington's biographer Louis Harlan has pointed out, even Washington knew the editorial had gone too far. He also seems to have been concerned about the effect it would have on his relations with Grimké. In an issue of the *Age* published only three weeks later, a small notice appeared on the editorial page, apparently referring to Grimké's work for *Alexander's*. It said: "It is interesting to see that Hon. A. H. Grimké, of Boston, is using his pen again. There are few men in our race who write more strongly and pointedly than is true of Mr. Grimké. He stands flatfooted in favor of all the rights of Afro-Americans and never flinches. *The Age* admires such characters, and we hope more and more in the future that we shall hear from Mr. Grimké through his pen." Because Grimké was using his pen to refer to Roosevelt and Taft in the manner of a "Brownsville ghoul," per-

21. Harlan and Smock, eds., *Washington Papers*, IX, 394; New York *Age*, November 14, 1907; Fox, *Guardian of Boston*, 108.

22. Harlan, *Booker T. Washington: Wizard of Tuskegee*, 324; New York *Age*, October 17, 1907.

haps the notice was Washington's way of apologizing, through Moore, for any personal implications the earlier editorial might have appeared to have.[23]

Grimké seems to have taken it that way, and he not only appreciated such efforts but showed that he himself was willing to maintain a relationship with Washington. In December, 1907, Grimké revived his old paper "Modern Industrialism and the Negroes" for his presidential address to the American Negro Academy. It was published a year later as an Occasional Paper, and Grimké again sent a copy to Washington. Washington wrote back a complimentary letter and added: "I have had no occasion to tell you, but I have always read whatever you have written with the greatest interest and profit. I am sorry that you are not writing still such articles as you formerly wrote for the New York Age for some of our publications, and I hope you may see your way clear at sometime in the future to again undertake the preparation of such articles." Whatever ghoulishness Washington may have seen in others, he continued to tell Grimké that he was not in that category.[24]

The two men maintained their cordiality, and Grimké wanted to keep a place for Washington in his life. But if he did find Washington's friendship valuable, it was soon to become plain that despite the friendliness and the flattery, Washington's use for Grimké was limited, and the relationship only occasionally went beyond such exchanges. Grimké called on Washington after the 1908 election on behalf of Whitefield McKinlay, who had asked Grimké for his help with Washington in obtaining a position (which he ultimately got) in the new administration. And Grimké still wanted to work with Washington on fund-raising for the Douglass home, even though the effort made very little headway. Thus, Grimké called on Washington to provide his services where he was most skilled—obtaining patronage appointments or fund-raising—but no longer relied on him as the anchor he had once been for political and racial activism. For this, Grimké had found a new center, composed of people who not only seemed to be in the process of constructing an organization but also shared his ideas.

In the aftermath of the election, Grimké resumed his usual round of activities. Despite Joseph Lee's death, he was spending a great deal of time in Boston, still seeing Bertha as a friend and, perhaps, as some-

23. Harlan, *Booker T. Washington: Wizard of Tuskegee,* 324; Harlan and Smock, eds. *Washington Papers,* IX, 384; New York *Age,* November 7, 1907.

24. Booker T. Washington to Archibald Grimké, December 16, 1908, in Washington Papers.

thing more than a friend, still leading a full social and intellectual life. He continued to be extremely active as a speaker. He went frequently to Howard University, where he addressed various groups on economic and social questions. He continued his association with the literary societies of both Washington and Boston, delivering addresses on a range of topics, some historical and some political. And, of course, he continued his work with the American Negro Academy. In 1908, he successfully championed the candidacy of J. Max Barber, the anti-Washington editor of the *Voice of the Negro,* for membership in the academy. He also had to deal with a proposal from Du Bois to merge the academy, along with the Afro-American Council and the Negro American Political League (an organization Trotter had started), with the Niagara Movement, which had fallen on hard financial times. Despite his affiliation with the movement, Grimké rejected the idea, chiefly on the ground that he wanted to maintain the scholarly purposes of the academy, which he felt might be compromised by any affiliation with a political movement such as Niagara. He may not have wanted anything more to do with Trotter either.[25]

Still, his commitment to the radical opposition had been made. It was to grow as the opposition itself took on clearer and more vital form.

25. Alfred A. Moss, Jr., *The American Negro Academy: Voice of the Talented Tenth* (Baton Rouge, 1981), 118, 191–92; *Horizon,* III (June, 1908), 5–6.

12

Independence

With the ending of the century's first decade and the opening of its second, Archibald Grimké's life took new and signficant turns. The founding of the NAACP in these years and Grimké's role in its founding gave him the firm orientation to racial activism that the disputes of earlier years had made impossible. Not that the disputes would end. Indeed, Grimké found himself at the center of bitter controversies over the next ten years, leading to periods of friendship and enmity at least as strong as those during the height of the Washington–Du Bois disputes. But the terms of debate were to be different and, from his point of view, were to pose far less significant barriers to effective action.

Archibald Grimké was in his sixties during the second decade of the twentieth century, but he was not slowed down, at least perceptibly, by age. His activities were undiminished, and his contributions were to be clearer and more concrete than they had ever been. When the decade came to a close—and Grimké's prestige had reached its zenith—he could point to much that he had done to affect the course of American race relations. This was not a small accomplishment when one considers the real and brutal challenges to black Americans during that time.

Grimké began the decade more convinced than ever of the strength of American racism. He had closed the preceding one with a lengthy exposition of his feelings, a lecture and, later, paper presented before the American Negro Academy, entitled "Negro Ideals and Ambitions," in which he stressed the hostility of white America to black aspirations. Citing "a change, a tremendous change" in "Negro consciousness, in his ideals and ambitions, by reason of his advance from the status of a mere piece of property in the republic to that of sovereign and equal citizenship under its government and laws," Grimké also decried the fact that only "a very slight change has been wrought in the white man's consciousness and sentiment." Noting exceptions, he asserted that "the whites as a class still cling to their one-sided version, to their un-American notion, that one white man is as good as another white man but better than any black man," and concluded; "There is an irrepressible conflict between the ideals and ambitions which the white man entertains for the Negro, and those which the Negro entertains for himself. The ideals and ambitions which the Negro entertains for himself are precisely those which the white man entertains for himself. And this the white man foolishly resents." Emphasizing the "doctrine of Jesus and of our American democracy, that one man is as good as another man," Grimké stressed the importance of white America's recognizing black America's ideals and ambitions.[1]

The paper repeated much that was familiar in Grimké's writing (Alfred Moss has suggested that the American Negro Academy chose not to print the address as an Occasional Paper largely because it had already printed three of Grimké's pieces and because of the similarity of this one to those published earlier), but it was also an important statement of Grimké's position at this time of his life, both politically and intellectually. Politically, it conveyed his persistent rejection of any goal other than absolute equality for black Americans, founded on basic rights of citizenship and on common aspirations. Intellectually, it expressed his thoroughgoing commitment to the same integrationist principles he had professed years before in the *Hub,* when he had written on the importance of balancing "racehood" with manhood. Obviously, there was no room in such a view for the separate development ideas of Booker Washington. Implicitly, however, the paper was also a commentary on his developing relationship with Du Bois.

Since before the turn of the century, though with no apparent connection to the relationship between Du Bois and Grimké, Du Bois had been stressing black distinctiveness. He emphasized the spiritual side of black character, with African roots, that both complemented and served as an alternative to mainstream American society and culture. Grimké had made little or no comment on Du Bois' views, but he must have known them well. Although Du Bois' first notable ex-

1. New York *Age,* December 10, 1908; Alfred A. Moss, Jr., *The American Negro Academy: Voice of the Talented Tenth* (Baton Rouge, 1981), 159–60; Archibald Grimké, "Alien or American; or, Negro Ideals and Ambitions," in Archibald H. Grimké Papers, Box 19, Folder 364, Moorland-Spingarn Research Center, Howard University, Washington, D.C.

position of black distinctiveness occurred in 1897, while Grimké was out of the country, that idea formed the core of his *Souls of Black Folk* and had gained enormous influence within the black literary and intellectual community. Such prominent figures as Benjamin Brawley and Arthur Schomburg built on Du Bois' work.

Grimké's "Negro Ideals" paper may have been a tacit response to Du Bois, spurred both by the spreading influence of Du Bois' ideas and by Grimké's own rapprochement with the man. The title of the paper referred to a phrase Du Bois had used in making his argument, contrasting distinctive "Negro ideals" with those of white America. Grimké, perhaps concerned to assert his independence, turned the phrase around, using it as an expression of his own fully integrationist faith, which gave no place to a distinctively black way of looking at the world. It would not be the first time that Grimké had subtly voiced a refusal to be guided by an overpowering factional leader; it would not be the last.[2]

The paper was foremost, however, a reassertion by Grimké of an approach to American race relations that was, in the narrowest sense, political and pragmatic and in confrontation with the most obvious ironies of the black experience in America. In the framework of events taking place over the next few months, he was to find new possibilities for working with a few of those good whites and with other black leaders in precisely the way the paper prescribed.

The initiative for this interaction came from a meeting held in the first week of 1909 in the apartment of William English Walling, a New York socialist and reformer originally from the South. Among those present were Mary White Ovington, a friend of Du Bois', who had had much to do with calling the meeting, and a social worker named Henry Moskowitz. Prompted by a variety of concerns, especially a violent race riot that had taken place in Springfield, Illinois, the preceding year, the three decided that a call should be issued on Abraham Lincoln's birthday for the creation of a citizens' body to fight American racial oppression, and they agreed to ask Oswald Garrison Villard for help. Villard wrote the powerfully worded "Call," which was endorsed by several leading figures, including Du Bois—who, recognizing problems in the Niagara Movement, had come to feel that an interracial organization was necessary for an effective fight against American racism—Grimké's friend E. H. Clement of the Boston

<hr />

2. See Sterling Stuckey, *Slave Culture: Nationalist Theory and the Foundations of Black America* (New York, 1987), 265.

Transcript, John Dewey, Jane Addams, Charles Edward Russell, William Dean Howells, Washington, D.C., clergyman J. Milton Waldron, and Francis—though not Archibald—Grimké. This "Call" invited "all the believers in democracy" to meet in a national conference, scheduled for late May, 1909, in New York, to discuss the problems of race in America.[3]

Francis Grimké had signed the "Call" but was unable to attend the conference, much to Villard's dismay. Instead, Archibald Grimké attended, though he played no major role in the conference proceedings. The conference itself was a great success. Several scientists spoke on racial equality, while others, including Du Bois, Trotter, Waldron, Ida Wells Barnett, and Grimké's old friend Albert Pillsbury, addressed the need for action against American racism. Despite the efforts of Villard, in particular, to break down factionalism on racial questions and to involve Booker Washington in the conference, it had a clearly anti-Washington tone, and Washington himself refused to take part.[4]

But of greatest significance for Grimké was his appointment to the Committee of Forty on Permanent Organization. Discussion of the committee's membership was contentious. A nominating subcommittee, hoping to gain Washington's support, had omitted Trotter, Waldron, and Ida Wells Barnett despite their prominence in the meeting. A good deal of ill will—some of it along racial lines—developed in the dispute, but, largely as a result of Charles Edward Russell's skill as presiding officer, the nominating committee's slate was approved with Russell's inclusion of Barnett and, later, of Waldron and a few others. The committee was charged not only with creating a permanent organization but also with laying plans for another conference to be held the following year.[5]

Over that next year, Grimké was an active member of the commit-

3. Mary White Ovington, *How the National Association for the Advancement of Colored People Began* (New York, n.d.), 1–2; Oswald Garrison Villard, *Fighting Years: Memoirs of a Liberal Editor* (New York, 1939), 193–94; Charles Flint Kellogg, *NAACP: A History of the National Association for the Advancement of Colored People, 1909–1920* (Baltimore, 1967), 12–13.

4. Kellogg, *NAACP,* 18–21; Louis R. Harlan and Raymond W. Smock, eds., *The Booker T. Washington Papers* (14 vols.; Urbana, 1972–89), X, 116–20; *Proceedings of the National Negro Conference 1909, May 31 and June 1* (N.p., n.d.); New York *Post,* June 2, 1909, Hampton University Peabody Newspaper Clipping File (Microfiche, ed.; Alexandria, Va., 1987).

5. Kellogg, *NAACP,* 28–30; Mary White Ovington, *The Walls Came Tumbling Down* (New York, 1947), 106–107; Henry Justin Ferry, "Francis James Grimké: Portrait of a Black Puritan" (Ph.D. dissertation, Yale University, 1970), 289.

tee. He took part in one of its first activities, a Garrison Memorial Meeting in Boston, held in October, where he spoke, along with his friend Maria Baldwin, among others. The meeting resulted in the establishment of the Boston Committee to Advance the Cause of the Negro—later to be the Boston branch of the NAACP—involving such friends of his as Pillsbury, Butler Wilson, and Francis J. and William Lloyd Garrison, Jr.[6]

He also participated actively in the committee's struggles to establish a structure for the organization and to define its foci, occasionally complaining that, sitting in the comfort of New York, the group was not really revolutionary. But he must have been pleased when, at Du Bois' urging, the committee decided to focus on disfranchisement as its central theme for the 1910 meeting.[7]

As in 1909, Grimké's role in the 1910 conference was small; he attended but did not speak. Nevertheless, he was affected by the proceedings. Among the more important results of the conference was the establishment of a permanent organization, the National Association for the Advancement of Colored People. Moorfield Storey, the former Mugwump, was named the first president of the association, and among the first officers were Walling, Villard, and John E. Milholland. The executive committee included such major figures as Pillsbury, Russell, Ovington, Mary Church Terrell, and Waldron. Grimké joined Trotter, Maria Baldwin, Francis Garrison, Kelly Miller, Charles Chesnutt, and Henry Moskowitz, among others, on a General Committee designed to encourage support for the new organization. And he affiliated with the Boston branch of the organization, one of the leaders of which was his friend and former partner Butler Wilson.[8]

Grimké's role in the founding of the NAACP was decidedly peripheral, and he did little over the next three years to enlarge that role. But his participation does show that he had now cast his lot with Washington's opponents. Once again, Du Bois was mentioning Grimké as one of black America's major leaders, something he had not done in years.[9]

6. Kellogg, *NAACP,* 31; William English Walling to Oswald Garrison Villard, n.d., in Records of the National Association for the Advancement of Colored People, Library of Congress; Archibald Grimké to Angelina Weld Grimké, October 26, 1909, in Angelina Weld Grimké Papers, Box 4, Folder 78, Moorland-Spingarn Research Center, Howard University, Washington, D.C.

7. Ovington, *Walls Came Tumbling Down,* 107; Kellogg, *NAACP,* 35–36.

8. Kellogg, *NAACP,* 43, 304–305; Stephen R. Fox, *The Guardian of Boston: William Monroe Trotter* (New York, 1970), 35–36.

9. W. E. B. Du Bois, *Writings by W. E. B. Du Bois in Periodicals Edited by Others,* ed. Herbert Aptheker (4 vols.; Millwood, N.Y., 1982), I, 408.

Whether Grimké was concerned about continuing factionalism as it might affect his own position is uncertain. Except for the implicit message of his defense of black political rights, Grimké had little to say either to or about Washington from this time forward. He did join Du Bois in the fall of 1910 in protesting Washington's efforts on a European tour to paint an optimistic picture of race relations in the United States, signing an "open letter" to the "People of Great Britain and Europe" drafted by Du Bois and presenting a series of facts intended to counteract Washington's positive assessment of the American situation.[10]

His relationship with Booker Washington was marked by increasing indifference. Although they continued to collaborate on the Douglass home, they had little to say to each other besides. Each man had apparently decided to let go of the other in what both realized was a losing battle. It is probably a measure of the relationship between the two men by this time that when, around Christmas, 1911, a large dinner was held in the District of Columbia in honor of Booker Washington, at which almost every local black leader was present, neither Archibald nor any other Grimké was on hand.[11]

But Grimké's position on the periphery of the fledging NAACP does not mean that he was entirely inactive, either in relation to the organization or in other public arenas. He continued, for example, to worry about the Brownsville incident, which was still unresolved. Following up on former senator Joseph Foraker's efforts to reopen the investigation of the incident, a Court of Military Inquiry had reaffirmed, in April, 1910, what had been established by earlier investigations. Grimké was deeply disappointed in the outcome and met with NAACP board member John Milholland to discuss it. They decided there was nothing to be done, but both were chagrined, Grimké lamenting to his daughter, "Oh, if our dear old friend & champion Foraker were in the Senate now to tear into bits the unjust, the contemptible findings of that packed & prejudiced court!" A few months later, the court did qualify fourteen of the men who had earlier been discharged for reenlistment—in effect exonerating them—an offer eleven accepted.[12]

He was also involved with the NAACP in protests against the con-

10. Harlan and Smock, eds., *Washington Papers,* X, 422–25.
11. Louis R. Harlan, *Booker T. Washington: The Wizard of Tuskegee, 1901–1915* (New York, 1983), 383–85, 400–404; Washington *Bee,* December 21, 1911.
12. Archibald Grimké to Angelina Grimké, April 12, 1910, in Angelina Grimké Papers, Box 5, Folder 79; James A. Tinsley, "Roosevelt, Foraker, and the Brownsville Affray," *Journal of Negro History,* XLI (1956), 59–61.

tinuing evil of lynching in the United States. In May, 1911, the District of Columbia branch sent a lengthy petition to President Taft, urging him to send a "Special Message to the Congress" decrying the evil and seeking legislation to prevent it, which Taft, of course, did not do. Grimké's was the first signature on the page; he was joined by such others as L. M. Hershaw, Mary Church Terrell, Carrie Clifford, and J. Milton Waldron.[13]

And he continued to speak out publicly on racial matters, often appearing with other NAACP figures. In November, 1910, he joined Butler Wilson in an appearance before the Twentieth Century Club, a civic club made up of Boston's most elite reformers, addressing the question of "racial peace," which both speakers said would come only with democracy and equality. A few months later, he delivered the Howard University commencement address, joining J. Milton Waldron, the dominant figure in the District of Columbia branch.[14]

He also continued his work with the American Negro Academy. In early 1911, in Washington, he presided over a meeting of the academy held to commemorate the centenary of Charles Sumner's birth, delivering the principal address. He was joined on the podium by Justice Wendell P. Stafford and Kelly Miller, and the program included a reading of a poem by Charlotte Grimké in honor of Sumner.[15]

His public activity is a testimony to his energy and dedication because this was also the beginning of a period, lasting through about the end of 1912, when much of his time was taken up with family and local matters. One of these involved a friend, Anna J. Cooper. A graduate of Oberlin, she earned an M.A. in mathematics as well as a bachelor's degree. Cooper had been principal of Washington's M Street High School from 1902 until 1906, when she was fired from the job after over a year of controversy. Having served in the intervening years as a professor of Latin and Greek at Lincoln University in Missouri, she had returned in 1910 to Washington, and to M Street, as a teacher of Latin. She wanted to regain her position as principal of the school.[16]

During her time in Washington, she had been close to the Grimké family and later wrote an account of its members, focusing mainly on Francis Grimké's wife, Charlotte. Francis had been one of her strong

13. Archibald Grimké *et al.* to William Howard Taft, May 31, 1911, in William Howard Taft Papers, case no. 1568, Library of Congress.

14. Indianapolis *Freeman,* June 10, 1911, in Hampton Newspaper Clipping File.

15. Boston *Guardian,* December 24, 1910, January 21, 1911.

16. Louise Daniel Hutchinson, *Anna J. Cooper: A Voice from the South* (Washington, D.C., 1981), 36, 43, 67–73.

supporters at the height of the controversy that cost Cooper her job. Socially, she was close to all the Grimkés, spending frequent evenings in the Grimké home on Corcoran Street, where she joined the family for tea and discussions of literature, art, and music.[17]

Archibald Grimké was often there, too, and, drawing on their friendship and on his position, Cooper called upon him for help in her efforts to get her position restored. He did what he could, chiefly trying to work with the school board president, James Oyster, who had great respect for his judgment. Though he ultimately failed to get her the job, the matter took up a great deal of his time and not a little of his energy.[18]

Grimké also had much cause for concern in regard to the well-being of his daughter, Angelina. On July 11, 1911, en route to Boston, she was aboard the Federal Express, which plunged down an eighteen-foot embankment, killing at least twelve passengers and injuring another fifty. Angelina was badly injured when the car in which she was riding "seemed to go to pieces." She was helped out of the car by a man whose wife was killed in the wreck.[19]

Angelina spent the summer convalescing in Boston, her father joining her there to take care of her. They did not return to Washington until the end of November, and it was later discovered that her spine had been fractured in the accident. As late as December, she remained under constant care, and it was predicted that she would require treatment for an indefinite period.[20]

The need to care for Angelina slowed down her father's public activity. It probably also took a toll on his social life, although he continued to visit actively friends both black and white: Pillsbury, Mrs. Wyman, a new friend, Rolfe Cobleigh, associate editor of the *Congregationalist,* the Butler Wilsons, the Edward Everett Browns—and Bertha Bauman's family, who were spending time in Boston. The preceding year had seen some complications in his relationship with Bertha

17. *Ibid.,* 71; Anna J. Cooper, *Personal Recollections of the Grimké Family* (2 vols.; N.p., 1951), I, 11–13.

18. Washington *Bee,* September 17, 1910; Unsigned to James F. Oyster, May 11, 1911, Anna Cooper to Archibald Grimké, May 26, 1911, Anna Cooper to James Oyster, July 9, 1911, in Archibald Grimké Papers, Box 4, Folder 90.

19. New York *Times,* July 12, 16, 1911; Angelina Weld Grimké to Archibald Grimké, July 13, 1911, in Archibald Grimké Papers, Box 3, Folder 65.

20. Boston *Guardian,* July 15, 1911; New York *Age,* November 30, 1911; John Dunlop to W. D. Griffin, December 7, 1911, copy, in Archibald Grimké Papers, Box 4, Folder 91.

because in the summer and fall of 1910 she had started to spend time with the Trotters. During that summer of 1910, Grimké and Trotter had again come into conflict. Trotter by now was on the outs with the local NAACP. Trotter and the Boston branch had decided independently to commemorate the Sumner centenary early in 1911, and neither would yield precedent to the other. Grimké, joined by Moorfield Storey, Francis Garrison, and Pillsbury, met with Trotter on behalf of the branch. Grimké urged Trotter to moderation, but there was to be neither compromise nor settlement. The national organization of the NAACP withdrew its interest from the celebration, but the branch went ahead, and in a replay of the 1905 Garrison centennial, Boston saw two commemorations of Sumner's birth.[21]

Bertha's friendship with the Trotters posed a real barrier to their relationship. At one point, Grimké told Angelina that he had not seen her for a while and did not expect to, unless by accident. "I certainly do not intend to call at the Trotters to see her," he said. His determination did not last long, however. Only a week later, he told Angelina that he had gone to Maude Trotter's for a dinner party, also attended by Bessie Trotter and Bertha. Even he seems to have been astonished by his presence there. The extent of his relationship with Bertha during the summer of 1911 is unknown because he was staying with Angelina and therefore not writing to her, but the following year, they still expressed some feeling for each other.[22] Whether Bertha had anything to do with it, he also began during 1911 to mend his relations with the Trotters—not only with Maude and Bessie but with Monroe as well. He began to interact with all of them not only socially but in public matters.

At the time of the rival Boston Sumner celebrations, Grimké was back in the District of Columbia, sponsoring his own commemoration at the American Negro Academy. Trotter gave extensive coverage to the meeting and to Grimké's address. He published a lengthy excerpt from Grimké's talk in the *Guardian* and gave the Washington, D.C., celebration the most positive possible treatment. Later in the spring, with the approach of the 1911 NAACP Conference to be held in Boston, Trotter, whose relations with that organization were improving, too, spoke favorably of Grimké as a Boston member of the National Committee. During the early summer, Grimké reciprocated,

21. Fox, *Guardian of Boston,* 131–32.
22. Archibald Grimké to Angelina Grimké, October 21, 28, 1910, in Angelina Grimké Papers, Box 5, Folder 79.

signing on—along with Angelina and Francis—as a contributor to the "Guardian Gold Testimonial" in tribute to Trotter and his paper.[23]

Shortly before Archibald and Angelina returned to Washington following her convalescence, this apparent rapprochement was strengthened by the unanimous vote of Trotter's New England Suffrage League and the National Independent Political League to invite him to be centennial orator at the Wendell Phillips centenary, scheduled for November 29, 1911, in Faneuil Hall.[24]

Grimké spoke, reiterating much that he had said about Phillips in earlier tributes to the great antislavery orator. The featured speaker in the all-day tribute to Phillips, Grimké had been preceded by Trotter, Francis J. Garrison, Albert Pillsbury, and others. The evening session, at which he spoke, was opened by John F. Fitzgerald, the mayor of Boston. Trotter's *Guardian* described Grimké's address as "memorable" and published a lengthy excerpt—his was the only one so honored—as well as a picture of Grimké. It is not clear why relations between Grimké and Trotter thawed, but for the moment, an old friendship had been revived.[25]

With the close of 1911 and into 1912, as Angelina's condition improved, Grimké continued his pattern of remaining active locally and at the periphery of larger movements. But his pace picked up noticeably about the middle of 1912, which was a presidential election year. That election pitted the incumbent Republican, William Howard Taft, against the progressive Democrat and white southerner Woodrow Wilson. It also saw an insurgent campaign under the banner of the Progressive party led by former president Theodore Roosevelt, by this time a bitter opponent of Taft and the old-guard Republicans. The ideological issues of the campaign were serious and significant. Roosevelt had moved to the left in the four years since he left office and proposed a program of economic, political, and social reform. Racial issues were no less serious, and the black leadership was deeply divided during the campaign.

Grimké, despite his previous feelings, went with Roosevelt, albeit with initial reluctance. In July, 1912, on the eve of the Progressive party's national convention, held in Chicago in early August, Grimké wrote to Roosevelt, noting his opposition to Roosevelt's earlier action.

23. Boston *Guardian*, December 24, 1910, January 21, March 18, August 5, 1911.

24. Emery T. Morris to Archibald Grimké, October 19, 1911, in Archibald Grimké Papers, Box 5, Folder 99.

25. Boston *Guardian*, December 2, 1911; Archibald Grimké, "Wendell Phillips," in Archibald Grimké Papers, Box 19, Folder 352.

But, he added, "I believe so entirely in the principles of the new movement and in your courage and sincerity as its leader that I have made
up my mind to let the dead past bury its dead and to cast my lot with
the new party in the living present." There was much in Roosevelt's
program that matched Grimké's views on such questions as the tariff,
relations of labor and capital, and an independent, Mugwumpian view
of party. Grimké did, however, urge Roosevelt to make a commitment to equal rights for black Americans.[26]

He participated actively in the campaign. He attended and took part
in the Progressive party's Massachusetts convention, held in Fanueil
Hall, where he succeeded in influencing the platform committee to
include planks on political equality and lynching. The committee,
made up of political unknowns, adopted a document inviting "men
and women of every race and color" to join the new organization,
urging enforcement of the Fourteenth and Fifteenth Amendments and
the equality of all before the law, regardless of race and color, and
deploring lynch law. Grimké felt the "victory" was something he had
accomplished "single handed" by his presentation to the committee,
and he exulted in the belief that "the country & the South will take
notice that the new party is a liberty party for all men, regardless of
race or color." The new party, like the Committee of Twelve earlier,
seemed to be a place where his ideas could have some influence.[27]

After Chicago, though he was shaken by Roosevelt's refusal to seat
black southern delegates at the convention, which did cost Roosevelt
some black support (notably Du Bois'), Grimké remained faithful to
the Progressive cause. Summering in Boston, Grimké tried to persuade his friends to go with Roosevelt, and he also served as a member
of the reception committee of the party chosen to greet Roosevelt on
a campaign visit to the city. He worked for Roosevelt until election
day and, after Wilson's victory, telegraphed the former president to
express his continuing support, noting that the Progressive party had
"come to stay" and that "the movement it represents will surely pre-
vail in the end," a telegram Roosevelt chose to acknowledge.[28]

26. Archibald Grimké to Theodore Roosevelt, July 20, 1912, in Archibald Grimké
Papers, Box 10, Folder 215.

27. Boston *Evening Transcript,* July 29, 1912; Boston *Globe,* July 28, 1912; Archibald Grimké to Angelina Grimké, July 27, 1912, in Angelina Grimké Papers, Box 5,
Folder 81.

28. Archibald Grimké to Angelina Grimké, August 18, 1912, in Angelina Grimké
Papers, Box 5, Folder 81; Laurence G. Brooks to Archibald Grimké, August 14, 1912,
Theodore Roosevelt to Archibald Grimké, November 8, 1912, in Archibald Grimké

There can be little doubt of the sincerity of Grimké's support for Roosevelt and that it was not simply a matter of strategy in a complicated setting of racial politics. His friend Richard Greener wrote to him after the election criticizing Grimké's "Roosevelt fetishism." But Grimké continued to defend his political choice, giving the fullest statement of his views in his presidential address to the American Negro Academy about a month and a half after the election, in a paper entitled "The Ballotless Victim of One-Party Governments."[29]

Focusing on the need to build a strong opposition to established southern state governments and describing the Republican party as hopeless in that regard, Grimké argued that the Progressives were the best hope for a southern political alternative. He defended Roosevelt's exclusion of southern black delegates at Chicago by noting both the inclusion of black delegates from the North and the need to build a southern party among those empowered to participate in the political process. Not a defense of even a temporary acceptance of southern disfranchisement, Grimké's paper argued that a genuine two-party system in the South was the best guarantee of recognition of suffrage for blacks. He concluded by declaring, as he had so often, that only suffrage would make possible any significant changes in living conditions for blacks in the region.

Response to the paper was strong and positive. Roosevelt wrote that Grimké's interpretation of his actions at Chicago was "absolutely right." Du Bois, after the publication of "Ballotless Victim," recognized the thrust of Grimké's argument and commended it highly, writing, "When anyone argues that political rights are not necessary to race advance, send him these eighteen pages of reason."[30]

But for all that was positive in the paper, it may also have been an expression of desperation. Viewing the current situation as a nadir characterized by political exclusion, Grimké could see nothing in the existing partisan structure on which to pin any hopes. It is probably

Papers, Box 10, Folder 215; August Meier, *Negro Thought in America, 1880–1915: Racial Ideologies in the Age of Booker T. Washington* (Ann Arbor, 1963), 188.

29. Richard T. Greener to Archibald Grimké, April 28, 1913, in Archibald Grimké Papers, Box 4, Folder 94; Archibald Grimké, *The Ballotless Victim of One-Party Governments,* Occasional Papers of the American Negro Academy, no. 16, 1913, in *American Negro Academy Occasional Papers 1–22* (New York, 1969).

30. Theodore Roosevelt to Whitefield McKinlay, April 29, 1913, in Archibald Grimké Papers, Box 5, Folder 102; *Crisis,* VII (1914), 202; Washington *Bee,* November 25, 1916.

significant that the 1912 election was the last in which he played any public role. He began to focus on other avenues for the action that would bring about justice and change. Four years later, he did not even bother to vote.

But Wilson's election was to bring significant and far-reaching changes to American racial life. During the campaign, many black leaders had worried with reason about Wilson's southern Democratic background. Even before Wilson took the oath of office, emboldened southern congressmen introduced legislation in the House and Senate advocating segregation in public transportation in the District of Columbia, segregation of federal empoloyees, and outlawing racial intermarriage. The NAACP was called to action early on these issues. In February, 1913, it opposed, through its Washington branch, legislation aimed at outlawing intermarriage, and Grimké drafted the branch's letter to members of Congress, quoting William Lloyd Garrison at length and urging that such laws lead "directly to concubinage, bastardy, and the degradation of the Negro woman." This effort, at least, was defeated.[31]

Still, the tide continued to roll, and before long federal segregation had become a major issue for black Americans and a central one in the federal city of Washington. It was to provide an important stimulus for the next stage of events in Archibald Grimké's life and career.[32]

31. W. E. B. Du Bois, *Dusk of Dawn: An Essay Toward an Autobiography of a Race Concept* (New York, 1940), 236; May Childs Nerney to William Monroe Trotter, February 19, 1913, in Records of the National Association for the Advancement of Colored People; Archibald Grimké to "My Dear Sir," March 8, 1913, in Archibald Grimké Papers, Box 25, Folder 488.
32. Kellogg, *NAACP,* 159–65; James Weldon Johnson, *Along This Way* (New York, 1933), 300–301; Villard, *Fighting Years,* 236–40.

13

NAACP

The policy of discrimination that marked Woodrow Wilson's first year in office posed serious problems for blacks throughout the United States, particularly for those in the city of Washington, where federal employment was an important support for black middle-class life. The young NAACP, and the District of Columbia branch, in particular, was the main organization in a position to deal with the problems the new administration was busily creating for black people. Before the year was out, by assuming the presidency of the branch, Archibald Grimké became the central figure in this effort.

Grimké took that role mainly because of serious difficulties inside the branch and a hope on the part of the national NAACP leadership that he could help ameliorate them. The sources of the problems confronting the D.C. branch in 1913 were many and various, but most important at the opening of the year were severe divisions within its ranks, chiefly involving the president of the branch at the beginning of the Wilson years, J. Milton Waldron, a Baptist minister and experienced activist. Problems with Waldron appeared on several fronts.

Much of the difficulty grew out of his political activities. During the 1912 campaign, Waldron had been an active partisan of Woodrow Wilson. After Wilson's election and inauguration, and despite the administration's segregationist stance, Waldron maintained his loyalty to the Democrat and was rumored to be seeking a position in the new administration. He appeared to be willing to go quite a way to get such a post. In a widely published address in Richmond, Virginia, Waldron expressed his faith in both the Democratic party and Wilson, even defending Wilson's policies, the white South, and, astonishingly, southern disfranchisement, arguing that by slavishly supporting the

Republican party, the black voter had "brought upon himself his own disenfranchisement." The comments were not well received by many members of the local branch.[1]

Other of his actions had also caused problems within the branch. Waldron had been accused of misusing branch funds, a charge he had to admit was true. He had also been a leader in a controversy in the District of Columbia schools, which had divided the branch's largely middle-class members, many of them school employees, as well. The controversy essentially involved a series of attacks by Waldron on the assistant superintendent for black schools, Roscoe Conkling Bruce, Harvard-educated son of Senator Blanche K. Bruce and former employee of Booker Washington at Tuskegee. The dispute centered on questions of hiring and promotion in the schools, with Waldron occasionally raising Bruce's former Tuskegee ties (which he had maintained since he had moved to the District) but focusing mainly on the man himself and on what he called "Bruceism" to accuse the assistant superintendent of favoritism and of trying to pack the schools with allies. Bruceites and anti-Bruceites were both well represented in the D.C. branch, further dividing the organization.

All these tensions and divisions—school, political, and organizational—came to a head in June, 1913, when Waldron was removed from the presidency to which he had been reelected only a couple of months before. The removal was accomplished at a general meeting of the D.C. branch, called to consider a recommendation of the Executive Committee presented by L. M. Hershaw, longtime radical and Bruce partisan, that Waldron step down. The meeting was, not surprisingly, full of dissension, and, in the aftermath, each side charged the other with having tried to stack the meeting with "new recruits." But with Hershaw as the leading spirit in the effort to remove Waldron, the Executive Committee's recommendation was adopted by the lopsided margin of 127 to 33.[2]

Archibald Grimké remained pretty much in the background of the controversy, though not ignored. During the period of greatest ten-

1. Washington *Bee,* January 4, 1913; Lewis Newton Walker, Jr., "The Struggles and Attempts to Establish Branch Autonomy and Hegemony: A History of the District of Columbia Branch National Association for the Advancement of Colored People, 1912–1942" (Ph.D. dissertation, University of Delaware, 1979), 26–27, 293.

2. Washington *Bee,* June 28, 1913; "Confidential Memorandum on the Washington Matter," June 22, 1913, and Clipping, n.d., both in Records of the National Association for the Advancement of Colored People, Library of Congress (hereafter cited as NAACP Records).

sion in the summer of 1913, he was out of the city, taking his usual summer sojourn in Boston. May Childs Nerney, secretary for the NAACP national office, met with Grimké just before he left and reported him to be "particularly disaffected" and "filled with disgust at the situation of the Local." According to her, so long as the branch remained in the hands of "self-seekers like Dr. Waldron," he would refuse to work actively with it and would identify himself with the Boston branch. William Monroe Trotter supported Waldron and took a more cynical view, writing of Grimké that "he lays around as a neutral to be called in when there is a row," presumably waiting to play a conciliatory role.[3]

He remained disaffected or on the sidelines waiting to be called in, depending on one's perspective, throughout the summer as the row continued. But he was not forgotten. Such people in the national leadership as Nerney and Villard had hoped for Waldron's removal, chiefly because of his political activity but also because he seemed to want to act too independently in his relations with the national body. And they looked fondly at Grimké as a possible replacement.

Nerney was especially persistent. As early as May, she had urged him to participate more actively in branch affairs. During the summer, while he was in Boston, she renewed her efforts, eventually approaching him on behalf of the national board, once Waldron had been voted out, about taking over the interim presidency of the D.C. branch, at least until a regular election could be held the following January. Somewhat to her surprise, he agreed to do so and took over the office in late September. Thus began what was to be the final stage of his public career, in which he was to be more active and more effective than he had ever been before.[4]

Upon assuming the presidency of the D.C. branch, Grimké had several tasks to deal with. One of these, obviously, was to try to make the branch more stable. With May Nerney's encouragement, he sought to stabilize the leadership, appointing experienced people who opposed Waldron, building bridges with Howard University's chap-

3. May Childs Nerney to Joel E. Spingarn, July 7, 1913, in Joel E. Spingarn Papers, Box 8, Folder 244, Moorland-Spingarn Research Center, Howard University, Washington, D.C.; William Monroe Trotter to F. H. M. Murray, n.d., in F. H. M. Murray Papers, Box 1, Folder 3, *ibid.*

4. May Childs Nerney to Archibald H. Grimké, July 9, 1913, Grimké to Nerney, July 28, 1913, in NAACP Records; Oswald Garrison Villard to Archibald Grimké, September 29, 1913, in Archibald H. Grimké Papers, Box 25, Folder 490, Moorland-Spingarn Research Center, Howard University, Washington, D.C.

ter, and even extending "the olive branch" to Waldron and his friends by subduing the more vocal criticism of the more ardent members of the anti-Waldron faction.[5]

Grimké apparently decided that he wanted to be more than an interim president. He quickly demonstrated a style of leadership that his brother Francis would later praise both for its outspokenness and for the way it showed Archibald's "ability of attaching people to himself and of holding them in perfect loyalty." Despite his initial reluctance about taking the post, he rapidly assumed leadership in the branch with great enthusiasm. He made it clear that any "olive branch" he might extend to the Waldronites would not compromise his own position. He well understood the circumstances under which he had become president, and he quickly sought to consolidate his position within the framework of those circumstances.[6]

One of his first steps was the creation, with the encouragement of the national office and within only a few weeks of taking the post, of a Committee of Fifty and More ostensibly to raise funds for the NAACP. The committee was packed with anti-Waldronites and, according to historian Lewis Newton Walker, Jr., was formed, in part at least, to forestall a return to power of the Waldron forces. The committee also brought together a mix of old and young activists, allies and opponents of Booker T. Washington, and old friends of Archibald Grimké. Among its members were his American Negro Academy colleague John Bruce, Whitefield McKinlay, Washingtonian Robert H. Terrell, and anti-Washingtonian L. M. Hershaw. Angelina Grimké was on the committee, as were the young Howard University philosopher Alain Locke and historian Carter Woodson. From the Washington schools came Roscoe Bruce, Charlotte Hunter, Garnet Wilkinson, and Lucy Moten. Jessie Fauset, later to become a leading literary figure associated with the *Crisis,* was also in the group. That Bruce, whose relationship with Booker Washington had begun to deteriorate, was not entirely comfortable with his place in what was still an anti-Washington body became evident when, in October, 1913, Grimké, on Bruce's urging, instructed May Nerney not to publish the names of the Committee of Fifty in the *Crisis* and when Bruce refused at the

5. May Childs Nerney to Archibald Grimké, October 6, 16, 21, 1913, in Archibald Grimké Papers, Box 25, Folder 491.

6. Francis J. Grimké, *Archibald H. Grimké, Born in Charleston, S.C., August 17, 1849. Died in Washington, D.C., February 25, 1930. A Brief Statement by His Brother, Rev. Francis J. Grimké, Pastor Fifteenth Street Presbyterian Church, Washington, D.C.* (N.p., n.d.), 3–4.

January, 1914, election to accept an office, though he wished to remain on the committee.[7]

Grimké also jumped headlong into fighting the problems posed by the Wilson administration. The issue of federal segregation occupied much of his time. During his first month in office, he learned that the Democratic caucus had passed a resolution to discharge all the colored employees in the Capitol and in the Senate and House office buildings and to replace them by whites—information he seems to have received from Rolfe Cobleigh, liberal associate editor of the *Congregationalist*—and began to work closely with Minnesota senator Moses Clapp, a friend of the NAACP, to prevent the action from taking place. Toward the end of October, he organized a mass meeting at the African Methodist Episcopal Metropolitan Church in Washington "To Protest Against Segregation—the New Slavery." He addressed the meeting, condemning Wilson for betraying his presumed promises of equal treatment made during the campaign, and was joined on the platform by Wendell Phillips Stafford, Villard, John Haynes Holmes, an NAACP national vice-president, and the Reverend Walter H. Brooks of New York, a member of the board of directors. According to the *Bee,* at least four thousand people crowded the meeting, with "twice as many on the outside of the church clamoring for admittance." Villard went outside to address those who could not get in. After bitter attacks on Wilson's policies, the meeting unanimously passed a series of resolutions protesting federal segregation as "medieval, Un-American, despotic and in violation of Republican institutions," and Grimké forwarded them at once, with a letter of his own, to Wilson and the members of the cabinet.[8]

Grimké also dealt with local matters in his role as branch president. Toward the end of November, a meeting was called under the leadership of President Wilson's daughter "to consider wider use of the school plant, a plan to correlate the city's recreational activities and the

7. Archibald Grimké to Roscoe Conkling Bruce, November 2, 1913, May Childs Nerney to Archibald Grimké, n.d., in Archibald Grimké Papers, Box 25, Folder 492; Bruce to Grimké, January 4, 1914, *ibid.,* Box 25, Folder 494; Washington *Bee,* January 7, 1911; Walker, "Struggles," 48, 55; NAACP Board of Directors, Minutes, December 2, 1913, in W. E. B. Du Bois Papers (microfilm), University of Massachusetts, Amherst.

8. Rolfe Cobleigh to Archibald Grimké, September 24, 1913, in Archibald Grimké Papers, Box 4, Folder 89; May Childs Nerney to Moses Clapp, September 27, 1913, in NAACP Records; Washington *Bee,* November 1, 1913; *Crisis,* VII (1913), 89–90; Archibald Grimké to Woodrow Wilson, October 29, 1913, in Woodrow Wilson Papers, Library of Congress.

location of swimming pools in the District of Columbia." Representatives of black civic organizations were excluded from that meeting
and from a subsequent one about two weeks later. Grimké, speaking
for the NAACP, protested that exclusion, noting the importance of
the meetings' deliberations to the city's black citizens and the extent
to which those citizens were "distressed and humiliated" by their exclusion from the planning process. Such local matters were to occupy
much of his time during his tenure as branch president.[9]

But even while he was involving himself in such work and putting
the affairs of the local branch in some order, he also began to make his
presence felt regarding the troubling internal issues in the national organization. Within a short time of taking the branch presidency, he
became an officer in the national body. The circumstances were as
turbulent as those under which he assumed his office in the District of
Columbia. They grew out of problems involving national NAACP
vice-president, strong Democrat, and erstwhile Grimké friend Alexander Walters. Walters' problems began in late October, following a
meeting with Secretary of the Treasury William G. McAdoo over the
placement of signs designating certain facilities "For Colored" in the
Treasury Department. The signs were removed after pressure from
Walters, Villard, Clapp, Ralph Tyler, and others. After the meeting,
however, it was rumored that Walters had agreed that segregation in
the department would be acceptable so long as the signs were removed. By November, Villard had become convinced that these reports were accurate, and he publicly accused Walters of supporting
segregation. Grimké wrote Villard almost immediately, asking for
evidence. Villard replied that he had met with Wilson and McAdoo,
both of whom had told him "flat-footedly that Bishop Walters had
favored segregation." The information had also been confirmed by
Wilson's secretary, Joseph Tumulty. Villard told Grimké he was willing to give Walters the benefit of the doubt. "It is possible," he said,
"that the Bishop seemingly assented by not protesting very loudly, as
we all have to do in the presence of high authority." Nevertheless,
feeling the heat, Walters resigned from the board and was replaced by
Archibald Grimké.[10]

Grimké was thus placed in a position to act significantly and almost
immediately in an early skirmish involving another internal conflict,

9. *Crisis,* VII (1914), 142.
10. Washington *Bee,* September 6, 1913; Oswald Garrison Villard to Archibald
Grimké, November 11, 1913, in Archibald Grimké Papers, Box 25, Folder 492.

one that continued throughout his tenure on the board. This was the strife between Villard and others on one side and the director of publicity, W. E. B. Du Bois, on the other. Du Bois and Villard had had difficulties going back to at least 1909, and, although they occasionally managed a temporary truce, they could never seem to remain at peace.[11]

They were in open conflict when Grimké joined the board in November, 1913, chiefly because Du Bois wanted greater autonomy as editor of the *Crisis* and Villard thought the publication should be clearly under the board's control. May Childs Nerney turned to Grimké for advice. She was not entirely happy with Du Bois and noted the need for "prying the publicity work loose from 'high brow' and personal influences." At the same time, she wanted to contain the problem within the board, saying, "This work is bigger than anyone in it but if I must choose the most essential officer, I shall have to choose the editor of the Crisis." Shortly thereafter, urging Grimké not to make up his mind until he had all the facts, she concluded, in a clear reference to Villard, "Dear me, isn't it a terrible thing to have both a personality and a grandfather."[12]

Grimké, however, did not entirely share Nerney's views. The issue came up at the board's November meeting, and harsh words were spoken. Du Bois had never felt very comfortable working with his white colleagues in the organization, and he was never convinced that they were dealing with him without prejudice in the dispute over the *Crisis*. He said as much in the meeting, and he said it not for the first time.[13]

Grimké had no illusions about white Americans, and he had recently received a letter from his old friend Pillsbury, who admitted to having been influenced by prejudice. But, prompted perhaps by his continuing distrust of Du Bois, Grimké quickly moved to dispute the editor. His exact words are unknown, but Nerney said that he gave "an eloquent and tactful rebuke to the attempt, always fatal, to put all our difficulties on the ground of race prejudice." That rebuke renewed the long-standing tension between Grimké and Du Bois. Du Bois showed his anger by ignoring Albert Pillsbury's request

11. Charles Flint Kellogg, *NAACP: A History of the National Association for the Advancement of Colored People, 1909–1920* (Baltimore, 1967), 108–109.
12. May Childs Nerney to Archibald Grimké, November 2, 29, 1913, in Archibald Grimké Papers, Box 25, Folder 492; May Childs Nerney to Archibald Grimké, December 4, 1913, *ibid.*, Box 25, Folder 493.
13. May Childs Nerney to Archibald Grimké, n.d., *ibid.*, Box 25, Folder 491.

that he publish in the *Crisis* Grimké's "Modern Industrialism and the Negroes." His refusal could not have been based on the ideas expressed in the paper because it contained much with which Du Bois could agree, both politically and philosophically. Such tension, with occasional respites, continued throughout Grimké's tenure on the board.[14]

Grimké gave a great deal of time and energy to the affairs of the NAACP, locally and nationally, and his activity outside the organization often reflected his involvement in it. He was still president of the American Negro Academy and, at the close of the year, presented his annual presidential address, titled "The Ultimate Criminal," an effort to lay the causes of crime in the black community to racial oppression. He was joined on the program by two of the leading figures in the anti-Waldron effort, Hershaw and Roscoe C. Bruce.[15]

At the close of 1913 and for some time to come, Grimké's activities were dominated by the NAACP. The year 1914 began auspiciously for both Grimké and the organization with a highly successful mass meeting on January 6, the birthday of Charles Sumner. The meeting was addressed by Senator Clapp, Wendell Phillips Stafford, Villard, and Grimké. Du Bois, despite his conflict with Grimké after the November board meeting, wrote in the *Crisis* that "no one at the meeting so eloquently expressed the real spirit of the association's work as Mr. Archibald H. Grimké, under whose brilliant leadership the Washington branch has become a powerful, cohesive body and a great source of strength to our organization." In his address to the meeting, Grimké stressed the importance of unity and cooperation and said candidly: "Segregation was the thing that did the work for us. The people became aroused and began to look around for the instrument that could help them. We took great pains to point out that there was only one instrument in fact . . . and that is the National Association for the Advancement of Colored People." It was for that reason, he said, that he had decided to devote the rest of his life to it.[16]

The D.C. branch was growing rapidly and achieving an influence that blurred the older national factionalism in black public affairs.

14. Albert E. Pillsbury to Archibald Grimké, November 26, 1913, *ibid.,* Box 5, Folder 100; May Childs Nerney to Archibald Grimké, n.d.; Stephen R. Fox, *The Guardian of Boston: William Monroe Trotter* (New York, 1970), 142–43.

15. Archibald H. Grimké, *The Ultimate Criminal,* Occasional Papers of the American Negro Academy, no. 17, 1915, in *The American Negro Academy Occasional Papers 1–22* (New York, 1969), 3, 5.

16. *Crisis,* VII (1914), 192.

Grimké's Committee of Fifty and More had brought together some old antagonists, and this fact was not lost on Booker T. Washington's more devoted lieutenants. Ralph Tyler, in a letter to Emmett Scott written at about this time, noted that the NAACP was growing rapidly and added that "in Washington its leaders are either avowed opponents of the Doctor or indifferent friends." Tyler heaped particular scorn on Roscoe Bruce—despite Bruce's efforts at anonymity—whom he described in a postmeeting letter to Booker Washington as "a grand high priest now in the N.A.A.C.P. movement, hurdling from his past friends who saved him to hoped for new friends." [17]

Tyler may have been right about Bruce. The assistant superintendent was still under fire. The Waldronites may have lost the NAACP battle, but they continued to vent their anger. Bruce now turned for support to Grimké and to his NAACP allies. He tried, for example, to get Grimké to help him in replacing a Waldronite on the school board by someone more friendly. It is not clear whether Grimké made any such effort, but the board member was not replaced. He also sent Grimké copies of virtually every piece of correspondence related to the schools. Bruce clearly pinned his hopes for survival mainly on his new friends. [18]

What Tyler was documenting, however, was not so much opportunism on the part of Bruce and others as changes in black politics in which Booker T. Washington was becoming increasingly irrelevant as a political force. As August Meier has noted, by 1914, prominent moderates and even Washingtonians were aligning themselves with the NAACP. Grimké continued to deal with Washington on the Douglass home—still achieving no success—but not much else. It is unlikely that anyone but Washington and such allies as Tyler had much concern for the old factional lines. [19]

Grimké was satisfied with the NAACP. He was elected to the branch presidency at the January 16, 1914, meeting, and found that working diligently and effectively on racial issues in the District of Columbia and in the federal government in early 1914 gave him greater prominence than he had ever known. In early March, he ap-

17. Louis R. Harlan and Raymond W. Smock, eds., *The Booker T. Washington Papers* (14 vols.; Urbana, 172–89), XII, 401–402, 405; Washington *Bee,* January 24, 1914.

18. Roscoe C. Bruce to Archibald Grimké, March 25, 1914, in Archibald Grimké Papers, Box 8, Folder 148.

19. Washington *Bee,* January 24, 1914; August Meier, *Negro Thought in America, 1880–1915: Racial Ideologies in the Age of Booker T. Washington* (Ann Arbor, 1963), 183–84.

peared before the House of Representatives Committee on Reform in the Civil Service, testifying in opposition to two bills introduced by Congressmen James B. Aswell of Louisiana and Charles B. Edwards of Georgia that provided for the segregation of black employees in the government service. Grimké found out about the hearing on the bill only at the last minute and had to appear without any preparation, but he did appear and with great effect.[20]

Grimké was ably supported by one member of the committee, Martin Madden of Illinois, but he was confronted by unconcealed hostility on the part of such southern representatives as Martin Dies of Texas and the chairman, Hannibal Godwin of North Carolina. In the hearing, Grimké spoke strongly against the principle behind the bills, asking if it represented the spirit of the republic. He responded bluntly to Martin Dies, his chief antagonist, who claimed that "the southern people are the best friends you have in the world." Citing case after case of humiliation and oppression wrought by southern whites upon black citizens and reminding the committee of the sacrifices black men and women had made for their country, he denied any truth to that hoary southern picture of race relations, arguing that the very bill he was there to oppose was evidence of how little friendship southern whites had for blacks.[21]

But his testimony was especially remarkable for its application of ideas and principles he had long expressed to the specific issues raised by the bills. When Dies asserted that "one of the races must be the ruling race, and the negro race as rulers is unthinkable," Grimké replied by noting that Dies's point was confounded by people like Grimké himself, who had "the blood of both races," and went on to call up ideas that went back in his thought to the "Negro Ideals" paper and even the women's suffrage address of the 1880s, arguing that white racial domination was as doomed to failure as rule by monopoly capital in the face of black resistance and the democratic forces of history.[22]

He made it clear that there was nothing of the accommodationist in him when facing these hostile white southerners. "The fact that you attempt to keep these people down shows there is something in them

20. Speech of Neval H. Thomas at the NAACP Annual Conference, Baltimore, May 4, 1914, copy in NAACP Records.
21. *Hearings Before the House Committee on Reform in the Civil Service, Segregation of Clerks and Employees in the Civil Service,* 63rd Cong., 2nd Sess., 18–19.
22. *Ibid.,* 19–20.

that you fear," he said, namely, that given a chance, black people would show their equality with whites. Not mincing words, Grimké confronted the hostile southern members openly and directly.[23]

The national organization was ecstatic at his performance. May Nerney wrote to him that people in the national office had been so excited by his "victory over the Bourbons" that they had "struck work for a half hour." And the testimony did succeed in getting the two bills "smothered" within the committee, although, of course, there was no guarantee that they would not be introduced again.[24]

The episode could only have strengthened Grimké's faith in the NAACP. As had happened with the Committee of Twelve almost ten years before, his testimony in Congress and the reaction to it had shown that he could speak his mind, representing the NAACP but basing his arguments on ideas that he had been developing for years, and receive respect both for those ideas and for himself. He would not become an organization man but would remain an individual within the organization—and an influential and independent individual.

A range of opportunities for further action quickly followed the Civil Service hearings. In early April, Grimké and the local branch learned of the introduction by Florida representative Frank Clark of yet another bill to outlaw intermarriage in the District of Columbia. The association voted to oppose the bill, and Grimké played an active role in its ultimate defeat, organizing protests and contacting congressional leaders.[25]

He also enjoyed other successes. When the Bureau of Printing and Engraving decided to segregate its dining facilities, Grimké went personally to officials and was able to prevent it, at least for a time. He protested planned appropriations for chronically underfunded black schools in the District of Columbia because no provisions were made for additional facilities and existing schools were badly overcrowded. Although Bruce, always feeling vulnerable, suggested that it might be best to "let well enough alone," Grimké tried to do something about the situation and was at least able to get a new high school to serve

23. *Ibid.*, 21.

24. Boston *Guardian,* March 21, 1914; Washington *Bee,* March 14, 1914; May Childs Nerney to Archibald Grimké, March 7, 1914, in Archibald Grimké Papers, Box 25, Folder 496; "N.A.A.C.P.: Some of the Year's Accomplishments," n.d., in Arthur Spingarn Papers, Library of Congress.

25. New York *Age,* April 2, 1914; May Childs Nerney to James C. Waters, April 15, 1914, Speech of Neval Thomas, in NAACP Records.

black pupils into the planning stages, largely by contacting the NAACP's "good friends" in Congress.[26]

Grimké was thus becoming an important and visible figure in the NAACP, active on key issues in Washington and doing an effective job. He had joined the board of directors and in January was made a national vice-president. He worked actively as a member of the board, contributing much time to its business. He soon became chairman of its Committee on Branches, chiefly responsible for evaluating applications from new local organizations that desired affiliation with the national body. He entered the May annual meeting of the NAACP in Baltimore as the man responsible for what had become the association's strongest branch. And at the convention, he was lavisly praised by a co-worker, Neval Thomas, for his leadership of the branch. At the Baltimore meeting, Grimké presented a reworked version of his address "Negro Ideals and Ambitions," which expressed a more optimistic vision of cooperation between blacks and whites in the future, in keeping with the spirit of the meeting. He organized, as well, a successful postconference meeting in Washington.[27]

At this meeting, held on May 6, 1914, he was joined on the platform by Justice Wendell Phillips Stafford, Senator Clapp, and Joel Spingarn. Grimké used the occasion to present a strongly worded attack on racism entitled, appropriately, "What Fools These Mortals Be," capturing themes he had used in his Civil Service testimony but in more colorful language. Citing the words of a former senator from Texas, Joseph Bailey, who had roundly asserted the inferiority of black people, he likened Bailey to King Canute, who had commanded the ocean's tide "thus far and no farther." Grimké said, "We laugh now at Canute's insane assumption of paramouncy in the one case, just as fifty years hence, the inflated Texan's insane assumption of unchangeable superiority for all of the whites and unchanging inferiority for all of the blacks will be laughed at by the men of that generation—provided, of course, that so small a man as is former Senator Bailey, is remembered at all at that time."[28]

Continuing his attack on Bailey, he noted "What a pitiful figure he actually cuts today by the side of those illustrious figures the Dumas,

26. Speech of Neval Thomas, in NAACP Records; "N.A.A.C.P.: Some Accomplishments," in Arthur Spingarn Papers; Roscoe C. Bruce to Archibald Grimké, March 10, 1914, in Archibald Grimké Papers, Box 8, Folder 148.

27. *Crisis*, VII (1914), 194; *Crisis*, VIII (1914), 86; Boston *Guardian*, May 9, 1915.

28. Archibald Grimké, "What Fools These Mortals Be," May 6, 1914, in Archibald Grimké Papers, Box 21, Folder 426.

father and son, or imagine, if you please, what a sorry figure his name
will cut a generation hence by the side of the names of Douglass, and
Du Bois and Washington, men who dreamed dreams and saw visions
of a new heaven and a new earth." The linking of Du Bois and Washington was both unexpected and significant, a sign of Grimké's sense
of the irrelevance of factionalism in the world Woodrow Wilson and
the NAACP were creating, even as it reinforced his expression of optimism that change was in the works.[29]

Motivated by such optimism, Grimké continued to work hard
against discrimination in the District of Columbia. Much of his effort
was behind the scenes and involved his attempts to defend individual
black federal employees. Shortly after the May meeting, for example,
he tried to get a thirty-year employee of the Treasury Department
returned to a position he had been segregated out of under the Wilson
administration. During the summer, he dealt with the case of the U
Street substation of the post office in Washington. It had been abol-
ished, which meant the loss of jobs for several black clerks. Grimké
went to the department and was able to get three of the clerks rein-
stated. Toward the end of the year, he succeeded, as well, in getting a
D.C. department store to reverse a newly adopted policy of segregat-
ing its restaurant. He was not always successful, of course, because the
Wilson administration worked steadily to create a segregated federal
city. But he could point to a few successes, and these encouraged him
to continue his efforts.[30]

His work did not go unappreciated. In the summer, Calvin Chase's
Washington *Bee,* which had lately been hostile to the NAACP—
reflecting its editor's capricious loyalties—described Grimké as "one
of the ablest, bravest and most active leaders of the New Abolition
movement," praising him for thinking "as a statesman," and noting
his accomplishments during the year—his appearance before the Committee on Reform in the Civil Service, his successes on behalf of the
post office employees, and his urging the construction of a new high
school. Later in the year, the "Sage of the Potomac" wrote in a *Bee*
column that Grimké was "clean as a hound's tooth, straight as a ver-
tical line," and argued that, as a result of Grimké's activities, "mebbe
after a while the Booker T. crowd and the N.A.A.C.P. folk will be
working hand in hand."[31]

29. *Ibid.*
30. Archibald Grimké to Hon. Charles S. Hamlin, May 14, 1914, in Archibald
Grimké Papers, Box 25, Folder 498; *Crisis,* VIII (1914), 237; *Crisis,* IX (1915), 136.
31. Washington *Bee,* July 25, December 12, 1914.

Not everyone was happy, however. In May, for example, and even after his testimony before the House committee and his rousing success with the post–Baltimore meeting, he met more than once with board member Charles Edward Russell, at May Nerney's request, to assure Russell that the Washington branch was active in the fight against federal segregation.[32]

Grimké was as thin-skinned as ever in the face of such dissatisfaction, especially when his own leadership in the fight against discrimination seemed to be questioned. This was evident in his reaction to the famous November, 1914, meeting between William Monroe Trotter and Woodrow Wilson at the White House, in which Trotter spoke strongly against the policies of the administration, and Wilson, who defended his segregationist policies, felt, not entirely fairly, that Trotter had been personally insulting to him. Trotter was both praised and condemned for his behavior at the White House, but there were some who thought he was trying to steal the NAACP's thunder on the segregation issue, engaging in spectacular action that undercut the work the association and Grimké had been doing since Wilson took office.[33]

Grimké was among Trotter's critics. A few days after the White House meeting, he made his feelings known when Trotter appeared before an enthusiastic crowd of two thousand people in the District of Columbia and gave his own version of the events and of the need for radical action. Grimké was at the meeting and was invited but refused to take a seat on the platform with Trotter. After repeated calls, he made his way to the rear of the hall. Obviously, he was not about to make himself a part of anything Trotter was doing or to make it appear, even implicitly, that he either needed or appreciated Trotter's help in fighting the Wilson administration.[34]

As Grimké's behavior indicates, the rapprochement with Trotter that occurred in 1911 had ended by 1914; by the time of the Wilson meeting, he was already angry with Trotter beyond any jealousy or resentment he may have felt over Trotter's spectacular play. The tensions in the relationship between the two men had been exacerbated a few months before the confrontation in Washington by the most unlikely of causes, the death of Charlotte Forten Grimké, his brother's wife. Although she had been ill for some time, her death was a blow

32. May Childs Nerney to Archibald Grimké, May 18, 1914, in Archibald Grimké Papers, Box 24, Folder 498; Fox, *Guardian of Boston,* 186–87.
33. Fox, *Guardian of Boston,* 185–86.
34. Washington *Bee,* November 21, 1914.

to the entire family, and when Trotter waited almost a month to take any notice of her death, Grimké was incensed. He felt that Trotter's behavior was both malicious and inexcusable. The episode did not do anything positive for the relationship between the two men.[35]

But nothing involving Trotter or anyone else in or out of the NAACP was a greater source of difficulty for Grimké at this time than the renewed eruption at the end of 1914 within the organization of the continuing dispute between two contentious NAACP national officers, W. E. B. Du Bois and Oswald Garrison Villard. At the close of 1913, after the stormy meeting in which Grimké had so eloquently expressed his views, an exasperated and exhausted Villard had stepped down as chairman of the NAACP board, largely as a result of his dispute with Du Bois, to be replaced by Joel Spingarn. Shortly after assuming the chairmanship, Spingarn wrote to Grimké, who had expressed concern that the dispute between Du Bois and Villard might split the association, to reassure him. Spingarn had, he said, met with Du Bois and frankly discussed the situation with him. According to Spingarn, he had made Du Bois aware of the dangers of continued fighting, and Du Bois had, Spingarn assured Grimké, made clear that he understood the need for unity in the organization.[36]

But the main issue of autonomy for the *Crisis* remained unresolved, and after almost a year, it was brought out into the open again. Du Bois still viewed those who who opposed him on the issue, especially Villard but now Nerney, too, as implacable opponents, and prejudiced ones at that. Grimké continued to side with Nerney and Villard. Still not trusting Du Bois, he approved of the association's control of the *Crisis* and had made clear his own views of the need for such control in a meeting with Nerney during the early stages of his membership on the board.[37]

Nerney was upset enough to propose at least one rather drastic solution to the issue, hoping to head off Du Bois on the race issue. Writing to Grimké in October about what she saw as the chief needs of the association, she suggested that she herself should step down from the post of secretary and that the executive head of the organization should be thenceforward "a colored man," a view Du Bois

35. Archibald Grimké to Angelina Grimké, August 20, 1914, in Angelina Grimké Papers, Box 5, Folder 83.
36. Joel E. Spingarn to Archibald Grimké, January 6, 1914, in Archibald Grimké Papers, Box 25, Folder 494.
37. May Childs Nerney to Archibald Grimké, March 13, 1914, *ibid.,* Box 25, Folder 496.

had suggested in the past. Her nominee for the post was Archibald
Grimké.[38]

She made a strong case for his qualification for the position, pointing out his reputation for fearlessness and integrity, his past work as a
lawyer, and his visible success with the D.C. branch. Nerney went to
Joel Spingarn with the idea, although for the time it was not pursued.
The matters involving Du Bois came to a head a couple of months
later, however, at the December meeting of the board of directors.
Grimké, who did not always go to New York to attend the meetings,
did attend this one, at which Du Bois presented a resolution designed
to increase his control over the *Crisis*. In a vote that was not on racial
lines, the resolution was soundly defeated, only Mary White Ovington and three other board members of the twenty present siding with
Du Bois.[39]

Grimké again spoke out against Du Bois, and according to Nerney,
his speech did more than anything to carry the day. "I am sorry for
the leader of the opposition," she wrote. "He was so confident of
victory and I fancy he was quite as unprepared for our landslide as
myself. This too was your fault I'm sure." Gratefully, she concluded,
"It's the second time you saved our Association and we all realize it."
This was not, however, to be the last time that Grimké would have to
choose sides as he sought to accomplish his purposes within the
association.[40]

38. May Childs Nerney to Archibald Grimké, n.d.
39. NAACP, Board of Directors, Minutes, December 1, 1914, in NAACP Records.
40. May Childs Nerney to Archibald Grimké, [December 6, 1914], in Archibald
Grimké Papers, Box 25, Folder 506; NAACP, Board of Directors, Minutes, December
1, 1914, in NAACP Records.

14

In Leadership

Despite the tensions carrying over from Grimké's first full year as a major figure in the NAACP, the new year of 1915 began with a flurry of activity that made clear his commitment to the organization and the significance of his place in it. Much of this activity resulted, of course, from the Wilson administration's never-ending onslaught against black America, which gave ample opportunity for both Grimké and the NAACP to function actively.

The first opportunity for both Grimké and the organization came early in the year, on the heels of the passage of legislation aimed at black Americans and at black people generally in the form of an amendment to a major immigration bill, passed by the Senate on December 31, 1914, providing for the exclusion of any further immigration by members of the "black or African race." Aimed at what was hardly a major group of immigrants to the United States, the amendment was introduced by Senator James Reed of Missouri, apparently because he thought its addition would kill the original bill, which he opposed. Nevertheless, its danger was recognized almost immediately by black leaders from every side.[1]

Archibald Grimké, as president of the D.C. branch of the NAACP, played an active role in fighting the amendment. Joined by such D.C. branch stalwarts as George W. Cook, Kelly Miller, and even the long-time Booker Washington ally Whitefield McKinlay, he lobbied members of Congress to mobilize opposition to the amendment or, at least, promise to change it should it get through the House. He met with

1. New York *Age,* January 7, 14, 1915; Atlanta *Journal,* April 20, 1912, in Hampton University Peabody Newspaper Clipping File (Microfiche ed., Alexandria, Va., 1987).

House leaders, drafted a brief which they distributed to every member the day before the vote, and, with his colleagues, called House members off the floor for consultations. In the end, Grimké had every reason to believe that effort had been worthwhile because the amendment was overwhelmingly defeated, 252 to 75, after only a short debate and despite strong support from southern Democratic representatives.[2]

Grimké had much to crow about after the amendment's defeat. He had worked hard on it, and even if the lopsidedness of the vote meant that the amendment likely would have failed anyway, he received much praise for his effort, especially from Joel Spingarn and others in the NAACP's national leadership. The victory also represented a triumph in what was to be a last fling on the old battleground over Booker Washington's leadership because Washington, not without justification, tried to gain a share of the credit. Washington, in the last year of his life, had gone into action to oppose the amendment as soon as the NAACP had and even contacted the Grimkés to express his concern, as well as lobbying Alabama representative John Burnett, a co-author of the original bill, to secure his opposition.[3]

Grimké, however, maintaining his aloofness from Booker T. Washington, had nothing to say about Washington's role and, significantly, described the House action as "a great victory for the National Association." For Grimké and others, even such erstwhile Washingtonians as Whitefield McKinlay, the real story was of a D.C. branch that could undertake so strong a role that Washington's efforts were effective primarily because of the force Grimké and the branch provided.[4]

But Grimké had little time either to savor the victory or to reflect on its implications because within a few days he was back at work against yet more hostile legislation. In mid-January, he wrote to Representative J. W. Smith asking for a hearing on a bill to prohibit intermarriages between the races in the District of Columbia. In February, he was confronted by the possibility of legislation to require Jim Crow

2. Archibald Grimké to Joel E. Spingarn, January 8, 1915, in Joel E. Spingarn Papers, Box 5, Folder 178, Moorland-Spingarn Research Center, Howard University, Washington, D.C.; New York *Age,* February 4, 1915; Louis R. Harlan, *Booker T. Washington: The Wizard of Tuskegee, 1901–1915* (New York, 1983), 416; *Crisis,* IX (1915), 190.

3. New York *Age,* January 7, 1915; Louis R. Harlan and Raymond W. Smock, eds., *The Booker T. Washington Papers* (14 vols.; Urbana, 1972–89), XIII, 213, 220; New York *Age,* January 14, 1915; Harlan, *Booker T. Washington: Wizard of Tuskegee,* 414–15.

4. *Crisis,* IX (1915), 190; Grimké to Spingarn, January 8, 1915; New York *Age,* February 4, 1915; Harlan, *Booker T. Washington: Wizard of Tuskegee,* 416.

cars in the District, which made it through the District Committee of the House of Representatives. Again, Grimké led an effort, consisting mostly of quiet lobbying, to defeat the proposals, and again he met with success because neither bill was finally considered for passage into law.[5]

In addition to responding to negative legislation, Grimké continued to be involved in the day-to-day activities of his position as branch president. He agitated for completion of a new high school building for black students in the District, a project he had sponsored almost from the beginning of his presidency. During the summer, especially, he was in close contact with Congressman L. C. Dyer of Missouri about delays in the construction. He also became involved in the cases of individual federal employees, usually with some success, as when, in the spring, he was able to get a permanent appointment for a black temporary employee who had been passed over for a permanent position at the same time that two white co-workers had been promoted.[6]

Effective as the NAACP seemed to be, however, and strong as Grimké was in cementing his leadership, there remained problems he could not escape. For example, Calvin Chase of the Washington *Bee* became a constant source of criticism early in 1915. It is not entirely clear why, because he had been friendly only a short time before. But he now expressed resentment over the NAACP's claim of victory in the immigration and Jim Crow car bills. After a public meeting on the car bill, Chase wrote that the organization could aptly be renamed the "National Association for the Advancement of Certain Colored Individuals," and, although he did not, on this occasion, single Grimké out by name, he would not always be so reserved.[7]

Far more threatening, however, were internal divisions, both locally and nationally. The Washington branch was beginning to have trouble within its ranks. Even as it scored major victories and continued to succeed at raising funds and gaining members, it was not a peaceful, stable body. Some of the tensions in the branch were per-

5. *Crisis,* IX (1915), 246; New York *Age,* February 25, 1915; Washington *Bee,* January 16, February 6, 1915.

6. L. C. Dyer to Archibald H. Grimké, June 14, 1915, Archibald Grimké to L. C. Dyer, July 3, 1915, both in Archibald H. Grimké Papers, Box 25, Folder 513, Moorland-Spingarn Research Center, Howard University, Washington, D.C.; E. M. Butler to Archibald Grimké, December 15, 1915, *ibid.,* Box 25, Folder 518; *Crisis,* X (1915), 201; *Crisis,* XI (1915), 35.

7. Washington *Bee,* February 27, 1915.

sonal. There were officers and members of the Executive Committee, notably L. M. Hershaw and one of the most active members, Neval Thomas, who did not like each other and who let their quarrels spill over into the activities of the branch. Moreover, and despite the absence of the Waldronites, the schools continued to affect the branch, with the chief lightning rod being Roscoe Bruce. The branch was still in the hands of Bruce's supporters, among them Grimké.[8]

Both Grimké and his daughter worried about the situation during the summer and into the autumn. By November, it seemed that a split was possible in the Washington branch, and Grimké was in the thick of it. Early in that month, a caucus of Bruce supporters met at Grimké's home to plot strategy. According to one report, the group adopted some very Booker Washington–like methods, including attempted suppression of anti-Bruce newspapers and purging the branch of anti-Bruce members so that the organization could line up as a body behind him. They also sought to influence Representative Martin Madden, with whom Grimké had worked on the immigration bill, to seek a change in the governance of the D.C. schools in a way that would strengthen Bruce and his position. Clearly, Grimké had become very jealous of his own position as head of the local body and was willing to fight to maintain his place.[9]

Ultimately, the issue seems to have blown over, but not without a great deal of bitterness and further tension surrounding the organization, both locally and nationally. And it also gave Calvin Chase of the *Bee* yet another pretext for maligning Grimké and the NAACP in one of the most vicious attacks ever made on Grimké. Grimké had recently addressed the combined graduating classes of the black public schools in the District, using the occasion to repeat his denunciation of American color prejudice and the obstinate white racism that refused to acknowledge the achievements of black men and women. It got a good reaction, the Washington *Sun,* for example, printing it in full, with a photograph and a flattering headline. The *Bee,* however, reported that the address was coolly received and noted that Roscoe Bruce had been acknowledged without enthusiasm by the audience.[10]

The *Bee* then stooped to a level that was both very personal and very ugly. Grimké had been a failure as a lawyer, the *Bee* stated, and

8. *Ibid.,* May 22, June 26, 1915.
9. Angelina Weld Grimké to Archibald Grimké, August 29, 1915, in Archibald Grimké Papers, Box 3, Folder 68; Washington *Bee,* November 20, 1915.
10. Washington *Bee,* May 25, June 26, 1915; Washington *Sun,* June 25, 1915, in Hampton Newspaper Clipping File.

had begun to associate with black people only "after he failed to succeed among the white." Chase declared that, under Grimké's leadership, the NAACP branch was "doing as much good for the colored people as a Georgia mob" and twice raised the painful issue of Grimké's marriage, many years earlier, to a white woman. How, Chase asked rhetorically, could Grimké champion the rights of black Americans "when he didn't think enough of the many millions of colored women in this country to make JUST ONE of them his wife." Even Chase would not match this level of hostility in the months to come, but it shows how bitter feelings could be, despite the success of the D.C. branch and Grimké's leadership in it.[11]

Problems remained, too, at the national level. The same jealousy Grimké had shown over his position of authority in local matters was responsible for some of the tension at the national level. And his own sharp tongue came into play when, despite his apparent closeness to May Childs Nerney, he was ready to attack for her attempting to interfere, as he saw it, in the most innocuous of ways, in the activities of the Washington branch. When, for instance, difficulties arose over the failure of Carrie Clifford, head of the branch's Juvenile Committee, to produce a "primer" for young people and she turned to Nerney for help, Nerney wrote to Grimké that she guessed she would have to do it herself. Grimké became inexplicably livid and accused her of wanting to "run the Washington Branch from New York," a charge he would level at others in the national office over the next few years.[12]

The difficulty with May Nerney was easily handled, but problems with Du Bois remained, for nothing had been resolved by Du Bois' defeat at the December, 1914, meeting of the board. Grimké by now was perceived as a leader of the anti–Du Bois group, a role Nerney encouraged. Du Bois himself may have shared the perception and acted toward Grimké in ways that were far from friendly. During the late spring, Du Bois paid Grimké back a little for his past opposition. The association had decided to distribute several pamphlets, including Grimké's American Negro Academy paper *The Ultimate Criminal*. Albert E. Pillsbury was happy with this and tried yet again to get Du Bois, as NAACP director of publicity and research, to distribute Grimké's old paper "Modern Industrialism and the Negroes" as well. According to Pillsbury, Du Bois refused to distribute the one—

11. Washington *Bee,* June 26, 1915.
12. May Childs Nerney to Archibald Grimké, n.d., in Archibald Grimké Papers, Box 25, Folder 508; Nerney to Grimké, April 23, 26, 1915, *ibid.,* Box 25, Folder 510.

although a small number of copies were finally distributed—or even to consider the other. The reason for Du Bois' nonaction seemed to Pillsbury to be largely personal. "It is not worth my while, nor probably yours, to speculate on his silence," he said.[13]

Du Bois, perhaps in a conciliatory gesture, offered Grimké an opportunity during July to write the editorial for the upcoming October number of the *Crisis,* the annual Children's Number. Grimké wrote a brief piece titled "Parents and Children," preaching the need for moral fitness in the battle against prejudice, which he sent to Du Bois the following month. It is a reflection of the state of affairs between the two men, however, that when Grimké sent his effort in he wondered to Angelina "how Du Bois will receive it."[14]

In addition, in September Du Bois tried to make amends for his failure to distribute Grimké's earlier works, singling out *The Ultimate Criminal,* which had been published by the American Negro Academy, for special praise. He described it as an "excellent statement," urged it on the readers of the *Crisis,* and quoted a lengthy paragraph from it.[15]

But this temporary peace, if such it were, did not end the tensions and problems involving Du Bois, the NAACP, and Grimké. Difficulties between Du Bois and the board were exacerbated in the late fall by an effort on the part of some of the officers—notably Joel Spingarn, Nerney, and Villard—to limit Du Bois' activities to editing the *Crisis,* insisting that he should be nothing more than a "paid employee."[16]

Grimké did not plan to get into the thick of this embroilment but

13. "NAACP Publicity," [1915], in W. E. B. Du Bois Papers (microfilm), University of Massachusetts, Amherst; A. E. Pillsbury to Archibald Grimké, May 17, 1915, in Archibald Grimké Papers, Box 5, Folder 100; Pillsbury to Oswald Garrison Villard, June 2, 1915, in Archibald Grimké Papers, Box 6, Folder 120; Alfred A. Moss, Jr., *The American Negro Academy: Voice of the Talented Tenth* (Baton Rouge, 1981), 176.

14. W. E. B. Du Bois to Archibald Grimké, July 16, 1915, in Archibald Grimké Papers, Box 25, Folder 513; Archibald H. Grimké, "Parents and Children," *Crisis,* X (1915), 288–90; Archibald Grimké to Angelina Weld Grimké, August 3, 1914, in Angelina Weld Grimké Papers, Box 5, Folder 84, Moorland-Spingarn Research Center, Howard University, Washington, D.C.

15. *Crisis,* X (1915), 252.

16. Elliott, M. Rudwick, *W. E. B. Du Bois: Propagandist of the Negro Protest* (New York, 1969), 171–74; Charles Flint Kellogg, *NAACP: A History of the National Association for the Advancement of Colored People, 1909–1920* (Baltimore, 1967), 107–108; B. Joyce Ross, *J. E. Spingarn and the Rise of the NAACP, 1911–1939* (New York, 1972), 76–77; *Crisis,* XI (1915), 25–27.

did try to play a conciliatory role. At a December meeting called to consider the issues of Du Bois and the *Crisis,* the move to limit Du Bois was decisively voted down. Although in principle he supported Spingarn, Nerney, and Villard, Grimké, in the interest of unity, ultimately voted with the majority. He spoke to Du Bois after the meeting, urging him to make peace with the other officers, to show a little more "tact," and to make a point of saying "something nice" about his co-workers in the pages of the *Crisis.*[17]

In the wake of the meeting, Grimké was again mentioned as a possible chief executive for the association—especially when, after their defeat, Spingarn, Nerney, and Villard threatened to resign (as Nerney ultimately did). He had strong support from Spingarn and even Du Bois, who had long wanted more black leadership in the group and, despite their disagreements, saw Grimké as the only candidate likely to have broad appeal. But Grimké declined the post, urging Spingarn's retention and choosing to maintain his leadership of the local branch.[18]

But the discussion probably was gratifying to Grimké and made him feel secure about his place in the NAACP, which he thought had become an effective organization. He seems to have relished his conflicts with the Wilson administration and its segregationist surrogates in Congress, gaining enough success to keep him excited. And he was as much rewarded as threatened by the various internal disputes within the NAACP, at least at the national level. He could point to much positive action by the association at the end of 1915.

Despite the fuss in the NAACP and the local issues that divided friends and colleagues, Grimké continued to pursue a private life that was both satisfying and full. He and his daughter remained extremely close. She had made a secure place for herself at the M Street High School, despite the problems within the school system. Her earlier difficulties seem to have been put behind her, and her rating sheets as a teacher were very good, sometimes excellent. She had also begun to expand her writing, trying her hand at drama. She sent one play, *Blessed Are the Barren,* to an agent, J. G. Underhill, a member of the NAACP board. Underhill gave her some encouragement, some

17. Archibald Grimké to W. E. B. Du Bois, December 29, 1915, in Du Bois Papers; NAACP, Board of Directors, Minutes, December 13, 1915, in Records of the National Association for the Advancement of Colored People, Library of Congress.
18. W. E. B. Du Bois to Joel E. Spingarn, Arthur B. Spingarn, and Mary White Ovington, December 16, 1915, in Arthur B. Spingarn Papers, Library of Congress; Joel E. Spingarn to Archibald Grimké, December 16, 1915, in Archibald Grimké Papers, Box 25, Folder 518; Kellogg, *NAACP,* 108–109.

praise, and some criticism, warning her that a career in drama could be very difficult.[19]

About the only note of sadness to enter his life at this time was the death during the summer of 1915 of the youngest Grimké brother, John. Archie and Frank had not seen him in years. Although they had invited him to visit Washington, he had refused to come and had little contact with his illustrious brothers. Angelina had never met him, seeing him for the first time "in his coffin." The family brought his body to Washington for burial in a family plot next to their mother.[20]

Life in Boston also provided him with both comfort and satisfaction. He must have been pleased when the Boston *Herald* picked up his pamphlet *The Ultimate Criminal,* presenting both a complimentary review and extensive excerpts and observing, in language Grimké could have appreciated for its irony, that he was a man "of distinguished ancestry which his white relatives, well known citizens of Boston, freely acknowledged" but was "stamped by the South as pariah and outcast."[21]

He also received respect and affection from old friends, including Nelly Stebbins, to whom he wrote a long, nostalgic letter upon the death of John, and Lillie Buffum Chace Wyman, with whom he began a schedule of correspondence and visiting at a higher level than before. These women seem to have represented for him a key tie with the past and with the community from which he had drawn so much sustenance as a young man. That he sent them everything he wrote may have been an effort to maintain the intellectual framework within which his career had begun.[22]

Despite the problems in the District of Columbia, he remained a figure of note there, too, both publicly and socially. He was always in demand as a public speaker. His 1915 graduation address before the public schools, of which Chase made so much, was an important one. On the day after Booker Washington's funeral in November, he was asked to deliver a memorial address at the Teachers' Institute in Wash-

19. Angelina Weld Grimké, Teacher rating sheets, in Angelina Weld Grimké Papers, Box 6, Folder 107; J. G. Underhill to Angelina Weld Grimké, February 9, 1915, *ibid.,* Box 2, Folder 20.

20. Ellen Stebbins to Archibald Grimké, July 13, 1915, in Archibald Grimké Papers, Box 6, Folder 109; Angelina W. Grimké, "A Biographical Sketch of Archibald H. Grimké," *Opportunity,* III (February, 1925), 44–47; Francis J. Grimké, *The Works of Francis J. Grimké,* ed. Carter G. Woodson (4 vols.; Washington, D.C., 1942), III, 12.

21. Boston *Herald,* June 2, 1915.

22. Lillie Buffum Chace Wyman to Archibald Grimké, July 4, 1915, in Archibald Grimké Papers, Box 7, Folder 126; Stebbins to Archibald Grimké, July 13, 1915.

ington, D.C., during a national symposium on public schools in which William Pickens, Du Bois, and Alain Locke also participated. Noting that he "was never a follower" of Booker Washington, he nevertheless praised Washington for having "the spirit of a conquerer as upward he climbed overcoming the brutal forces and barriers of American race prejudice."[23]

And he continued to hold his place of honor as president of the American Negro Academy, although during 1915 he became embroiled in his first real controversy in that position. The trouble began in 1914, when Grimké and others on the academy's Executive Committee rejected a proposal by F. H. M. Murry to present a paper before the group. Murray, William Monroe Trotter's man in the District of Columbia, angrily denounced the body, writing to John Cromwell that it was under the leadership of "self-seekers and fakers" and singling out Grimké as chief among them. He pointed out that of all the publications of the academy, including its Occasional Papers, a disproportionate number were by Grimké—a charge that, as historian Alfred Moss has pointed out, was not without foundation.[24]

But neither Grimké's prestige nor his leadership could be compromised. Murray's complaint faded away, and when the academy held its annual meeting in December, 1915, Grimké delivered his presidential address and was reelected to the presidency without opposition. Joined on the program by Hershaw, Arthur Schomburg, and William Pickens, Grimké offered a reworking of his much earlier paper "The Heart of the Race Problem," retitled, more explicitly, "The Sex Question and Race Segregation" and issued a short time later as an Occasional Paper.[25]

Finally, the thorn in his side that was the Frederick Douglass home was removed. He had never stopped working on the project with Booker Washington. But he had met with little success and was relieved when, about the middle of 1916, the entire project was taken over by the National Association of Colored Women's Clubs under Mary Talbert's leadership. A few more years were to pass before the mortgage was paid, and Grimké remained involved in the project, but someone else was now directing it with a good prospect for success.[26]

Grimké's public life mostly revolved around the NAACP. He was

23. Archibald Grimké, "Booker T. Washington," 1915, *ibid.,* Box 19, Folder 359; Program, Teachers' Institute, November 17–19, 1915, *ibid.,* Box 39, Folder 772.

24. Moss, *American Negro Academy,* 179–81.

25. Washington *Bee,* January 8, 1916.

26. New York *Age,* August 17, 1916; *Afro-American,* April 8, 1916, in Hampton Newspaper Clipping File.

an active member of the national board of directors, although he only occasionally made the trip from Washington to New York to attend the meetings. His lack of attendance seems to have been owing more to not wanting to make the trip than to the unpleasant internal politics of the board. He was entering his late sixties, and the trip could not have been easy, especially if he did not feel his presence was essential. But he did serve on the Annual Report Committee, chaired by Du Bois, and on the Nominating Committee for the board with Florence Kelly and Joseph P. Loud. The continuing tension between him and Du Bois was evident when, near the end of 1916, Du Bois asked him, as a member of the Nominating Committee, to urge that certain people be nominated for the board. Grimké apparently failed to respond, and none of the names Du Bois suggested was on the final slate.[27]

The organization underwent a significant change toward the end of 1916, when James Weldon Johnson was hired to be the national organizer, thus bringing it closer to the desire of some of the officers to increase the number of blacks in leadership positions. Much has been said about Johnson's appointment, which, though made with Du Bois' support, grew most immediately out of the way in which he had impressed Chairman of the Board Joel Spingarn at the Amenia Conference in late August, 1916. Spingarn had sponsored this conference at his New York estate in an effort to bring together former allies of the late Booker Washington with Washington's opponents and to heal old divisions. Johnson was a former ally of Washington's, though he had been close to the NAACP since at least early 1915. His appointment in the wake of the conference thus had symbolic as well as practical significance.[28]

Grimké did not attend the Amenia Conference. He had been invited repeatedly by Spingarn, who had invited Angelina and Francis Grimké as well. But Archie decided not to go—none of the Grimkés went—simply telling Spingarn that he found the time of the meeting inconvenient. Perhaps he was motivated by political reasons. Trotter was there, and Grimké may not have wanted to spend several days

27. W. E. B. Du Bois to Archibald Grimké, November 1, 1916, in Archibald Grimké Papers, Box 26, Folder 529.

28. Kellogg, *NAACP*, 133–34; Eugene Levy, *James Weldon Johnson: Black Leader, Black Voice* (Chicago, 1973), 176–86; W. E. B. Du Bois to James Weldon Johnson, November 1, 1916, in James Weldon Johnson Correspondence, Folder 136, James Weldon Johnson Collection, Benecke Rare Book and Manuscript Library, Yale University, New Haven, Conn.

isolated with a man for whom he still had bad feeling. But the reason
may have been entirely personal and a matter of inconvenience, as he
said. He was attending national board meetings irregularly, and his
decision to skip Amenia may have reflected both his age and a sense
that the issues the conference was to address were not as pressing as
they once had been.

In addition, the Amenia Conference would have seriously cut into
his summer sojourn in Boston. Since about 1913, he had devoted less
of his time in Boston to public life as a respite from the intense activity
his presidency of the D.C. branch required. This summer turned out
to be particularly satisfying, as he continued to build on longtime
friendships and to enjoy the pleasure they brought. In addition, although he had been seeing Bertha Bauman socially for several years,
in the summer of 1916 he spent more time with her than he had in
several years and took more delight in her company. While his colleagues were working through their problems at Amenia, Grimké was
enjoying some very happy evenings with Bertha and her family, re-
vitalizing a relationship that was now almost a decade old. Although
there is no evidence that his desire to be with Bertha was the reason
he avoided Spingarn's conference, there is no doubt that the pleasure
of her company made Boston a much more convenient place to be.[29]

But the Boston sojourn was merely a sojourn. Life in the District
of Columbia remained as hectic as ever and Grimké's leadership as
prominent. Early in the year, for example, along with local NAACP
leaders in other cities, he led an unsuccessful effort to get D. W. Grif-
fith's recently released film *The Birth of a Nation,* a racist work based
on Thomas Dixon's novel *The Clansman,* banned from the city. He
was more successful in representing the local branch in February at a
hearing of a subcommittee of the House Committee on the District of
Columbia called to consider two new bills on old subjects, one to
prohibit "intermarriage of whites and Negroes" in the District, the
other to segregate the city's streetcars.

The bills were ultimately defeated, but the hearing was eventful.
The chairman of the full committee, Ben Johnson of Kentucky, had
been reluctant to allow Grimké and other black citizens to speak and
had been willing to create the subcommittee only after the interven-
tion of George Holden Tinkham of Massachusetts. Tinkham was ap-

29. Archibald Grimké to Joel E. Spingarn, June 27, August 9, 1916, in Joel Spingarn
Papers, Box 5, Folder 179; Archibald Grimké to Angelina Grimké, August 16, 23, 1916,
in Angelina Grimké Papers, Box 5, Folder 85.

pointed to it, along with Carl Vinson of Georgia. Vinson, who came to the meeting only after Grimké and several other colleagues from the branch had been made to wait for a time, made his orientation clear when he loudly objected to the presence of "a lot of niggers and mongrels" and left Tinkham to take the testimony alone. Tinkham promised that a transcript of any testimony would be made available to the full committee, making the exercise something other than a waste of time. Grimké's testimony focused on the intermarriage bill and was in essence a condensation of "The Heart of the Race Problem."[30]

On two important occasions, Grimké allowed family interests and NAACP activities to overlap. In early 1916, he got in a fight over the new high school he had worked so hard for. His sister-in-law, Charlotte Forten Grimké, had died in July, 1914, and Archibald Grimké proposed that the new high school be named for her. He succeeded in getting the D.C. branch of the NAACP to endorse the suggestion. Chase was outraged. Churlishly, he editorialized that Mrs. Grimké's name "has no particular claim on the colored people in this city," ignoring her record in abolition, activism, and civic matters— including a stint on the school board. Urging that the school be named for the poet Paul Laurence Dunbar, Chase asked his readers to write letters to the *Bee* in support of that choice so that he could forward them to the school board and, more important, to the District commissioners, who had final say in the matter.[31]

Some heavy politicking ensued, and Grimké persuaded the school board to endorse naming the school after Charlotte Grimké no doubt using the same NAACP connections that were keeping Roscoe Bruce in office. The District commissioners, however, were persuaded by Chase's letter-writing campaign, which went heavily in favor of Dunbar, and decided that the new high school would be named in honor of the poet. When it opened about a year later, Grimké was on hand to deliver the featured address on Dunbar's life and work.[32]

Later in the year, he again made use of his NAACP position and connections to assist the embryonic theatrical career of his daughter, Angelina. She had revised her play *Blessed Are the Barren*, retitling it *Janet* and then *Rachel*, her final choice. The play focused on its title character, Rachel, a sensitive and highly educated young women

30. Boston *Herald,* March 6, 1916.
31. Washington *Bee,* December 27, 1915, January 8, 1916.
32. *Ibid.,* January 13, 1917.

driven mad by the horrors of a racist society. In early March, 1916, Grimké's D.C. branch sponsored two performances of *Rachel* at the Miner Normal School. The performances were well-received, even gaining a favorable review in the Washington *Post* (although, of course, Chase's *Bee* was less kind). Grimké arranged for the play to be performed in Boston and asked Joel Spingarn to try to organize still more NAACP-sponsored performances. Again, he met with success when a performance was sponsored by the New York branch, patronized by most of the New York members of the NAACP's national board.[33]

The latter event must have been particularly gratifying, assuring Grimké that despite tensions, he held a secure place in the national association. Nevertheless, even while Grimké was finding his place in the NAACP a source of satisfaction and effectiveness, new issues were developing that would soon place him back in the center of controversy and tension.

33. Angelina Weld Grimké, *Rachel: A Play in Three Acts* (Boston, 1920); Program for *Rachel,* in Angelina Grimké Papers, Box 13, Folder 226; Helen Heizer to Archibald Grimké, September 14, 1916, copy, in Angelina Grimké Papers, Box 5, Folder 85; *Crisis,* XI (1916), 284; Washington *Post,* March 19, 1916; Washington *Bee,* March 11, 1916; Roy Nash to Archibald Grimké, October 23, 1916, in Archibald Grimké Papers, Box 26, Folder 528; W. E. B. Du Bois to Joel E. Spingarn, March 15, 1916, in Joel Spingarn Papers, Box 4, Folder 139; Roy Nash to Arthur B. Spingarn, March 27, 1917, in Arthur Spingarn Papers; Gloria T. Hull, *Color, Sex and Poetry: Three Women Writers of the Harlem Renaissance* (Bloomington, 1987), 119; Kellogg, *NAACP,* 145.

15

War

The next two years were to be among the most difficult and frustrating of any Archibald Grimké had known in public life. He faced many familiar problems, both in the NAACP and in other areas, but with the further complications posed by the entry of the United States in April, 1917, into World War I.

The D.C. branch was prospering, and his leadership was intact. He did lose his temper at one meeting when, criticized over a minor issue, he accused his colleagues of offering him little help and even threatened to resign. But this disruption was short-lived, and, perhaps to make him feel better, Carrie Clifford's youth group gave him a testimonial tribute. Even Calvin Chase's Washington *Bee* was coming back to his side, writing about both Grimké and the NAACP in flattering terms. Chase actually said, at one point, "We wish we had many more men of the stamp of Mr. Archibald Grimpke" and recommended Grimké, among others, for the presidency of Howard University, should its white president, Stephen Newman, decide to step down, as had been predicted.[1]

Grimké was active in the District community on several fronts. He organized a special meeting of the American Negro Academy to honor Frederick Douglass' birth, giving an address on Douglass' work as a reformer and an agitator. He served as a life trustee for the Douglass

1. *Crisis,* XIV (1917), 305; Carrie W. Clifford to Archibald Grimké, June 14, 1917, in Archibald H. Grimké Papers, Box 26, Folder 536, Moorland-Spingarn Research Center, Howard University, Washington, D.C.; Stansbury Boyce to Francis J. Grimké, November 14, 1917, in Francis J. Grimké Papers, Box 2, Folder 39, Moorland-Spingarn Research Center, Howard University, Washington, D.C.; Washington *Bee,* February 3, June 23, 1917, March 2, 1918.

home, helping Mary Talbert and the National Association of Colored Women's Clubs. He was gratified when, at the beginning of 1918, the home was at last "redeemed," the mortgage paid off. In honor of this success, Grimké nominated Talbert, albeit unsuccessfully, for the 1918 Spingarn Medal—the award given by the NAACP and instituted in 1914 by Joel Spingarn for the highest achievement by a black American—an award she was to receive in 1922.[2]

Nevertheless, the bulk of his public activity was taken up with the NAACP, either in his role as branch president or as a national officer and a member of the board. As president of the D.C. branch, he dealt with the usual problems of federal segregation and related issues. Grimké began 1917 fairly optimistic about the likelihood of hostile legislation in the Congress. The prediction turned out to be inaccurate because the session saw the usual round of bills intended to prevent racial intermarriage and to mandate Jim Crow streetcars, as well as to segregate black federal employees. But these bills posed little real threat of passage.[3]

Grimké also continued the branch's efforts on behalf of black schools in the District of Columbia. Early in 1917, he contacted Senator Moses Clapp to try to get support for the purchase of additional land for Dunbar High School, specifically to remedy the lack of "playground facilities." Such facilities were extensive at the white Central High School. Later, both he and Roscoe Bruce, representing the branch, persuaded Washington senator Wesley Jones, another friend of the NAACP, to join them on a tour of the two school campuses to compare facilities. Grimké remained concerned about funding for the schools, noting toward the end of the year that even though black pupils made up about one-third of the District's student population, funding for black schools was only about 10 percent of the total allocation.[4]

2. Program for the dedication of Dunbar High School, January 15–19, 1917, in Archibald Grimké Papers, Box 39, Folder 773; Mary B. Talbert to Archibald Grimké, January 18, 1918, *ibid.,* Box 6, Folder 118; Bishop John Hurst to Archibald Grimké, November 5, 1917, *ibid.,* Box 26, Folder 541; Washington *Bee,* January 13, 1917; *Crisis,* XV (1918), 164; Twin City *Star,* February 27, 1917, in Hampton University Newspaper Clipping File (Microfiche ed.; Alexandria, Va., 1987).

3. Roy Nash to G. Gould Lincoln, January 11, 1917, in Archibald Grimké Papers, Box 26, Folder 531; *Crisis,* XIV (1917), 41.

4. Archibald Grimké to Senator Moses Clapp, January 26, 1917, in Archibald Grimké Papers, Box 8, Folder 150; Roscoe C. Bruce to Senator Wesley Jones, April 11, 1917, *ibid.,* Box 26, Folder 534; Archibald Grimké to Louis Brownlow, December 26, 1917, *ibid.,* Box 26, Folder 542.

He also had the usual round of individual cases of federal discrimination to deal with, and in the early fall, after he had returned to Washington, he confronted an effort in Congress to segregate blacks in the Capitol building, which occurred when a black woman was denied admission to the Senate gallery and two men were refused service in the Senate restaurant on grounds of color. He took the matter up with Senator Jones, who contacted Senator Lee Overman, under whose control the restaurant came. Both Overman and Charles P. Higgins, the sergeant-at-arms of the Senate, assured Jones and Grimké that segregation was not the policy. Jones, however, promised to keep an eye on the facilities to ensure that this was, indeed, the case.[5]

And he continued to work for the progress of the organization. In April, the association launched a Moorfield Storey Drive to increase its membership, and the District of Columbia branch, under Grimké's leadership, responded with unparalleled enthusiasm, growing from a base of about a thousand members to almost seven thousand, about 20 percent of the total national membership.[6]

In March, he joined with Storey, Bishop John Hurst, Joel Spingarn, Villard, and Du Bois in a composing a memorial to Woodrow Wilson, urging that in his inaugural address Wilson "say something against the barbaric system of lynching which prevails in various parts of this country," a vain request. In May, the NAACP held its annual conference in Washington with Grimké, as president of the D.C. branch, presiding.[7]

At this May, 1917, meeting he found it necessary to respond to the involvement of the United States in the European war. The NAACP meeting came only a short time after America's entry into the war, and everyone was fully aware of the implications it had for all black Americans and thus for the association. Grimké, addressing the meeting, condemned the continuing wrongs against blacks in the United States and, stressing a point he would pursue many times in the

5. Washington *Bee,* September 22, November 3, 1917; Archibald Grimké, Petition to the United States Senate, September 26, 1917, in Archibald Grimké Papers, Box 26, Folder 539; James Weldon Johnson to Archibald Grimké, October 15, 1917, in Archibald Grimké Papers, Box 26, Folder 540.

6. Washington *Bee,* April 20, June 22, 1918; *Crisis,* XVI (1918), 173; John R. Shillady to Archibald Grimké, May 6, 1918, in Archibald Grimké Papers, Box 27, Folder 547.

7. *Crisis,* XIII (1917), 284; *Crisis,* XIV (1917), 131; NAACP, Minutes of the Board of Directors, December 10, 1917, in W. E. B. Du Bois Papers (microfilm), University of Massachusetts, Amherst; Washington *Bee,* May 12, 1917; New York *Age,* May 24, 1917.

months to come, observed that "foreigners, even though engaged in war against the United States, could go where none of us would dare go, though dressed in uniform." Grimké saw the dilemma of fighting and dying for a country that had done its black citizens so much wrong.[8]

The dilemma these words represented was widely appreciated within the NAACP and by all its officers. Some, notably Mary White Ovington and Villard, were opposed to the war. But everyone was aware of the issue Grimké had posed—how to participate in a war on behalf of a country that practiced the worst discrimination against those upon whom it would call to fight. The dilemma was exacerbated by the primary goal of the association—to work for the integration of black citizens into American society. The war, as many NAACP leaders understood, provided yet another opportunity for black Americans to prove their merit to the rest of the country, to demonstrate their patriotism, and to further their claim to equal political and civic rights.

For the most part, NAACP leaders, including Grimké, felt constrained to give public encouragement to black American loyalty in time of war and focused their attention on ensuring that those black Americans involved in the war effort should receive fair and equal treatment. This was not a trivial matter. As early as April, 1916, blacks had begun to complain of discrimination within the service and of their exclusion from certain branches of the military. Once America had entered the war, these problems became more pressing as a range of immediate, essentially practical issues began to emerge. Some involved day-to-day patterns of discrimination against individuals. These soon came to the attention of the NAACP and of Archibald Grimké. He did what he could in such cases, addressing protests and appeals to the appropriate authorities.[9]

But larger issues arose as well that went back before the war but became particularly complex now that war had been declared. These more severely tested Grimké's mettle, and he showed himself not entirely comfortable with the role the association had chosen to play in this difficult time.

One of the first such tests to arise was the issue of black officers in

8. New York *Age,* May 24, 1917.
9. Charles Flint Kellogg, *NAACP: A History of the National Association for the Advancement of Colored People, 1909–1920* (Baltimore, 1967), 256–60; Washington *Bee,* April 1, 1916.

the American forces. At the outbreak of war, there were no camps for training black officers and, according to law, they could not be trained with white officers. Before war was declared but appeared imminent, NAACP chairman Joel Spingarn, who had already enlisted in the military, had begun to work on his own to create a camp that would provide separate training for black officers. He believed that a separate camp was better than providing no training for black men.[10]

Grimké was aware of Spingarn's effort and was not entirely happy with it, recognizing the purpose of the camp but seeing it as a compromise with segregation. He told Spingarn of his feelings and also that he felt support of such a camp posed a problem for the organization. He was not alone, and Spingarn received enough pressure that ultimately he told Grimké he would resign his chairmanship, separating his efforts from the organization, despite his desire for NAACP support.[11]

Grimké asked Springarn not to resign, stressing his respect for the chairman's leadership and signing his letter, "With warm regards for you personally (but not the Camp)." When it became clear that most people in the NAACP leadership supported both Spingarn and the camp, Grimké put aside his feelings to serve on a delegation with Spingarn, James Weldon Johnson, and others to try to convince Secretary of War Newton Baker—successfully—to establish the camp.[12]

But Grimké had never been a real organization man, and before long he rebelled against the association line on the war and even, perhaps, his own role in carrying it forward. He gave voice to his feelings only a couple of months after the meeting with Baker, making remarks far more radical than those of any other NAACP leaders at the

10. Kellogg, *NAACP*, 250–51; B. Joyce Ross, *J. E. Spingarn and the Rise of the NAACP, 1911–1939* (New York, 1972), 84–87.

11. Joel E. Spingarn to Archibald Grimké, April 3, 1917, in Joel E. Spingarn Papers, Box 5, Folder 179, Moorland-Spingarn Research Center, Howard University, Washington, D.C.; James Weldon Johnson, *Along This Way* (New York, 1933), 318–19; Joel E. Spingarn to James Weldon Johnson, October 19, 1933, in James Weldon Johnson Correspondence, Folder 454, James Weldon Johnson Collection, Beinecke Rare Book and Manuscript Library, Yale University, New Haven, Conn.

12. Joel E. Spingarn to Archibald Grimké, April 3, 1917, and Grimké to Spingarn, April 4, 1917, in Joel Spingarn Papers, Box 5, Folder 179, Howard University; Roy Nash to Joel E. Spingarn, May 17, 1917, in Joel E. Spingarn Papers, Folder 21, Johnson Collection; W. E. B. Du Bois to Joel E. Spingarn, September 25, 1917, in Joel E. Spingarn Papers, Folder 9, Johnson Collection; New York *News*, May 3, 1917, in Tuskegee Institute News Clippings File (microfilm), Manuscripts and Archives, Yale University, New Haven, Conn.; *Crisis*, XIV (1917), 131; Kellogg, *NAACP*, 255.

time. Breaking his recent pattern of focusing on his private life during his annual summer visit to Boston, he traveled across the river to Cambridge, where he had been asked to speak. There, he urged a meeting of young black men to go into war industries rather than into the military, leaving the fighting to the whites while building a place for themselves in industrial occupations at home. They had nothing to gain, he said, by joining a military system that discriminated against them and potentially demanded their lives. By avoiding the war, he suggested, black young men would be able to produce "a hardy race of young black people to perpetuate their species while the whites would only have a war-crippled stock." No one else in the NAACP had urged that blacks not participate in the war, and only a few other black spokesmen had done so. And even Grimké would have little to say about it in the months to come, as the impossibility of the strategy became clear. But such words show his bitterness about wartime discrimination, including the need to accept a separate camp, and his discomfort with a strategy of compromise on the part of the NAACP.[13]

An episode occurring only about a week after the Cambridge address increased his bitterness and his sense that compromise with the war was at best a fruitless strategy. Racial violence broke out in Houston, Texas, that resulted, first, in the conviction and execution of thirteen black soldiers for causing the difficulties and, later, in the condemnation of sixteen others for the same crime. Grimké, in keeping with his place in the D.C. branch, became involved in the case almost at once, serving as the organization's chief contact with the War Department on it, communicating regularly with Emmett Scott, Booker Washington's former secretary, who had been appointed to a post in the War Department to deal with racial matters emerging during the conflict.[14]

In February, 1918, in support of the organization's efforts to help the condemned men, Grimké, representing the District of Columbia branch, wrote to President Wilson urging clemency for the remaining group of condemned men. "This unhappy affair," he wrote, "had its inception in the determination of an overwhelming majority of the

13. *Afro-American*, August 8, 1917. On other black opponents to the war effort see Theodore Kornweibel, Jr., *No Crystal Stair: Black Life and the Messenger, 1917–1928* (Westport, Conn., 1975), 18–19.
14. Johnson, *Along This Way*, 322–25, NAACP, Minutes of the Board of Directors, January 14, 1918, in Du Bois Papers; James Weldon Johnson to Archibald Grimké, November 13, 1917, in Archibald Grimké Papers, Box 26, Folder 541.

white people of the community in which it occurred, to treat colored people according to the standards erected to maintain relations subsisting between master and slave, and not between freemen." There were no immediate results, although at the end of August Wilson commuted the sentences of ten of the remaining condemned men to life imprisonment—the other six were executed. This was hardly the response Grimké had hoped for.[15]

But more expressive of his feelings about the issue and its significance for black Americans was a poem he wrote about the incident, "Her Thirteen Black Soldiers." It was a lengthy poem, stressing that the soldiers had responded bravely to America's call for service, only to meet death by hanging:

> For her at her bidding they marched ready to die,
> For her they gave their bodies to wind and rain and cold,
> For her they marched without turning or tiring to face her enemies
> For her they charged them and their cannon,
> For her they leaped over danger and breastworks
> For her they clutched out of defeat, victory,
> For her they laid their all at her feet, her thirteen black soldiers.
> And she hanged them in anger and hate,
> And buried them in nameless disgrace.

Indicating an "American colorphobia" that made soldiers, even in uniform, "but common niggers," Grimké used his poem to convey the picture of a violently racist country that could never appreciate the loyalty and courage of black Americans.[16]

Grimké saw little about the war that did not make him angry about American hypocrisy, and he encountered little in his contact with the war that did not increase his frustration. He used the occasion of the annual American Negro Academy meeting in Washington in December, 1917, to telegraph President Wilson, who had just organized American railroads under the control of the national Railroad Administration, asking him on behalf of the academy to use his newly assumed authority to "abolish by Executive order all discrimination among passengers based on race and color."[17]

Not surprisingly, the president did not respond either in word or

15. Washington *Bee,* February 23, 1918; New York *Age,* September 21, 1918.

16. Archibald Grimké, "Her Thirteen Black Soldiers," in Archibald Grimké Papers, Box 8, Folder 156.

17. Lillie Buffum Chace Wyman to Archibald Grimké, September 4, 6, 1917, in Archibald Grimké Papers, Box 7, Folder 126; Archibald Grimké to Woodrow Wilson, December 27, 1917, in Woodrow Wilson Papers, Library of Congress.

deed. And this set the tone for Grimké's role as NAACP leader until the Armistice in November, 1918, and beyond. The futility represented by the unanswered telegram, the Houston incident, the nature of opportunity represented in the form of a separate camp for black officer training, and the continuing discrimination in and out of the military all had their effect on Grimké, especially after the relative success he had met earlier in his NAACP career. Throughout 1918, he continued to soldier for the NAACP, but he met frustration more often than success, within and outside the NAACP. Perhaps for this reason, as he neared the end of his seventh decade, he began to express a more radical turn of mind, which would put him into conflict with the national organization as well as with society as a whole and, particularly, with Du Bois.

Nevertheless, he did not shirk his duties for the NAACP. The school funding issue remained a major priority for him. More directly related to the war, Grimké continued to hear and to try to deal with cases of discrimination within the military and the federal Civil Service and usually met with the same troubling results. He heard often from individuals who had scored well on the Civil Service examination only to be denied employment, as in the case of one young woman who placed seventh on the list and saw eighty white women hired and not one black. Late in the year, he heard from a YMCA worker at Camp Humphreys in Virginia, who described a situation in which white noncommissioned officers sought to terrorize black troops. The sergeants were said to carry pistols all the time and had been told by their superiors to "shoot the 'damn niggers' if they can't rule them any other way." Several men had, in fact, been shot. Grimké tried to deal with such complaints, although he achieved only rare successes.[18]

Grimké worked hard on these and other cases and received much praise for his actions on behalf of blacks. The *Bee* was on his side much of the time, and its "Sage of the Potomac" gave him the greatest praise, writing that Grimké had "rejuvenated" the NAACP,

> made it make a noise like activity, get an expression like sincerity, and write "deeds, not words," all over its constitution and by-laws. He is never too occupied but what he can lay down Homer's Iliad and go out into the moisture of the night to poke some anti-negro brute under his fifth rib for

18. Emma F. Roy to Archibald Grimké, February 19, 1918, in Archibald Grimké Papers, Box 27, Folder 544; W. F. D. Bardeleben to Archibald Grimké, December 11, 1918, *ibid.,* Box 27, Folder 554.

discriminating against some squeeze print. He is never too tired but what
he can sit up, with eyes open, and listen to a tale of woe from some salve-
colored individual who ain't got no more brains than to think he ought to
have a white man's chance.

Praising, as well, Grimké's selflessness, the Sage said, "Some day,
when the Hamites here get awake to all he has done for them . . . they
will go up to Congress and ask them to derrick the Goddess of liberty and put a figure of Archibald up there on the top of the Capitol 'doom.'"[19]

No doubt Grimké appreciated the praise, but the war had brought
him plenty of frustration and concern about the way the country was
going. Nothing was likely to have produced more frustration than his
involvement in the NAACP's ongoing campaign against lynching. Although, like the organization itself, he remained uninvolved in—or
on the periphery of—a campaign begun about this time to support an
antilynching bill in the Congress sponsored by Representative L. C.
Dyer of Missouri, Grimké did help in the continuing agitation to get
President Wilson to take a public stand against lynching, an effort
begun by the national NAACP Anti-Lynching Committee, of which
he was a member. Writing on behalf of the D.C. branch, he declared,
"A people less loyal than those represented by this Association would
ask if it were worth while to send their sons and brothers to make the
world safe for democracy when America, their home, is not safe for
them." Responding to pressure, as well as to reported disaffection
among black troops over racial problems on the home front, Wilson
did, in mid-July, make such a statement.[20]

It was not precisely what Grimké had wanted, although the
NAACP counted it as a victory and distributed fifty thousand copies
of the president's statement to the public. Deploring the "mob spirit"
in general, Wilson lumped together a variety of manifestations of that
spirit, including harassment of people with German surnames. Grimké
saw the statement for what it was in the setting of the Wilson administration and as of a piece with the war effort generally. Later in the
year, he denounced it harshly, declaring that Wilson had never intended to do anything about lynching if the victims were black Ameri-

19. Washington *Bee,* April 27, 1918.
20. Archibald Grimké to the President, July 1, 1918, in Archibald Grimké Papers,
Box 27, Folder 549; Robert L. Zangrando, *The NAACP Crusade Against Lynching,
1909–1950* (Philadelphia, 1980), 44–45; Henry Blumenthal, "Woodrow Wilson and the
Race Question," *Journal of Negro History,* XLVIII (1968), 11.

cans. Echoing a sentiment he had expressed in the opening days of the war, Grimké said: "the German can travel in a Pullman, he can eat in a first-class hotel. And he can enjoy all other luxuries for which he is able and willing to pay, while we who shed our blood for democracy are treated worse than dogs."[21]

Thus as 1918 went along, he became even more outspoken about the war and especially about its relationship to the problems of black Americans. His remarks brought him to the attention of those concerned about disloyalty and subversion in time of war. All during 1918, blacks in Washington were under close surveillance by federal agents, with special attention to the NAACP, which was more than once charged with "causing some dissatisfaction among members of the negro race." Major Walter H. Loving, an army musician who had been the focus of controversy over military racial policies earlier in the century, was doing security work for the military in Washington during much of the war, and word reached him that Grimké had advised teachers at Dunbar High School to refuse to report acts of disloyalty on the part of their co-workers. The government had been encouraging such reports in its fight against "dissatisfaction." Roscoe Bruce was accused of having been responsible for the charge but denied it vehemently, both to Loving and to Grimké. Loving went to see Grimké to discuss it, and Grimké readily admitted to having spoken exactly as charged. Although he told Loving that he was less concerned about disloyalty than about discord among the teachers, his remarks reflected a less than positive attitude toward the government's loyalty campaign. Loving left the meeting pleased, writing to his superiors that "from this interview we have made a friend of one whom we had thought was an enemy of the government," but Loving's superiors remained concerned about the thrust of Grimké's remarks and retained a garbled version in their files. The federal agent responsible for compiling the report on Grimké wrote that Grimké was "connected with Dunbar High School," adding, "so far as can be judged from reports, he is a negro."[22]

21. New York *Times,* July 23, 27, 1918; Washington *Evening Star,* December 26, 1918.

22. Roscoe Conkling Bruce to Walter Loving, February 27, 1918, in Archibald Grimké Papers, Box 27, Folder 544; Walter Loving to Chief, Military Intelligence Section, March 5, 1918, in Walter H. Loving Papers, Box 1, Folder 10, Moorland-Spingarn Research Center, Howard University, Washington, D.C.; Washington *Bee,* January 26, 1918; R. F. Cotten, Special Report, RE: Alleged Negro Activity, Washington, D.C., January 25, 1918, Casefile OG 369936, and James L. Bruff, Memorandum RE: Officers

But it was this consistent, outspoken disaffection with the war effort more than any government file it might have produced that put him into a collision with others among the NAACP leadership, particularly Du Bois. Grimké thought the NAACP and Du Bois were temporizing in the face of increasing atrocities. The events leading to a collision developed slowly but steadily from the beginning of the year to about midsummer.

An immediate pretext for the collision was Grimké's effort to get his poem "Her Thirteen Black Soldiers" published. He sent it first to the *Atlantic,* which turned it down quickly, saying, in essence, that the evidence against the soldiers was convincing, and, moreover, the soldiers would have been hanged had they been white rather than black. He then sent the poem to Du Bois for publication in the *Crisis.* Du Bois had strongly condemned what had happened at Houston, but he did not publish Grimké's poem. His decision had nothing to do with its literary merit or even with the version of the case Grimké presented. Rather, it was a question of loyalty. Du Bois initially accepted the poem, planning to run it in the June number. In May, however, he returned it to Grimké, telling him: "We have just been *specially warned* by the Department of Justice that some of our articles are considered disloyal. I would not dare, therefore, to print this just now." [23]

Du Bois was certainly telling the truth. The *Crisis,* like other black publications, was under surveillance for much of the war. Du Bois had expressed reservations about the war effort, both before and after America's entry into the conflict, even though he endorsed the separate camp. The question had been raised about whether the *Crisis* should be allowed in military camps. Spingarn went to bat for the magazine, and by June, shortly after he had turned down Grimké's poem, Du Bois had given assurances to Spingarn, to convey to the appropriate authorities, that he would "make his paper an organ of patriotic propaganda hereafter." Du Bois was obviously worried, and he worked closely with Spingarn to combat suspicions. [24]

---

and Directors of the National Association for the Advancement of Colored People, July 13, 1918, Casefile 10218-154, Records of the Military Intelligence Division, both in Federal Surveillance of Afro-Americans (1917–25): The First World War, the Red Scare and the Garvey Movement (microfilm), Manuscripts and Archives, Yale University Library, New Haven, Conn.

23. *Crisis,* XIV (1917), 284–85; *Crisis,* XV (1917), 14–19; Editors of the *Atlantic* to Archibald Grimké, February 15, 1918, in Archibald Grimké Papers, Box 8, Folder 146; W. E. B. Du Bois to Archibald Grimké, April 18, May 4, 1918, in Archibald Grimké Papers, Box 8, Folder 156.

24. Joel E. Spingarn to Col. C. C. Churchill, June 10, 1918, Casefile 10218-154,

The relationship between Du Bois and Grimké became irreconcilably hostile after this point. They had begun that year on relatively good terms, experiencing one of the rare rapprochements that occasionally marked their relationship. Grimké had, for example, sent warm greetings to Du Bois on the latter's fiftieth birthday, thanking Du Bois for "all the brave & big things that you have done for the race," and had served on the Dinner Committee formed in honor of Du Bois' life and career. Du Bois, for his part, had repeatedly singled out Grimké for praise in the pages of the *Crisis*.[25]

But Du Bois could have done nothing to confirm more clearly the feelings Grimké had begun to have even at the time of the separate camp issue than to return Grimké's poem for the reasons he gave. Du Bois' submission to higher authority and his refusal to publish the poem, which he had initially acknowledged to be an eloquent protest against an obvious racial injustice, was a sign that was hard for Grimké to miss, and it was to inform his view of Du Bois in a series of challenging events that took place shortly after the poem was returned to Grimké.

Relations between the two men thus returned to normal and even worsened after the problem of Grimké's poem. Some glimmerings of the difficulties between them, both philosophical and personal, surfaced about a month after Du Bois rejected the poem at a conference of black editors called by Emmett Scott to address the question of loyalty, an issue that concerned Grimké. Scott invited a diverse group, ranging from the tractable Fred Moore of the *Age* to the steelier William Monroe Trotter and such others as Du Bois, Kelly Miller, Roscoe Bruce, George W. Cook, and Grimké. Joel Spingarn addressed the group, along with Secretary of War Newton Baker, chairman of the Committee on Public Information George Creel, and Assistant Secretary of the Navy Franklin Roosevelt. The conference concluded with a call for loyalty, both in the military and in American society as a whole.[26]

How enthusiastically Grimké took his place at the conference is

Records of the Military Intelligence Division, in Federal Surveillance of Afro-Americans; W. E. B. Du Bois to Joel Spingarn, Charles Studin, and John Shillady, July 3, 1918, in Du Bois Papers; Kellogg, *NAACP,* 271–72.

25. Archibald Grimké to W. E. B. Du Bois, January 28, 1918, in Du Bois Papers; Program, "In Honor of the Fiftieth Birthday of W. E. Burghardt Du Bois. A Dinner Given By His Friends and Admirers at the Civic Club, New York City, Monday, February 25, 1918," in Joel E. Spingarn Papers, Folder 10, Johnson Collection.

26. Chicago *Defender,* July 6, 1918, in Hampton Newspaper Clipping File.

hard to tell. He may have been there as a favor to Scott, who was his chief contact for dealing with the cases of discrimination that came to his attention. But he had an agenda of his own, joining other representatives of the D.C. branch, especially Bruce, in trying to get the conference to issue a powerful, detailed resolution condemning discrimination, particularly disfranchisement. Grimké did not succeed this time, and Du Bois played the leading role in ensuring that loyalty, not protest, would be the main theme in the final statement. This, too, looked like temporizing to Grimké, and the conference made even plainer the disagreement of the two men on the demands of the war.[27]

Hostility between the two men came to a head later in June and in July, when an internal debate erupted in the NAACP over Du Bois' exact role in the organization and in the war effort. Du Bois, working with Spingarn, had put the Crisis squarely behind the war effort, particularly with a noted editorial, "Close Ranks," which appeared in the July issue. In this much cited piece, Du Bois urged, "let us, while this war lasts, forget our special grievances and close our ranks shoulder to shoulder with our own white fellow citizens and the allied nations that are fighting for democracy."[28]

Grimké could not share the sentiments expressed in "Close Ranks." Shortly after the editorial appeared, he called the District of Columbia branch together to state its opposition to what Du Bois had written, calling it "untimely and inconsistent with the work and spirit of the Association." Giving a formal declaration of support to the war effort and taking a more moderate stance toward it than Grimké's the branch concluded, nevertheless, that "we see no reason for stultifying our consciences by pretending or professing to be ignorant of, or indifferent to the acts of indignity and injustice continually heaped upon us, or by admitting that they are to be excused or forgotten until they are discontinued."[29]

Grimké's anger was soon to be exacerbated. At the time "Close Ranks" appeared in the Crisis, as historian Mark Ellis has shown, Du Bois was actively seeking a military commission to work with Spingarn to address racial problems in the American armed forces. Du

27. Washington Bee, July 27, 1918; New York Post, July 1, 1918; Cleveland Gazette, May 31, 1919.

28. Crisis, XVI (1918), 111; Joel E. Spingarn to Col. C. C. Churchill, July 6, 1918, Casefile 10218-154, Records of the Military Intelligence Division, in Federal Surveillance of Afro-Americans; Mark Ellis, "'Closing Ranks' and 'Seeking Honors': W. E. B. Du Bois in World War I," Journal of American History, LXXIX (1992), 106.

29. Crisis, XVI (1918), 218.

Bois claimed that the offer was independent of the editorial, but Grimké was among many who suspected a connection.[30]

Grimké's reaction became apparent when Du Bois went to the NAACP board of directors, expressing his desire to take the commission—he would be a captain in Military Intelligence, working with Spingarn—but asking that he be allowed to retain "general oversight" of the *Crisis*. With the agreement of Spingarn and Ovington, he asked the board to let him do both and to continue to pay him a supplementary salary because his pay as a captain would not equal what he had been earning as *Crisis* editor. Whatever support he had from other members of the board, he did not have the support of Archibald Grimké, and Grimké moved into open opposition to Du Bois.[31]

The board met to discuss the matter on July 8, 1918, with Grimké not only in attendance but also assuming the chair. Du Bois presented his proposition feeling that, based on his earlier contacts with board members, it was very likely to be approved. It was not, and Grimké led the opposition. Telling members of the board that Du Bois' acceptance of the commission would "disrupt the Washington branch and spread suspicion and discouragement," he was able to persuade enough members that it would not be wise to create a real core of opposition. Instead of approving Du Bois' proposal, the board passed a motion that the editor of the *Crisis* should "be able to give his full time and attention to the important work" and that "it is inadvisable that Dr. Du Bois undertake to combine the duties of . . . editor of the Crisis with that of service as a commissioned officer."[32]

Du Bois and Spingarn were enraged. Spingarn again threatened to resign and to "notify all those who remain in it that the organization is dangerously unpatriotic and anti-American." He also tried to see Grimké to persuade him to change his mind.[33]

But Grimké was not about to be persuaded, and if Du Bois had support—from Spingarn, of course, and from assistant to the secre-

30. Elliott M. Rudwick, *W. E. B. Du Bois: Propagandist of the Negro Protest* (New York, 1969), 204; Ellis, "'Closing Ranks,'" 107–108.

31. Rudwick, *Du Bois*, 204; W. E. B. Du Bois to the Board of Directors, July 2, 1918, in Du Bois Papers; Richmond *Planet,* September 7, 1918, in Tuskegee News Clippings File.

32. NAACP, Minutes of the Board of Directors, July 8, 1918, and W. E. B. Du Bois to Joel E. Spingarn, July 9, 1918, in Du Bois Papers.

33. Joel E. Spingarn to Charles Studin, July 10, 1918, and W. E. B. Du Bois to Mary White Ovington, July 11, 1918, in Du Bois Papers; W. E. B. Du Bois to Joel E. Spingarn, July 19, 1918, in Joel E. Spingarn Papers, Folder 10, Johnson Collection; *Crisis,* XVI (1918), 216.

tary of war Emmett Scott—Grimké did, too, particularly from the Washington branch, where it was widely felt that Du Bois had been willing to sell out the interests of the race and to give his full support to the war effort in the interests of a military title and a military paycheck. With Neval Thomas as his chief ally, Grimké again raised the issue at a meeting of the branch toward the end of July, a few weeks after the board had refused to accept Du Bois' proposal. Spingarn was present to defend Du Bois, who also had the support of L. M. Hershaw, but Grimké and Thomas carried the meeting. The branch voted to censure Du Bois, referring to him as a "traitor" and "Benedict Arnold," and issued him an ultimatum. Either he could edit the *Crisis* or cast his lot with the military. As the board had earlier resolved, he could not do both.[34]

Things calmed down a bit after this July confrontation. Grimké went to Boston, where the NAACP seems to have been somewhat out of his mind. He spent some of his time with Bertha. By now, Angelina was becoming worried about the relationship. She wrote to him that she was afraid Bertha had "baffled him to death"; but he assured her that the relationship was only platonic. Her words may have had some effect, however, because this summer of 1918 seems to have been his last to enjoy Bertha's company. At least, it was the last in which he spoke of it to Angelina.[35]

But he did not lose his fire on political questions. He did not moderate his views on the war or the place of black Americans, nor would he after the Armistice. Early in December, he encouraged the Washington branch to adopt a statement, "What will the Negro Get Out of the War?" taking yet another not too subtle swipe at Du Bois by concluding that "no group can be rated intelligently loyal, that is not at the same time conscious of . . . citizenship rights." A few weeks later, addressing the American Negro Academy, he reiterated his earlier statements about the war effort and declared that after the role blacks had played in it, they should demand "equality of right and equality of opportunity."[36]

34. Emmett Scott to W. E. B. Du Bois, August 13, 1918, in Du Bois Papers; Washington *Bee,* July 20, 1918; Cleveland *Gazette,* May 31, July 5, 1919; Rudwick, *Du Bois,* 204–205; Chicago *Defender,* July 20, 1918, in Hampton Newspaper Clipping File; Ellis, "'Closing Ranks,'" 110.

35. Archibald Grimké to Angelina Grimké, August 8, 1918, in Angelina Weld Grimké Papers, Box 5, Folder 86, Moorland-Spingarn Research Center, Howard University, Washington, D.C.

36. "What Will the Negro Get Out of the War? Statement Adopted at Meeting of

Given Grimké's stance toward the war and, implicitly, toward Du Bois' position on it, it is not surprising that the ill will engendered by Du Bois' refusal to publish Grimké's poem and exacerbated by Du Bois' commitment to the American war effort continued to the end of the year and beyond. From the beginning of the war, Du Bois had drawn significant links between the war effort and the "darker races," especially the peoples of Africa, whose situation could not be separated from the conflict among colonial powers that was, he believed, the essence of the war. At the close of the war, he worked hard for a Pan-African conference at which the interests of all people of African descent could be represented and expressed, a meeting to be held in Paris in February, 1919. The project was dear to Du Bois and had the support of the NAACP. Only Grimké expressed misgivings, "reminding" the board at its December meeting, which he attended, that, "it will not be desirable to permit a diversion of efforts on Africa lest American questions be subordinate, his view being that the Association should more and more concentrate on the rights and wrongs of the American Negro." In this instance, he was not supported, and Du Bois was helped to make the trip. But he was not reconciled with Du Bois either.[37]

Columbia Branch, National Association for the Advancement of Colored People, December 11, 1918," in Du Bois Papers; Washington *Evening Star,* December 26, 1918.

37. Rudwick, *Du Bois,* 210–12; NAACP, Minutes of the Board of Directors, December 9, 1918, in Du Bois Papers.

16

Spingarn Medalist

In the year following the close of World War I, Archibald Grimké turned seventy, an age that might have marked a peaceful retirement after a long and arduous career. Befitting a man who had worked so diligently, he began to receive honors and praise from various quarters, including the NAACP's prestigious Spingarn Medal. But he did not withdraw from the battles that had occupied his time for so long. He remained in the fight against racism. At the same time, his feud with Du Bois continued unabated and broadened to include others in the NAACP national office. The District of Columbia branch, moreover, though continuing to be enormously successful, became a source of conflict as well as pride. Even the American Negro Academy, of which he had so long been president, posed difficulties for him.

The close of World War I could not be said to have brought peace for black Americans, for the NAACP, or for Archibald Grimké. Despite the heroism of black soldiers, and despite Woodrow Wilson's finally issuing a statement on lynching, racial violence was a powerful feature of American life in the year after the war, lynching abated little, and serious riots occurred in several places, including Chicago, Omaha, Longview, Texas, Phillips County, Arkansas, Philadelphia, and even Washington D.C.[1]

Grimké addressed these problems by organizing a successful mass meeting in Washington to protest lynching and by responding to the Arkansas riot, chiefly by keeping the NAACP's concerns in the case

1. New York *Evening Mail*, January 23, 1919, New York *Sun*, October 3, 1919, in Hampton University Peabody Newspaper Clipping File (Microfiche ed.; Alexandria, Va., 1987); James Weldon Johnson, *Along This Way* (New York, 1933), 341.

before the federal authorities. (He was not directly touched by the Washington riot because at the time it occurred he and Angelina were spending the summer in Boston, and even Frank was away in Philadelphia; others in the branch did keep him apprised of the events).[2]

But he did not need spectacular episodes of racial madness to remind him of the kind of world postwar America had become. Even apart from the riots, America, and Washington, D.C., in particular, was a difficult place for blacks in these last years of the Wilson administration, and Grimké remained as active as ever in dealing with problems of segregation and discrimination in the capital, as well as with the affairs of the D.C. branch. He continued to address individual cases of discrimination in federal employment and facilities, and he continued to fight for more nearly equal appropriations for the District's black schools. He also fought an effort to reorganize the District school system by putting the responsibility for all the city's high schools, white and black, under a single director, which, he argued, would reduce "the responsible head of the colored schools to the status of clerk or messenger boy," undercutting the authority of his ally, Roscoe Bruce.[3]

He also faced renewed threats to the health of the branch. These threats grew, once again, out of problems in the schools, focusing on Bruce's leadership. They emerged when a scandal broke out involving a Dutch anthropologist named H. M. B. Moens, who was accused to taking nude pictures of black female students in the District for his "research." He was said to have been aided by former branch vice-president Charlotte Hunter, a teacher, with the support of Bruce. These charges prompted calls for Bruce's resignation.[4]

Grimké was not personally involved in the Moens affair, but Calvin Chase of the Bee and J. Milton Waldron, nursing old grievances, accused him of trying, as president of the branch, to protect his friends Hunter and Bruce and of using the branch in the effort. Although there was some dispute about the truth of the charge, the branch

2. Constance McLaughlin Green, *The Secret City: A History of Race Relations in the Nation's Capital* (Princeton, 1967), 190–92; Washington *Bee,* July 26, 1919; New York *Age,* July 26, 1919; S. M. Kendrick to Archibald Grimké, July 25, 1919, in Archibald H. Grimké Papers, Box 28, Folder 561, Moorland-Spingarn Research Center, Howard University, Washington, D.C.

3. Archibald Grimké to William P. Dillingham, January 2, 1919, in Archibald Grimké Papers, Box 27, Folder 554; Archibald Grimké to George E. Hamilton, March 10, 1919, *ibid.,* Box 27, Folder 557.

4. Washington *Bee,* May 3, June 28, 1919; New York *Age,* May 3, 1919.

supported Bruce and Hunter throughout the debacle. In addition, Grimké had cultivated close ties to newly elected school board president John Van Schaick, an NAACP member, who had to deal with the case. When Van Schaick exonerated Bruce in the affair (although Hunter was forced to resign her teaching post), the suspicions of those who had attacked the branch seemed to be confirmed. The result left Chase and the rejuvenated Waldron dissatisfied, and they continued to snipe at Bruce, the branch, and Grimké's leadership for some months to come.[5]

But these local problems paled beside the more tumultuous issues and relationships involving Grimké and the national office of the NAACP, which had been developing since the early days of World War I. At one level, relations could not have been better between Grimké and the national organization, as shown by the praise he received as winner of the fifth Spingarn Medal, presented at the association's annual meeting held in Cleveland in June, 1919. Although the medal was awarded to him officially, "for seventy years of distinguished service to his country and his race," what was especially important to most people was his leadership of the District of Columbia branch, which remained the organization's largest and most active. Mary Ovington seems to have been chiefly responsible for Grimké's selection for the award, despite any disagreements they had in the past. She submitted a lengthy letter to Bishop John Hurst of Baltimore, chairman of the Selection Committee, focusing on Grimké's work with the D.C. branch and urging the appropriateness of honoring Grimké in his seventieth year. Other candidates for the medal had strong support on the committee, including Emmett Scott for his work in the War Department, Carter Woodson for his efforts on behalf of the study of Negro history, and Du Bois for the Pan-African Congress. But none seems to have posed a serious challenge to Grimké (Du Bois was to receive the medal in 1920, Woodson in 1926; Scott was not to be so honored). The committee, consisting of Hurst, Oswald Garrison Villard, and John Hope, readily chose Grimké.[6]

5. New York *Age,* October 4, 1919; District of Columbia, Board of Education, "Results of an Investigation, authorized by the Board of Education, into the Educational and Administrative Efficiency of Roscoe Conkling Bruce, Assistant Superintendent of the Colored Schools of the District of Columbia," October 8, 1919, in Roscoe Conkling Bruce, Sr., Papers, Box 4, Folder 101, Moorland-Spingarn Research Center, Howard University, Washington, D.C.

6. Mary White Ovington to Bishop John Hurst, May 1, 1919, John Hurst to John Shillady, February 28, April 17, 1919, Office Secretary to Joel E. Spingarn, April 29,

NAACP practice was to keep the name of the medal recipient secret until the moment of its announcement at the award ceremony. This could not be safely done in Grimké's case, however, because of his age and the location of the meeting in Cleveland so Ovington let him know well in advance, and Grimké, aware of the honor involved, was happy to make the trip.[7]

He received his award on the evening of June 27, 1919. President Charles Thwing of Western Reserve University presented it to him, with a few remarks commending Grimké for a career "not of force but of intelligence, of thoughtfulness, of graciousness." Grimké was overcome. Ovington later recalled that upon the medal's presentation, Grimké and the association's secretary, John Shillady, "almost fell into one another's arms." Then he responded, also briefly. Thanking the association, he told the assembled delegates that he had never worked "for the purpose of getting a medal," that the conditions he had fought against in Washington were so intolerable that he had had no choice but to try to remedy them. He expressed his pride in the work he had tried to do and the recognition he received.[8]

But all was not well between Grimké and other national leaders. Tensions remained from the events of the previous year involving Du Bois' "Close Ranks" editorial and his commission, which had developed into a conflict between the national office and the entire District of Columbia branch, Grimké included. These were serious enough that in early 1919, Spingarn created a committee made up of Grimké, Moorfield Storey, Charles Studin, Bishop John Hurst, and others to "take under advisement the structure of the Association, its constitution, the constitution and by-laws provided for branches, the relation of branches to the National Office." Grimké's appointment was, perhaps, an effort to co-opt this vocal critic.[9]

If so, the effort was not a success. Grimké was still too angry to become a good organization man, and his anger was fueled further when Du Bois, who had begun to narrow the philosophical difference

1919, Office Secretary to James H. Dillard, May 12, 1919, in Records of the National Association for the Advancement of Colored People (hereafter cited as NAACP Records), Library of Congress.

7. Mary White Ovington to Archibald Grimké, June 9, 1919, in NAACP Records.
8. Mary White Ovington, The Walls Came Tumbling Down (New York, 1947), 167–68; "Presentation of the Spingarn Medal, and Response of Archibald H. Grimké," in NAACP Records.
9. Joel E. Spingarn, letter dated January 24, 1919, in NAACP Records.

between himself and his critics over the "Close Ranks" affair, chiefly because had been appalled by the discrimination he saw exercised against black soldiers by white American military authorities during his trip to Paris for the Pan-African Congress, criticized Emmett Scott for failing to use his War Department post to act positively against that discrimination.

Grimké felt that because of his wartime message Du Bois had no right to speak and wrote a strong letter in support of Scott's work, saying he had acted conscientiously to try to rectify the problems that came to him. Grimké's Washington colleague Neval Thomas responded even more strongly and in a way that drove the wedge deeper between Grimké and Du Bois. In an open letter to Scott but aimed at Du Bois, he wrote, "Whenever our devoted president, Mr. Archibald Grimké . . . wanted to present the grievances of our brave soldiers, it was to you, and not to the editor of The Crisis, whom we are paying $5,000 per year, that we came, and we never came in vain." Accusing Du Bois of preaching "complete surrender," he pointedly concluded, "Du Bois, instead of giving you support in The Crisis, was [filling] the editorial columns with Christmas stories."[10]

Matters were still further complicated because Grimké was trying to help Thomas get a seat on the national board of directors. In the beginning, Thomas' prospects looked good, although he had a way of being his own worst enemy. Early on, he organized a letter-writing campaign to the board on his own behalf. Grimké was asked to "put a quietus" on it, which he did. Once the dispute with Du Bois over Scott came out into the open, it created more problems for Thomas' candidacy. Other board members were put off by Thomas' words, feeling that the attack on Du Bois was an attack on the NAACP itself. Both Shillady and John Haynes Holmes wrote to Grimké asking him to try to persuade Thomas to issue a public apology.[11]

Grimké was able to get Thomas to write the apology, but he was not happy about the process, relating it to his other problems and ultimately asking, rhetorically: "Has it come to this, that no amount of devoted service to the NAACP is able, in the minds of our Board of Directors, to excuse severe criticism of Dr. Du Bois? It begins to

10. New York *Age,* May 24, 1919; Cleveland *Gazette,* May 10, 1919.
11. John R. Shillady to Archibald Grimké, March 25, 1919, in Archibald Grimké Papers, Box 27, Folder 557; Shillady to Grimké, May 10, 1919, John Haynes Holmes to Grimké, May 26, 1919, *ibid.,* Box 27, Folder 559; Archibald Grimké to John R. Shillady, March 27, 1919, John Haynes Holmes to Shillady, May 3, 1919, in NAACP Records.

look so." He continued to work for the nomination, bringing pressure to bear from others in the Washington branch. It soon became clear that, despite Du Bois' opposition, the association could not afford to antagonize its most important branch, and Thomas was elected. When Thomas attended his first board meeting, however, Du Bois refused to speak.[12]

But the Thomas affair was only one problem involving Grimké, Du Bois, and the national office. Another issue had to do with the NAACP's decision to pay Du Bois' expenses for the first Pan-African Congress, which Grimké had fruitlessly opposed from the beginning. Grimké was not, however, willing to let the matter rest, and he brought it up at the February meeting of the board. When it became clear that he was in a decided minority, he left the meeting in a huff, returned to Washington, and sent in his resignation from the board and from his national vice-presidency.[13]

Grimké's actions caused a dilemma for the national office. Du Bois had been promised the money and had already begun his travels. Yet the importance of the Washington branch had to be taken into consideration, as well as Grimké's resignation, which could damage relations with the branch, given its loyalty to him in most disputes involving Du Bois. Ovington was of a mind to accept Grimké's resignation; others in the national office were not. Shillady, along with James Weldon Johnson and Walter White, put pressure on Grimké to withdraw the resignation, and on the eve of the March meeting, where it was to be considered, he did so. But he was not reconciled either to the situation or to his place on the board and, toward the close of the year, was still considering giving up his position.[14]

The bad blood between Grimké and Du Bois remained even when Du Bois, assenting to what his critics had said at the time of the

12. W. E. B. Du Bois to the Nominating Committee, June 19, 1919, Archibald Grimké to John R. Shillady, June 11, 1919, in NAACP Records; Minutes of the Board of Directors of the NAACP, July 11, 1919, in W. E. B. Du Bois Papers (microfilm), University of Massachusetts, Amherst; Neval Thomas to Archibald Grimké, October 13, 1919, in Archibald Grimké Papers, Box 28, Folder 564.

13. Mary White Ovington to W. E. B. Du Bois, February 11, March 7, 1919, in Du Bois Papers; Joseph Loud to Archibald Grimké, March 4, 1919, in Archibald Grimké Papers, Box 27, Folder 557.

14. Ovington to Du Bois, March 7, 1919, Minutes of the Board, July 11, 1919, in Du Bois Papers; Mary White Ovington to Archibald Grimké, February 14, 1919, in Archibald Grimké Papers, Box 27, Folder 556; John R. Shillady to Archibald Grimké, March 5, 1919, in Archibald Grimké Papers, Box 27, Folder 557; Washington Bee, December 27, 1919, January 24, 1920.

"Close Ranks" controversy, began to sound positively Grimkéan in his comments on wartime and postwar discrimination. He wrote, for instance, "A nation with a great disease set out to rescue civilization; it took the disease with it in virulent form and that disease of race-hatred hampered its actions and discredited its finest professions." Given Grimké's view of Du Bois' motives at the time of the "Close Ranks" editorial, such an about-face on Du Bois' part probably did as much to confirm as to assuage his suspicions. [15]

On several occasions, the hostility between Grimké and Du Bois spilled out into the open. When Du Bois returned from France, he was invited to address Washington's Bethel Literary and Historical Association describing his experiences. One account noted that Grimké and the other officers of the D.C. branch, though in the audience, were "conspicuous by their absence from the platform and by their silence when the address was laid before the society for discussion." [16]

More pointed was Grimké's refusal to let bygones be bygones even when he received the Spingarn Medal. After expressing his gratitude to the association, he concluded his remarks by saying, "I haven't done anything very startling," adding, "I would rather have this medal than a distinguished service cross from the hands of President Wilson." The latter remark could well have been an inference to Du Bois' willingness to divide his loyalties by accepting a wartime commission. [17]

Du Bois was not at all happy that Grimké was awarded the Spingarn Medal. The ceremony provided an opportunity for peacemaking on the part of many in the national office. Villard, for example, made brief remarks, including oblique references to earlier difficulties by saying that Grimké's work had been so valuable the association hoped he would not "retire" from it. Du Bois, however, showed his displeasure during the Cleveland convention. According to the reporter for the Cleveland *Gazette,* referring pointedly to Du Bois' quest for a commission a year before, "Many noted the 'Captain's' temperamental exhibition at the meeting, Monday evening, when called upon by the audience for a speech," which he refused to give. The exhibition was laid directly to the fact that the organization's tribute was going to the man most responsible for Du Bois' failure to get the commis-

15. W. E. B. Du Bois, "An Essay Toward a History of the Black Man in the Great War," *Crisis,* XVIII (1919), 87.

16. New York *Age,* May 10, 1919.

17. Ovington, *Walls Came Tumbling Down,* 167–68; Cleveland *Plain-Dealer,* June 28, 1919, in Hampton Newspaper Clipping File.

sion—and extra salary. Du Bois did not report Grimké's pointed remarks in his terse but unavoidable account of the award, which appeared in the *Crisis*.[18]

The hostility was further increased after the Cleveland meeting, in the fall of 1919, by Grimké's initiation of collaboration with a new set of colleagues. This initiation was marked most visibly by a renewed controversy over "Her Thirteen Black Soldiers," Grimké's poetic expression of his anger over the execution of the Houston soldiers, which a worried Du Bois had refused to publish in the *Crisis*. In late 1917, a new magazine, the *Messenger,* had been established by two young black radicals, A. Philip Randolph and Chandler Owen. Socialist in its drift and openly antiwar, the magazine had reacted as strongly to Du Bois' message of closing ranks as Grimké had. Grimké seems to have been attracted to the *Messenger* early in its life. By February, 1919, he was being quoted in the magazine's advertising, linking it with Max Eastman's radical *Liberator,* a journal he also admired, as one of those magazines that "dare to speak out NOW when others grow silent and submit to be muffled," a celebration of the magazine's outspokenness during the war years, even in the face of government persecution, and thus another not too subtle reference to the NAACP's official organ.[19]

Randolph and Owen had initially classed Grimké with other black leaders of the "old school"—Du Bois, Kelly Miller, William Pickens, James Weldon Johnson, and others—whose work had to be judged a failure and who were "too old to be reformed." Grimké's longtime friend E. H. Clement, to whom Grimké had sent a copy of the magazine, wrote back: "I have never felt so venerable and super-annuated since seeing everybody among my contemporaries in defense of Negroes' rights dismissed in the Messenger's columns as 'old gentlemen.'" But they soon changed their assessment, at least of Grimké. Though worrying that age had made him too conservative, they noted his willingness to listen to socialist ideas and praised his "dogged resolution" in fighting segregation as president of the NAACP's Washington branch. Their changing view was also the product of the role Grimké and his poem played in their continuing conflict with *Crisis* editor Du Bois.[20]

18. Cleveland *Gazette,* July 5, 1919; *Crisis,* XVIII (1919), 193.

19. Jervis Anderson, *A. Philip Randolph: A Biographical Portrait* (New York, 1973), 104; *Crisis,* XVII (1919), 202; Theodore Kornweibel, Jr., *No Crystal Stair: Black Life and the Messenger, 1917–1928* (Westport, Conn., 1975), 3–4, 33–34.

20. E. H. Clement to Archibald Grimké, November 28, 1919, in Archibald Grimké

Grimké was not willing to let the poem disappear and, in the fall of 1919, sent it to the *Messenger,* along with the rejection letters he had received from the *Atlantic* and from Du Bois. Victor Daly, one of Randolph and Owen's colleagues, recognized the usefulness of the materials and wrote to Grimké that they wanted to print not only the poem but the letters as well. Grimké willingly gave his permission, and all were duly printed in the October, 1919, issue. The editors described Grimké as "the most influential Negro in the NAACP" and endorsed his view, expressed in the poem, that the soldiers would not have been hanged had they been white. They also declared that the *Crisis'* failure to print the poem "throws further light upon Du Bois" and, improving on one of Calvin Chase's choicer lines from some years back, asked rhetorically, "Is the N.A.A.C.P. for the advancement of colored people or for the advancement of certain people?"[21]

The *Messenger* editors may have been using Grimké and his poem in their vendetta against Du Bois. They referred to it several times in years to come and, as late as 1925, quoted from the correspondence in an attack on Du Bois. But the poem, once published, made an impression of its own, and some of the attention it attracted was problematic. As a socialist magazine that vocally opposed the "Close Ranks" philosophy Du Bois had expressed in 1918, the *Messenger* and its editors came under constant scrutiny from the Justice Department. Grimké's poem provided new grist for the investigatory mill, one agent saying at the time of its publication that it "really comprises an exoneration of the negro soldiers in their lawlessness at Houston, Texas, and constitutes an incitement to further action of the kind." In a long report on "subversive" material in Negro publications, "Her Thirteen Black Soldiers" was singled out by Justice Department investigators as evidence of the *Messenger*'s dangerous radicalism.[22]

Some readers, however, liked the poem. In 1921, William Pickens

---

Papers, Box 28, Folder 565; *Messenger,* II (January, 1918), 23–24; *Messenger,* II (October, 1919), 18, 20.

21. Victor Daly to Archibald Grimké, September 10, 1919, in Archibald Grimké Papers, Box 28, Folder 563; *Messenger,* II (October, 1919), 8, 25–26.

22. *Messenger,* VII (1925), 209–10; Robert A. Bowen to William H. Lamar, October 1, 1919, Casefile B240, U.S. Postal Service, Records Relating to the Espionage Act, World War I, and Report on Negro Publications, n.d., Casefile OG 357, Records of the Federal Bureau of Investigation, both in Federal Surveillance of Afro-Americans (1917–25): The First World War, the Red Scare, and the Garvey Movement (microfilm). Manuscripts and Archives, Yale University Library, New Haven, Conn.

wrote to Grimké that he had heard a young black woman, a student at Hunter College, recite the poem to the accompaniment of "gentle music," a recitation he found very moving. A month later, he wrote to Grimké's asking for a copy, suggesting with what one suspects was unintended irony that it be made available to the NAACP for "general distribution." Du Bois felt differently, although he did not respond immediately to Grimké's new and pointed connection with the *Messenger* and its editors.[23]

If Du Bois did not respond immediately to Grimké's new choice of friends, others did, and in the most unlikely place, the American Negro Academy. The poem itself was not at issue, but the *Messenger* connection was, precipitating the end, in 1919, of his association with that group. According to the historian of the academy, Alfred Moss, dissatisfaction with Grimké's leadership had been building for some time over a range of issues, including his domination of the Occasional Papers series. The dissatisfaction erupted into real controversy when Grimké decided to extend an invitation to A. Philip Randolph to address the 1919 meeting. Other members objected violently on the basis of Randolph's radicalism and the *Messenger*'s unremitting attacks on such other academy members as Du Bois, Miller, and John E. Bruce. One member, Jesse Moorland, objected so strenuously to the invitation that he asked that his "name shall not be allowed to appear in any of the printed proceedings of this meeting" and threatened to resign from the group.[24]

Grimké was removed from the presidency at the 1919 meeting. Whether there was a contested election is not apparent because, as Moss points out, no records have survived from the meeting. There was, however, little obvious conflict or bitterness. Archibald Grimké was joined in leaving his post by his brother Francis, who had been treasurer since the academy's founding. Archibald assumed the title of president emeritus, and each received a ceremonial farewell from the group. Still, neither Grimké was to have much to do with the academy in the years to come.[25]

Archibald Grimké delivered his final presidential address to the academy at the 1919 meeting. Titled *The Shame of America; or, The*

23. William Pickens to Archibald Grimké, March 1, 1921, in Archibald Grimké Papers, Box 28, Folder 581; Pickens to Grimké, April 8, 1921, *ibid.*, Box 28, Folder 582.

24. Alfred A. Moss, Jr., *The American Negro Academy: Voice of the Talented Tenth* (Baton Rouge, 1981), 212–13; J. E. Moorland to Archibald Grimké, December 20, 1919, in Archibald Grimké Papers, Box 28, Folder 566.

25. Moss, *American Negro Academy,* 142–47.

Negro's Case Against the Republic, it was published as an Occasional Paper in 1924—perhaps, Moss suggests, to erase any bad feelings that might have remained after his removal from office. A new version of the 1900 "Negro's Case Against the Republic," the paper focused on what Grimké saw as a gap between American professions and deeds, stressing the hostility of white Americans to the conditions of blacks from revolutionary times to the present.[26]

But *The Shame of America* was more than simply a representation of an earlier paper. It showed the direction Grimké's thought was beginning to take on the heels of the disappointments and frustrations of the preceding two or three years. Emphasizing the problems he had spent so much time trying to solve during the war, Grimké spoke yet again of the hypocrisy of an America that would ask young men to die for a society in which they had no rights. Then, using a term that was to have increasing currency during the postwar era and that Randolph and Owen did much to promulgate, Grimké asserted that the black soldier returning from France, who "saw the incredible meanness and malice of his own country by the side of the immense genius for Liberty and Brotherhood of France," had come back "a new Negro," ready to "challenge injustice in his own land and to fight wrong with a courage that will not fail him in the bitter and perhaps bloody years to come."[27]

Grimké certainly did not see himself as a "New Negro." He was too old, and he described his proper role as one of offering assistance. But the speech was important because it indicated that Grimké had come to feel that a new generation would have to take the reins of leadership in the struggle for racial justice.

The years 1918 and 1919 had been extremely difficult for Archibald Grimké. Even in the depths of peacetime Wilsonianism, he could point to a few successes—jobs protected and retained, segregationist legislation defeated or at least stalled, the growing prestige of the District of Columbia branch. But the war and its aftermath brought mainly frustration from failed causes and especially from directions that the NAACP chose to pursue, particularly during the war. He mentioned Garrison and Sumner, not surprisingly, in his American Negro Academy address. But it had become inescapably obvious that

---

26. *Ibid.,* 280; Archibald H. Grimké, *The Shame of America; or, The Negro's Case Against the Republic,* Occasional Papers of the American Negro Academy, no. 21, 1924, in *The American Negro Academy Occasional Papers 1–22* (New York, 1969).

27. Grimké, *Shame of America,* 16–17; see also Archibald H. Grimké, "Negro Citizenship," *Howard University Record,* XIV (1920), 176; Kornweibel, *No Crystal Stair,* 49.

the creation of a "new abolition" movement and the realization of a new emancipation were not close at hand.

His surrender of leadership of the American Negro Academy also marked the beginning of his surrender of public life. During the last decade of his life, he was to grow increasingly detached from various forms of activism, appearing occasionally before official bodies, dealing with a few local issues, but more and more leaving the work to others. He did not withdraw completely until his health forced him to, but he was ever more inclined to place his hopes with that coming generation of "New Negroes" whose emergence he celebrated in *The Shame of America*.

17

The Closing

The next three years saw Archibald Grimké's progressive disengagement from public life and particularly from the activities of the NAACP. After 1919, he attended only one more meeting of the board of directors—in May, 1920—though he remained a board member through 1923. He also played a decreasingly active role as the organization's point man on matters involving federal legislation and the national government. Beginning in 1920, it was more common for the organization to send its first black secretary, James Weldon Johnson, to Washington to handle matters of national significance. Although he remained firmly entrenched in the District of Columbia branch, by the mid-1920s he noticeably lessened his activity there, too. He retired from the post in 1925, retaining only the honorific titles of president emeritus of the branch and national vice-president.

He was ready for others to take over the work. Age was beginning to wear on him, and he disliked more than ever traveling on the association's business, though he continued his visits to Boston, and often pleaded ill health when asked to participate in various activities. Even at the local level, he called on such lieutenants as Neval Thomas to handle organizational and public duties connected with the D.C. branch.

His negative feelings about the NAACP were to continue strong as he approached the end of his career. The association, especially at the national level, did little to make him feel better about his place in it. The Du Bois feud went on hold for a couple of years—the two men seem to have stopped having anything to do with each other—but it was to resurface with powerful consequences around the middle of 1923. Ultimately, Grimké's tensions with the organization were exacerbated when it sent Johnson and others to engage in work that in the past had been primarily his.

Finally, the racism of the larger society appeared as intractable as ever in the twilight of Grimké's career, supplementing any other causes that might have been at work to bring his career to an end. Certainly, it was reflected in much that he said and did in the first half of the 1920s.

As the decade began, however, he was hard at work on the affairs of the association, continuing to act on its behalf as the locus of his battle for racial equality. At the beginning of 1920, for example, both he and the association were entering a major contest growing out of an effort on the part of the NAACP and others to secure strong federal legislation against lynching. In May, 1919, after the abortive earlier effort in which the NAACP did not take an interest, Missouri representative L. C. Dyer again introduced such a bill in the Congress. The bill, closely based on a proposal that had been devised in 1902 by Grimké's old friend Albert Pillsbury, reached the House Judiciary Committee in January, 1920.[1]

As president of the District of Columbia branch, Grimké was very active on behalf of the bill, helping to gather witnesses from Washington's black community to appear before the committee and testifying himself in its favor. He was typically unreserved in his testimony, comparing the postwar spate of racial violence to the "Turkish atrocities in Armenia" and to the actions of the Germans in Belgium during the war. He attacked what he saw as congressional indifference in terms that reflected both his own radicalism and his awareness of the ironies of the Red Scare raging in America at this time, by saying, "Is it the fault of such people when they ask Democrats and Republicans, the two parties in power, for help and they do not get it, while there are people who do promise to give it to them, attempt to give sympathy, call them bolsheviki, call them socialists, call them I.W.W., call them anything you choose, but there they are connecting with the rankling feeling of wrong of the colored people." Grimké did not take the leadership for the association on the issue. Johnson, Arthur Spingarn, and a few others in the national leadership did that. But he did speak his mind in this first effort to get the much-needed legislation passed, supplementing the work of his New York colleagues.[2]

1. Eugene Levy, *James Weldon Johnson: Black Leader, Black Voice* (Chicago, 1973), 240–42.
2. *Crisis*, XIX (1920), 324; *Hearings Before the House Judiciary Committee, on H.R. 259, 4123, and 11873, Antilynching*, 66th Cong., 2nd Sess., Serial 14, p. 55.

And he did take the leading role for the association when, about two weeks after his testimony on Dyer's bill, he went back before the House Judiciary Committee to testify against a Red Scare bill to support federal action against presumed sedition. The bill came quickly to the attention of the NAACP because one provision cited as objectionable any material "wherein and whereby appeal is made to racial prejudice the intended or probable result of which appeal is to cause rioting or resort to force." As Grimké pointed out, the clause could easily be turned against blacks because militant black rhetoric, exercised in the South, was likely to "incite" rioting on the part of racist whites. The proposed legislation would leave blacks voiceless in the region, Grimké argued, putting a "stranglehold" on any possibility of protest against racial oppression. Arousing a storm of opposition in addition to that of the NAACP, the legislation failed to gain congressional approval.[3]

But Grimké began pulling away from such relatively mainstream NAACP projects, in part because of age, in part because of alienation. Perhaps the most important evidence of the latter factor was his increasing involvement with A. Philip Randolph and Chandler Owen, who represented precisely the radicalism he had discussed before the House Judiciary Committee in the hearings on the Dyer bill.

Grimké had come under scrutiny for radicalism for his activities during the war and, in April, 1920, he was again officially linked to radicalism by a special committee of the New York State legislature—popularly known as the Lusk Committee, for its chairman, Clayton Lusk—which cited his public endorsement of the *Messenger* and listed him in the index, with unsurprising inaccuracy, as "president of the National Association for the Advancement of Colored People, and a radical."[4]

The mention in the Lusk report may have been more a tribute to the committee's paranoia than to Grimké's activities, but his association with Randolph and other black radicals was becoming closer. In early 1920, Randolph, Owen, Victor Daly, and W. A. Domingo, among others, called for a convention to be held in Washington in

3. *Hearings Before the House Judiciary Committee on S. 3317, H.R. 10650 and 12041, Sedition*, 66th Cong., 2nd Sess., Serial 16, pp. 263–64.
4. New York State Legislature, Joint Committee Investigating Seditious Activities, *Revolutionary Radicalism: Its History, Purpose and Tactics, with an Exposition and Discussion of the Steps Being Taken to Curb It; Being the Report of the Joint Legislative Committee Investigating Seditious Activities, Filed April 24, 1920* (4 vols.; Albany, 1920), I, 1, II, 1482, 2004, II, General Index to Part I, p. 91.

May to create the Friends of Negro Freedom, a new socialist black organization, as an alternative to what they saw as the too conservative NAACP. Grimké was the first to respond to the call, which contained an economic radicalism similar to views he had earlier developed and an unswerving dedication to full racial equality that he admired. He told Randolph, "I think the time is ripe for a new organization such as you have in mind," and assured him, "I am with you in this work." He attended the meeting and became, briefly, an officer in what turned out to be a short-lived organization.[5]

But Grimké's words were especially important as a measure of his dissatisfaction with the NAACP. One could easily overstress that measure because Grimké was not the only NAACP officer involved with the new organization and, especially, the *Messenger*. The magazine had been warmly endorsed by others within the NAACP leadership, including Mary White Ovington, John Haynes Holmes, William Pickens, and Neval Thomas.[6]

But its significance should not be underestimated either. There was still a strong conservative outlook represented on the board, and Grimké was often seen as chief among those opposing it. Even before the Friends of Negro Freedom meeting, when the *Messenger* published an uncomplimentary article on the NAACP, one of Grimké's colleagues on the board, Herbert Seligmann, contacted him, asking him to use his influence to tone down the magazine's criticism. Seligmann wrote: "I think it is distinctly up to you to bring this point forcibly to the attention of the editors of the *Messenger*."[7]

He learned the strength of that conservatism more fully about the time the Friends of Negro Freedom meeting was scheduled, when several board members, led by William English Walling and including Joseph Loud and Moorfield Storey, urged the body to go on record denouncing "un-American" agitation among blacks. Grimké, encouraged by Holmes, was moved to attend the May meeting at which the proposal was to be considered, the last he ever attended, assisting in its defeat. But the conservatives were able to get through another resolution that made clear the organization's orientation, which was to pursue the goal of equal rights "through the press, the platform, the

5. *Messenger,* II (April–May, 1920), 16.
6. *Ibid.,* 6.
7. William Pickens to Archibald Grimké, September 17, 1921, in Archibald H. Grimké Papers, Box 28, Folder 587, Moorland-Spingarn Research Center, Howard University, Washington, D.C.; Herbert J. Seligmann to Archibald Grimké, March 22, 1920, *ibid.,* Box 28, Folder 569.

ballot box, legislative bodies and the courts, and by every tried and tested legal and constitutional method of education and agitation, and by no other method." Grimké could, perhaps, agree with the letter of the resolution: he joined in a unanimous vote approving it. One may wonder if his subsequent nonparticipation had to do with a concern about its spirit.[8]

The early part of 1920, then, saw Grimké both deeply involved and marginalized in the affairs of the NAACP, at least at the national level—asked to do what he could on issues raised by national legislation and federal policy, viewed as something of a dissident so far as the organization itself was concerned. He encouraged both impressions as he acted diligently in his role of congressional liaison for the association while pursuing apparently new organizational ties with Randolph, Owen, and their friends.

Little of this affected his activities in the branch. There, too, problems existed, but they were different, requiring different action. The most pressing issue to face him as branch president during this time grew, as usual, out of the schools. The controversy over the Moens case had never died down after Bruce's exoneration by the school board in 1919. Bruce's more vocal critics had been revitalized toward the end of that year by the nomination of school board president John Van Schaick to be a commissioner for the District of Columbia. Van Schaick had the support of Grimké and the D.C. branch, and when his name came before the Senate for confirmation, Bruce's critics took advantage of the situation to vent their ire at Van Schaick, Grimké, the branch, and Bruce. The resulting controversy, augmented by other issues, was hot, nasty, and ultimately caused Van Schaick to lose the post.[9]

Grimké weathered the verbal storm, but one effect of the Van Schaick controversy was to produce in February, 1920, a long-demanded investigation of the schools by the Congress, which Bruce's opponents hoped would finally result in his removal. Undertaken by a select committee of the Senate, the investigation was supposed to focus on every aspect of school policy and administration, but the

8. John Haynes Holmes to Archibald Grimké, April 19, 1920, *ibid.*, Box 28, Folder 570; Levy, *Johnson,* 274; Minutes of the Board of Directors, NAACP, May 10, 1920, in Records of the National Association for the Advancement of Colored People (hereafter cited as NAACP Records), Library of Congress.

9. Washington *Bee,* January 17, 31, February 28, 1920; Washington *Post,* January 13, 14, March 4, 1920.

hearings came down to a grilling of Van Schaick and his allies, with the main emphasis on the black schools. Grimké had little to do with the more controversial aspects of the hearings, although he testified before the committee on funding problems. But he did have to face the controversy, when in the aftermath, Van Schaick asked Bruce to resign.[10]

Grimké quickly became Bruce's chief spokesman in the affray and wrote a long and angry letter to F. W. Ballou, superintendent of schools. In the letter, Grimké reviewed Bruce's situation and described the plot to remove him as originating not from unhappy parents but from a cabal of Waldronites and those southern Democrats who had run the investigative hearings. He did not wish either Bruce or the branch to succumb to this opposition.[11]

The argument Grimké made in his letter to Ballou was not new. Both Bruce and Coralie Cook, a branch member and school board ally, had made it in the hearings, explaining Bruce's persecution as a desire for revenge dating from the defeat of the Waldronite faction in the D.C. branch in 1913. Whether Grimké had a hand in developing that argument for the hearings is impossible to say, but his use of it in the letter to Ballou shows he could accept it. And it helps to explain why, even after it became clear that Bruce could not be saved, Grimké continued to work for him, to try to provide him with a graceful exit from his position.[12]

Grimké knew that retirement or resignation would be accurately interpreted as an admission of guilt on Bruce's part and a triumph for a group that had been unfriendly to the D.C. branch for years. Working with Kelly Miller, he arranged for a negotiated settlement in which Bruce agreed to apply for an extended leave of absence, in return for which the board would not pursue forcible removal or any charges that might arise following the Senate investigation. Bruce was far from satisfied with the result, but he knew that Grimké had done everything possible to help him. A year later, after taking a position as rural supervisor of schools in Huntington, West Virginia, he wrote to Grimké expressing his gratitude and saying, "There are but two

10. *Hearings Before the Select Committee of the United States Senate, Pursuant to S. Res. 310, Public School System of the District of Columbia,* 66th Cong., 2nd Sess., 1235–46; Archibald Grimké to Frank W. Ballou, March 21, 1921, copy, in Archibald Grimké Papers, Box 28, Folder 581.

11. Grimké to Ballou, March 21, 1921.

12. *Hearings Pursuant to S. Res. 310,* 1046.

photographs on my wall. One is my Father, the other of you who have been so fatherly to me."[13]

Grimké, too, remained upset about the matter. He never did feel that the motivations for the attack on Bruce were other than base and calculating, products of hostility to himself and the branch as well as to the assistant superintendent. And he did not like a more general issue it raised. Bruce had been accused of insubordination, among other things, and, as Grimké said at one point: "In a Southern community like Washington no charge against a man of color in official position has such strategic value as this charge of insubordination. Undoubtedly for this reason it was finally decided upon as the ground of attack upon Mr. Bruce." He thought that, if anything, Bruce had been too docile: "Booker Washington trained him, perhaps, too well."[14]

The Bruce fight was the last really difficult, time-consuming issue he involved himself in as branch president and NAACP officer, although over the next two or three years, he continued to play some role within the NAACP at both the national and local levels, representing it before congressional committees, addressing controversies arising around a variety of issues. He also went at least twice in 1921 to meet with the newly elected president, Warren Harding, on behalf of the NAACP, once as part of a delegation trying to obtain pardons for soldiers still in jail after the Houston incident, once to invite Harding to address a meeting of the District of Columbia branch scheduled for October. Harding declined, but his response to Grimké went beyond a refusal to appear. "I may be dreaming," Harding said, "but it seems to me that the colored man of the South has his only opportunity by falling in the ranks behind the leadership of white men, until such a time as he may be able to control the Legislature." These words indicated that he intended to pursue a lily-white policy so far as the South was concerned and to make no effort to change the existing southern order. (About a month later, Harding, speaking in Birmingham, Alabama, decried any "aspiration for social equality" on the part of blacks, stressing the "fundamental, eternal, and inescapable difference" between the races. The speech provoked a strong letter of protest from Lillie Buffum Chace Wyman in the *Nation*.) Grimké's staunch supporter in the D.C. branch, Coralie Cook, professed shock

13. Archibald Grimké to Charles W. Eliot, May 23, 1921, in Archibald Grimké Papers, Box 28, Folder 583; Roscoe C. Bruce to Archibald Grimké, March 26, 1922, *ibid.*, Box 29, Folder 593; Washington *Bee*, May 28, 1921; *Crisis*, XXIII (1921), 34.
14. Grimké to Eliot, May 23, 1921.

at Harding's words. How, she asked, "could Harding look at a man like him and say the things he did?" But, of course, Grimké looked very different to Warren Harding than he did to Cook.[15]

He also did a little work for the NAACP in its ongoing effort to have the Dyer bill passed. Although Grimké and others had testified strongly on its behalf in 1920 and the Republicans had managed to get the bill through committee, the House had not acted when the legislation was submitted to it in May, 1920. The subsequent election of a Republican president encouraged Dyer and the NAACP to try again. Dyer resubmitted the bill to the new Congress. It went through the Judiciary Committee and was reported favorably in October to the full House. Walter White wrote to Grimké suggesting that James Weldon Johnson would be in Washington for the duration of the battle and would work closely with Grimké and the D.C. branch to carry the fight before the House. But, though Grimké met with some individual congressmen to try to gain their support, most of the work from this point was carried on by Johnson. The bill made it through the House, only to die in the face of a threatened southern filibuster in the Senate. Although this did not mean an end to the attempt to secure antilynching legislation, Grimké was to have no part in any subsequent efforts.[16]

While playing a minor role for Johnson on the Dyer bill, Grimké was taking a more active part in a pair of local issues. One of these, arising in April, represented the beginning of segregation at such facilities as public parks in the District of Columbia. On Easter Sunday, 1922, Colonel Charles Sherrill, a southerner appointed by Harding to be supervisor of public buildings and grounds, ordered the posting of signs designating picnic areas in Rock Creek Park "For Colored Only" or "For White Only." The following Tuesday, Grimké led a delegation from the branch to meet with Sherrill to protest the signs. Remarkably, they were removed.[17]

15. Harding quoted in *Messenger,* III (November, 1921), 275–76; Coralie F. Cook to Angelina Weld Grimké, August 17, 1921, in Angelina Weld Grimké Papers, Box 1, Folder 3, Moorland-Spingarn Research Center, Howard University, Washington, D.C.; *Light,* October 21, 1921, *Nation,* January 25, 1922, in Hampton University Peabody Newspaper Clipping File (Microfiche ed.; Alexandria, Va., 1987).

16. Walter White to Archibald Grimké, October 21, 1921, in NAACP Records; Levy, *Johnson,* 244–50.

17. Washington *Tribune,* April 22, 1922, Washington *Eagle,* April 22, 1922, in Tuskegee Institute News Clippings File (microfilm), Manuscripts and Archives, Yale University Library, New Haven, Conn.

About a month later, however, Sherrill made another segregation-ist move, this time in his organization of the dedication ceremony for the new Lincoln Memorial, scheduled for May 30, 1922. Engraved invitations were sent to all members of Washington's black elite. But when the invitees arrived at the site, they discovered that a special section had been set aside for blacks, far from the platform and back in the weeds. A few of the black guests left the ceremony in disgust, among them Whitefield McKinlay and Emmett Scott. Others stayed on, embarrassed and angry.[18]

Grimké, representing the District of Columbia branch, wrote to William Howard Taft, chief justice of the Supreme Court and presi-dent of the Lincoln Memorial Commission, to protest the segrega-tion. Taft denied that he had ordered segregation and claimed that, to the contrary, he had told Sherrill it was not to occur. Sherrill also denied any intentional segregation but added that he could not see why "any Colored person . . . should object so strenuously to sitting next to other Colored people," a disingenuous denial. Of course, little could be done after the fact, and the problem of Sherrill's leadership was to become still more severe over the next year or so.[19]

These efforts, however, hardly matched Grimké's level of activity of earlier years. By about the end of 1921 and into 1922, he was approach-ing the end of his career. Events were to push him still nearer to it.

Whatever frustrations Grimké felt as a partisan of the NAACP and its cause, he had always been a good president of the D.C. branch and had done much to make it the largest, most successful branch in the association. Despite occasional turmoil, the branch had grown steadily and had successfully attracted members and raised funds. By 1921, much of the work of recruitment and fund-raising had been taken on by an executive secretary Grimké had appointed, Shelby Davidson, a former government employee and attorney. Still, Grimké remained a deeply interested observer.[20]

He became especially interested when, toward the end of 1921, Da-

18. Washington *Tribune,* June 3, 10, 1922; New York *Age,* June 17, 1922.

19. Archibald H. Grimké to William Howard Taft, June 7, 1922, in William How-ard Taft Papers, Library of Congress; Washington *Tribune,* June 10, 1922, Chicago *Defender,* July 1, 1922, in Tuskegee News Clippings File; New York *Age,* Decem-ber 23, 1922.

20. Lewis Newton Walker, Jr., "The Struggles and Attempts to Establish Branch Autonomy and Hegemony: A History of the District of Columbia Branch National Association for the Advancement of Colored People, 1912–1942" (Ph.D. dissertation, University of Delaware, 1979), 138–39; New York *Age,* April 16, 1921.

vidson got into a nasty fight with the national office over what portion of funds raised by the branch were to be retained locally and what portion were to be sent to New York. Davidson thought the national office was taking too much, and Grimké enthusiastically agreed. The controversy raged for several months, but when, by the fall of 1922, it became clear that Davidson and the branch were fighting a losing battle, Grimké, in anger, again submitted his resignation from the board and from the vice-presidency.[21]

There was little sentiment on the board to accept Grimké's resignation, and though the matter was discussed at the November meeting, the board voted not to do so. Mary White Ovington wrote him the official letter, but a couple of days later she followed it with a private one in which she showed her understanding of his situation. "I wonder," she said, "if the war hasn't hit you as it has me and made work seem more futile than formerly. When a few people can ruin the world the education of the masses to intelligence doesn't seem as much a cure-all as it did. I wonder whether the more we think the less hopeful we are bound to become." She urged Grimké "to take a long view of things" and put his grievances with the board behind him, recognizing the respect and affection he had from her and others.[22]

Grimké was not placated, however, and tensions involving him, the national office, and the District of Columbia branch festered over the next few months. Angry over the funding controversy, he was also unhappy with the attitudes of others in the NAACP national office on other grounds. He had, for instance, recently had an argument with Villard over a racist advertisement that appeared in the Nation, of which Villard was the editor. When angry, he could be uncooperative as when James Weldon Johnson asked him in September to hold a meeting of the Committee on Branches, of which Grimké was a most inactive chairman, to discuss funding questions. Grimké not only refused, saying he did not feel like it, but noted gratuitously that the only real funding problem lay in excessive salaries and rents for the national office. It was not a reply designed to further reconciliation with those in New York.[23]

21. Walker, "Struggles," 141, 145; Arthur B. Spingarn to James Weldon Johnson, October 7, 1921, in Arthur B. Spingarn Papers, Library of Congress.

22. Mary White Ovington to Archibald Grimké, November 17, 19, 1922, in Archibald Grimké Papers, Box 29, Folder 601.

23. Archibald Grimké to Oswald Garrison Villard, August 13, 1923, Villard to Grimké, August 14, 1923, in Oswald Garrison Villard Papers, Houghton Library, Harvard University, Cambridge, Mass.; James Weldon Johnson to Archibald Grimké, Sep-

The matter came to a head in October, 1923, when Grimké's term on the board of directors was about to expire, along with those of such other directors as Holmes, John E. Milholland, Joel Spingarn, and Moorfield Storey. The usual practice in the association was to form a committee, which normally renominated those whose terms were expiring or proposed replacements, if any were necessary. For 1923, the Nominating Committee consisted of Du Bois, Charles Studin, and Bishop John Hurst. Du Bois decided to take advantage of the situation to remove Grimké from the board, citing the overrepresentation of the District of Columbia branch and Grimké's failure to attend meetings. He was obviously still smarting from past conflicts, noting that Grimké was "continually indirectly attacking the Association," which he felt a board member should not do.[24]

Du Bois had his way, and Grimké's name was not among those submitted to the board at the November meeting, nor was there any discussion of the omission. He was asked to remain a vice-president, but this was to be simply an honorary title in recognition of his past services. Grimké's parting from the board was, however, far from amicable. There seems to have been some ill will toward him on the part of some board members. A resolution offered in January expressing gratitude for his services was not passed, and, indeed, the official record offers only silence in response to his departure. Apparently Grimké, despite his earlier attempts to resign, was angered by his removal, as were many in the District of Columbia branch. Branch leader James A. Cobb wrote to Arthur Spingarn, expressing the group's dismay, and Spingarn replied, somewhat inaccurately, that the sole reason for Grimké's removal was his age—NAACP founder John Milholland had been dropped for the same reason—and at the annual meeting the association had expressed its gratitude to both men.[25]

Grimké thought about severing all connection with the organiza-

---

tember 25, 1923, Grimké to Johnson, September 29, 1923, in Archibald Grimké Papers, Box 29, Folder 610.

24. W. E. B. Du Bois to Bishop John Hurst, October 18, 1923, W. E. B. Du Bois to Charles Studin, October 20, 1923, in W. E. B. Du Bois Papers (microfilm), University of Massachusetts, Amherst.

25. John Hurst to Archibald Grimké, November 1, 1923, in Archibald Grimké Papers, Box 29, Folder 612; Minutes of the Board of Directors, November 12, 1923, in NAACP Records; Proposed resolution, January, 1924, in Du Bois Papers; James A. Cobb to Arthur B. Spingarn, January 5, 1924, Spingarn to Cobb, January 8, 1924, in Arthur Spingarn Papers.

tion and threatened to resign not only from any national offices but from the branch presidency as well. Cobb was afraid that the branch would fall apart without Grimké's leadership and enlisted Spingarn's aid in trying to keep Grimké in the post, at least for another year. This, he suggested, would provide time for the branch to calm down and then for an orderly transition, including the opportunity for Grimké to select his own successor. This Grimké agreed to do, retiring at the end of 1924 and naming his friend Neval Thomas to succeed him. Grimké was named president emeritus of the branch.[26]

During his last year in office, Grimké did very little in the way of formal work for the NAACP. He was asked to preside at a session of the national meeting in May but declined. He did take on a few individual cases, but these were scattered and hardly put him at the center of even branch activity. About his last public act was to serve as a member of a fourteen-person delegation, headed by James Weldon Johnson and including A. Philip Randolph, to meet with President Calvin Coolidge and present him with a petition to pardon the fifty-four men still imprisoned as a result of the Houston riot. Coolidge instructed the War Department to begin a new inquiry into the cases and, astonishingly, progress began to occur almost immediately. Over the next three years, all but twenty of the men were released, and, in March, 1927, the president ordered the release of the remainder of them within the next year. An event that had figured strongly in Grimké's career was at last brought to a conclusion.[27]

The tapering off of Grimké's public life in the NAACP was matched by a more general tapering off in his other public activities. Even his writing career, in which he had invested so much effort, virtually came to a halt. He did publish letters of support for the *Messenger* and made brief contributions to magazine symposia. In the *Messenger,* for example, he responded to a 1922 poll on Marcus Garvey. Not surprisingly, he had little good to say about Garvey, whose program he described as "collosal folly." In 1926, he was again contacted by Randolph, who, the preceding year, had embarked on the job of organizing the Pullman porters into a union. Grimké commended Randolph for the effort but took no part in the project.[28]

26. James A. Cobb to Archibald Grimké, January 12, 1924, in Archibald Grimké Papers, Box 29, Folder 614; New York *Age,* January 24, 1925.

27. *Crisis,* XXVII (1924), 210–11; *Crisis,* XXVIII (1924), 70; New York *Age,* March 12, 1927.

28. *Messenger,* IV (December, 1922), 550–51; *Messenger,* VIII (February, 1926), 57; Jervis Anderson, *A. Philip Randolph: A Biographical Portrait* (New York, 1973), 166–67.

He was also contacted on two occasions, at about the time he was severing his connections with the NAACP, by Henry Goddard Leach, editor of the *Forum,* a widely read journal of opinion, and asked to take part in symposia organized by Leach and based on responses gathered from a broad range of scholars and public figures. In November, 1923, he was asked to comment on the continued relevance of the Monroe Doctrine. In company with several others, Grimké, drawing on ideas he had expressed since his Santo Domingo days, described the doctrine as a cloak for imperialism: "Trade rivalry has converted us into a nation in pursuit of raw materials and markets. . . . We seek now not opportunities to defend our weak neighbors but how best to exploit them in the interest of our vast industrialism and money power." The following year, Leach asked him to contribute to a forum on the movement of black Americans from South to North, which Grimké did. His reply was not quoted in the magazine, but he was cited among those who argued that the migration was inevitable because of oppression in the South.[29]

But perhaps Grimké's most revealing piece of writing during his last year in public life was not published. It was his part in an exchange with the Harvard philosopher William Ernest Hocking. Grimké had met Hocking at the home of mutual friends in Boston in 1924 and sent him a copy of *The Shame of America.* Hocking had responded by sending Grimké a letter detailing his view of the significance and indelibility of racial differences. Expressing sympathy for justice and fairness in the treatment of black Americans, he nevertheless urged that "each race has its peculiar genius, and builds up its culture according to that genius." The view was not far from Du Bois', but Hocking showed the danger inherent in Du Boisian views, which Grimké had noted years earlier in his paper "Negro Ideals and Ambitions." Hocking pointed to such "indelible" differences to stress the irreconcilability of peoples and to justify a continuation of segregation and white rule in the South "for, let us say, the next hundred years."[30]

Grimké responded by reiterating many of his earlier arguments on behalf of black suffrage. But he then turned directly to Hocking's assumption of the indelibility of race and, more significantly, to his at-

29. Archibald Grimké to Henry Goddard Leach, November 6, 1923, in Archibald Grimké Papers, Box 29, Folder 610; Grimké to Leach, October 8, 1924, *ibid.,* Box 29, Folder 621; *Forum,* LXXI (1924), 106–107; *Forum,* LXXII (1924), 853.

30. Alfred A. Moss, Jr., *The American Negro Academy: Voice of the Talented Tenth* (Baton Rouge, 1981), 280–81; William Ernest Hocking to Archibald Grimké, June 18, 1924, Archibald Grimké Papers, Box 5, Folder 96.

tempted celebration of racial differences, making explicit the consequences he saw in "keeping alive the national consciousness of those
differences which react so disastrously upon the colored people."
Hocking's ideas demonstrated, he said, that so long as the consciousness of difference was preserved, so would a sense of racial superiority
and inferiority, helping to entrench what he called "a caste system in
the republic along the color line."[31]

Grimké argued pessimistically that so long as a color line existed in
the American mind, it would exist in American society. He had implied such a view earlier when analyzing the irrational forces supporting American racism. He had taken up the idea more directly a few
years before the Hocking exchange when, in a letter to Pillsbury, he
mused that the only solution he could see to the race problem was the
obliteration of the color line through "amalgamation," a process
which white men seemed bent on accomplishing, their protestations
to the contrary notwithstanding. The law of nature, he said, would
take care of what human law could not, a point he reiterated in the
letter to Hocking.[32]

But the implicit rejection of Du Boisian ideas of racial distinctiveness was no less important, especially in the mid-1920s, a period of
heightened black consciousness. Given shape and voice by the literary,
artistic, and ideological movement known as the Harlem Renaissance,
this heightened consciousness built on the Du Boisian ideas of a distinctive racial genius, searching history, folklore, and experience for
modes of expression that were uniquely black, celebrating difference
to a degree previously unknown in black thought. By the mid-1920s,
the ideology of the Harlem Renaissance dominated the African-
American intellectual community. Whether he had that in mind as he
framed his response to Hocking, Grimké, by his remarks, put himself
far outside its scope.

Even in the mid-1920s, Grimké remained a concerned and original
thinker. The main currents of African-American thought had, however, gone in different directions, leaving him as marginalized to that
world as he had become in the practical politics of the NAACP. Perhaps this, too, helps to explain why, even as a writer, his retirement
from the active life of the NAACP was also a retirement from the

31. Archibald Grimké to William Ernest Hocking, August 8, 1924, in Archibald
Grimké Papers, Box 5, Folder 96.
32. Archibald Grimké to Albert Pillsbury, September 27, 1921, *ibid.,* Box 28,
Folder 587.

public arena. He still had things to say, but he could not be sure that anyone would listen.

In any event, Grimké grew virtually silent. His daughter, Angelina, writing about him in early 1925, shortly after his retirement from the branch presidency, said that, at seventy-five, he had decided "his work is over," and, although she did not agree, he seems to have acted on this decision. His name is conspicuous by its absence from public life after the last months of 1924.[33]

Throughout the 1920s, Grimké maintained contact with old friends. Lillie Chace Wyman remained particularly close; he often visited her in Boston and used the occasion of his visits to create informal reunions of those within his old abolitionist-based network of friends and companions—Pillsbury, for example, editor Edward Clement of the Boston *Transcript,* and, of course, Nelly Stebbins. He also seems to have had another rapprochement with William Monroe Trotter, who wrote him in September, 1921, a long letter recalling the past, apologizing for failing to invite Grimké, a "summer sojourner," to a picnic being held in Trotter's honor, and assuring him of his friendship.[34]

He also renewed a friendship with T. McCants Stewart, which extended back to their boyhood in Charleston. In the intervening years, Stewart had achieved prominence as an attorney and jurist, lived in Liberia serving as a justice of the Supreme Court there, and in the 1920s, settled in the Virgin Islands. Telling Grimké of his inability in all his travels "to escape the *domination* of the white man," he also wrote that Grimké's photograph had years ago stood with Heureaux's on the Stewart piano and twitted him about his graying hair. He thought, he wrote in the summer of 1922, of returning to America, but he died in the Virgin Islands early in the subsequent year.[35]

Archibald Grimké was not the only one who was growing old and leaving public life. The mid-1920s saw the retirement or death of many of those he had worked with and known for years, the "first generation of college-bred colored men," as Kelly Miller remarked in a column noting the deaths of such figures as Robert Terrell and Wil-

33. Angelina W. Grimké, "A Biographical Sketch of Archibald H. Grimké," *Opportunity,* III (February, 1925), 47.

34. Lillie Buffum Chace Wyman to Archibald Grimké, September 17, 1919, in Archibald Grimké Papers, Box 7, Folder 126; William Monroe Trotter to Archibald Grimké, September 10, 1921, *ibid.,* Box 6, Folder 119; Stephen R. Fox, *The Guardian of Boston: William Monroe Trotter* (New York, 1970), 253, 255.

35. T. McCants Stewart to Archibald Grimké, July 10, 1922, in Archibald Grimké Papers, Box 6, Folder 114.

liam Sinclair and the retirement of the Grimké brothers, Francis also having cut back on his activities during the mid-1920s.[36]

In the summer of 1928, Archibald Grimké's health failed. He told his brother, "Frank, I guess the crisis has come." It had not, his brother recalled, for he was to live for almost two more years. But he never regained his health, and he spent most of the time left to him in bed. In November, he gave Angelina power of attorney, and by April of the following year he was under the constant care of two nurses. He was mentioned at about this time in connection with a dispute at his alma mater, Lincoln University, about the hiring of black faculty, but this was more his brother's cause. Archibald Grimké was physically incapable of doing anything more than endorse his brother's sentiments. His suffering was, apparently, not great, at least not unrelieved, but he was, for much of that time, basically helpless.[37]

Both Francis and Angelina Grimké, who had retired from teaching in 1926, largely as a result of injuries she had suffered in the train crash fifteen years before, cared for him constantly during his long final illness. Angelina played the role of a third nurse in caring for him day and night. Francis, the minister, worried deeply about the state of his brother's soul. He reflected that not once during the illness had a "word escaped his lips as to the outlook beyond the grave," although he was assured of his brother's goodness and even of his faith.[38]

The effort to care for him caused problems within the house-

36. Unidentified clipping, May 15, 1926, in Kelly Miller Papers, Box 3, Folder 77, Moorland-Spingarn Research Center, Howard University, Washington, D.C.; Francis J. Grimké, Resignation statement, 1923, in Francis J. Grimké Papers, Box 1, Folder 7, Moorland-Spingarn Research Center, Howard University, Washington, D.C.; New York *Age,* June 27, 1925.

37. Francis J. Grimké, *Archibald H. Grimké, Born in Charleston, S.C., August 17, 1849. Died in Washington, D.C., February 25, 1930. A Brief Statement by His Brother, Rev. Francis J. Grimké, Pastor Fifteenth Street Presbyterian Church, Washington, D.C.* (N.p., n.d.); Power of Attorney, November 14, 1928, in Archibald Grimké Papers, Box 2, Folder 56; Albert Pillsbury to Archibald Grimké, June 13, 1929, in Archibald Grimké Papers, Box 5, Folder 101; Francis J. Grimké to James Weldon Johnson, April 29, 1929, in James Weldon Johnson Correspondence, Folder 175, James Weldon Johnson Collection, Beinecke Rare Book and Manuscript Library, Yale University, New Haven, Conn.; William H. Crogman to Francis J. Grimké, February 28, 1930, in Francis Grimké Papers, Box 2, Folder 72; Francis Grimké to Charles A. Booker, March 14, 1928, in Francis Grimké Papers, Box 2, Folder 37. On Archibald Grimké's association with the Lincoln issue, see Arnold Rampersad, *I, Too, Sing America* (New York, 1986), 70–71, Vol. I of Rampersad, *The Life of Langston Hughes,* 2 vols.

38. Francis Grimké, *Archibald H. Grimké;* Francis J. Grimké, *The Works of Francis J. Grimké,* ed. Carter G. Woodson (4 vols.; Washington, D.C., 1942), III, 405.

hold, leading to violent confrontations between Angelina and Francis Grimké over matters of finance and bitter recriminations that were to extend for some time after Archibald Grimké's death. Apparently the tensions had been there for some time. Francis sensed that Angelina had been jealously trying to come between the two brothers, unsuccessfully, he felt, for years. But the anger seems to have surfaced often during those trying days of Archibald Grimké's final illness.[39]

Finally, about the middle of February, 1930, the crisis did come. Grimké clung to life for about ten days, with a tenacity that, his brother remarked, surprised even his doctor and the nurses. Then, late in the afternoon on February 25, 1930, he died.[40]

His passing was briefly commemorated by the NAACP. A memorial service later in the year honored both Grimké and Neval Thomas, who also died in 1930. Kelly Miller eulogized Grimké; Roscoe Bruce, Thomas. Grimké's daughter, whom he left well provided for, continued to fight with her uncle and moved out of their common home a short time after her father's death. She later moved to Brooklyn, where she died in 1958. Francis lived another seven years, remaining active, particularly in his protests against American racism, until very near his death. In 1938, the District of Columbia named a school in Archibald Grimké's honor. Angelina traveled to Washington for the occasion and read a poem she had composed shortly after his death.[41]

Grimké has not been widely remembered in the years since his death. Certainly, as a leader, his influence did not match that of Du Bois or Washington. But he was a major figure during his time, and his thought and actions were considered of great significance by his contemporaries. His life was a testimony to his efforts to confront both the demands and limitations posed by the racist world in which he had to live.

39. Francis Grimké, *Works,* III, 413; Grimké family financial agreements, *ca.* 1930, in Angelina Grimké Papers, Box 8, Folder 119.

40. Francis Grimké, *Archibald Grimké;* Angelina Grimké, notes on father, in Archibald Grimké Papers, Box 2, Folder 51.

41. Program, District of Columbia Branch, NAACP, Joint Memorial Service in Honor of the late Archibald H. Grimké and Neval H. Thomas, October 19, 1930, in Angelina Grimké Papers, Box 3, Folder 47; Angelina Weld Grimké, "For the Dedication of the Grimké School," n.d., in Grimké MSS., Johnson Collection.

Index